KAREL ČAPEK

LIFE AND WORK

Also by Ivan Klíma
in English Translation

Between Security and Insecurity
(Prospects for Tomorrow), essays
Judge on Trial, novel
Love and Garbage, novel
Lovers for a Day, collected stories
My First Loves, stories
My Golden Trades, stories
My Merry Mornings, stories
No Saints or Angels, novel
The Spirit of Prague and Other Essays
Ultimate Intimacy, novel
Waiting for the Dark, Waiting for the Light, novel

KAREL ČAPEK

LIFE AND WORK

by Ivan Klíma

Translated from the Czech by
Norma Comrada

CATBIRD PRESS
A Garrigue Book

Translation of *Velký věk chce mít též velké mordy: život a dílo Karla Čapka*

First English-language edition

CATBIRD PRESS
16 Windsor Road, North Haven, CT 06473
800-360-2391; catbird@pipeline.com
www.catbirdpress.com

Our books are distributed to the trade by Independent Publishers Group

Translator's Acknowledgments
Much – enormous – credit herewith to Lída O'Donnell, who devoted so much time and heart to serving as sounding board and decoder par excellence.

Library of Congress Cataloging-in-Publication Data

Klíma, Ivan.
[Velký věk chce mít též velké mordy. English]
Karel Čapek – life and work / by Ivan Klíma ; translated from the Czech by Norma Comrada.
"A Garrigue book."
ISBN 0-945774-53-2 (alk. paper)
1. Čapek, Karel, 1890-1938. 2. Authors, Czech–20th century–Biography. I. Title.
PG5038.C3 Z752413 2002
891.8'6252–dc21

2002001594

CONTENTS

Publisher's Preface

Karel Čapek was not the twentieth century's greatest playwright, novelist, story writer, journalist, children's writer, biographer, humorist, essayist, illustrator, or translator, but he was very good at all of these, and among his twenty-five years of mature output (he died at the age of forty-eight) there are several major works, and numerous short pieces, that are truly great.

But what distinguishes Čapek, other than his versatility, and what makes him so difficult to capture, is the way he worked on many levels at the same time. His writing has attracted relatively little scholarly attention because on the surface most of it seems so simple, so light. Compared to his Prague contemporary Franz Kafka, for example, most of Čapek's writing seems transparent, almost artless.

A principal reason for the surface simplicity of Čapek's writing was his deep belief in democracy, a very fragile idea in the country where he lived (and increasingly in Central Europe), which first attained its freedom and democracy when Čapek was twenty-seven, when he was just about to become a world-famous writer. What this meant in practice is that Čapek wanted his ideas, and the works in which he presented them, to be accessible to all who could read. But as an artist, and in many ways an avant-garde artist, he did not want to give up his interest in such things as cubism, changing the Czech literary language, and exploring philosophical concepts. He knew that different readers would appreciate different aspects of his work, and that most readers would only enjoy the surface, but he put it all there for anyone to plunge into, as deeply as they were willing or able.

What lay beneath the light exterior of Čapek's writing? Let's take the example of the mystery stories he wrote for his newspaper and collected as *Tales from Two Pockets*. In these stories Čapek entertained with his wonderful storytelling while (1) deconstructing the detective story (by dropping various conventions or rules in all but one of the forty-eight stories) before such stories had even appeared in his language; (2) creating a singularly inventive overall structure for the second volume of stories; (3) sketching out sections of his novel trilogy, which was his next major work; (4) experimenting with the use of colloquial Czech in literature, which normally used a very different, formal Czech; (5) providing a range of perspectives on such questions as what is truth, what is justice, and what is mystery; (6) using his hobbies and obsessions as fascinating background material for the stories' details, something he rarely did elsewhere in his fiction; and (7) making out of these highly varied, mostly unrelated stories – some comic, some dramatic, some deeply troubling – a work greater than even its wonderful parts. In short, the sophistication of these apparently harmless stories is at least equal to that of Kakfa's and, much closer in style, Chekhov's.

Even in the short columns Čapek did for newspapers, a description of himself from the point of view of his cat could be not only cute and clever, but also, without any direct hint, a commentary on perspective in art and life – the central notion of Čapek's work, I feel, and indispensable to his humanism. We can infer from the fact that this very lack of perspective exists in both Čapek's Newts (in his most famous novel, *War with the Newts* (1935)) and in the people who blindly exploit them, that his subject wasn't cats, but rather what we need to have truly pluralistic democracy. The twentieth century's horrors were perpetrated by those who failed to read, or who despised, the work of Karel Čapek, who lacked the perspectives he offered and who wanted no one else to obtain them.

It is this complexity underlying the simple and Čapek's interest in multiple perspectives that lead everyone who writes about him to see him so differently.

Ivan Klíma's focus on the way Čapek's personal and, especially, love life affected his writing, and on the tension between his art and his philosophical and political ideas, is fresh and valuable. And his extensive quoting from Čapek's letters, columns, and commentaries on his works as well as from his family's letters and memoirs provides a great deal of information that has never before appeared in English translation. It is also important that Klíma is the first Czech writer to honor Čapek with a full-length study (in fact, this is his second; his first was his dissertation, which was published in 1962). Growing up in Čapek's enormous shadow, the writers of Klíma's generation did not on the whole admire Čapek's work. He was an author to react against, not to embrace.

William Harkins, an American scholar who wrote a fine book on Čapek in 1962, had, like Čapek, a background in philosophy, and there is little overlap between his book and Klíma's. Nor is there much overlap between Klíma's chronological study and the chaotic but equally personal "essay" by Slovak critic Alexander Matuška (1964). Bohunka Bradbrook's recent book on Čapek takes an overview of the critical views of Čapek and focuses on the various forms he wrote in. These are the other books on Čapek in English, and you would have to read all of them to approach a full understanding of Čapek. But this book is an excellent place to start.

By the way, this is not a book written for Czechs that Catbird Press simply picked up from a Czech publisher. We commissioned it, and Klíma wrote it with foreign readers in mind. So he does not assume any prior knowledge of Čapek's life or works.

Robert Wechsler

Czech Pronunciation Guide

b, d, f, m, n, s, t, v, z - like in English
c - like ts in oats
č - like ch in child - Čapek = Chop'-ek
ch - one letter; something like ch in loch
d' - soft, like d in duty (see ě below)
g - always hard
h - like h in have, but more open
j - like y in you
l - like l in leave
ň - like n in new (see ě below)
p - like our p, but without aspiration
r - rolled
ř - pronounce r with tip of tongue vibrating against upper teeth, usually approximated by English speakers by combining r with s in pleasure
š - like sh in ship
t' - soft, like t in tuesday (see ě below)
ž - like s in pleasure

a - like u in cup, but more open - Karel = Kah'-rehl
á - hold it longer
e - like e in set, but more open
é - hold it longer
ě - after b, m, n, p: usually approximated by English speakers by saying the consonant plus yeah; after d and t, soften the consonant by placing tongue at tip of upper teeth
i, y - like i in sit, but more closed
í, ý - hold it longer, like ea in seat - Klíma = Klee'-mah
o - like o in not, but less open
ó - hold it longer, like aw in lawn
u - like oo in book
ú, ů - hold it longer, like oo in stool
ou, au, and eu are Czech dipthongs

Rule No. 1 - Always place accent on the first syllable of a word.
Rule No. 2 - Pronounce all letters.

Introduction

Sixty years and more after his death, the arguments are forgotten, along with the polemics, the passions, the accusations, and the envy – but the work remains. More of Čapek's work has survived than has that of the majority of his Czech contemporaries. It is interesting that, even though Čapek became famous first and foremost for his plays, today he seems to speak to readers more with his novels and stories, and even his journalism: his perceptive essays on the spiritual problems of Europe, the role of the intelligentsia, and the dangerous trends leading to totalitarian thought, as well as his splendid columns about everyday things and ordinary people, about their interests, hobbies, and passions.

Finally, the results of his ability to perceive those tendencies in human behavior that threaten our civilization remain fascinating to this day; his *War with the Newts*, for instance, belongs for all time among those works that have lost nothing in their ability to urgently address readers.

Čapek was an author inspired more often by ideas than by individuals' fate, and yet, as I try to demonstrate, his work often reflects his own problems and traumas, his personal anxieties and hopes. His talent was many-sided, and he had everything that makes a writer a writer: the ability to see in things and events what ordinarily goes unnoticed, and to write about them with a vivid wit and with a freshness that can be appreciated to this day. He was skilled at describing even commonplace events in the most unexpected ways, and at giving a new sense to old stories. He had the gift of epic narrative as well as lyrical observation. He kept a close eye on the consequences of our actions and on the suicidal streaks of our civilization. He also had an extraordinary linguistic sense, and a close reading of his works still delights the reader with its richness, precision, and of course the language itself – as if it had not been touched by time.

Čapek died at a tragic moment in Czechoslovak and European history. That may be why, among those who study and write about his work, it has become the established view that his fate, too, was tragic, and so they have placed him in the pantheon of those great Czech personages traditionally considered martyrs. I believe the truth is just the opposite. Even though Čapek surely, as we all do, had his difficult moments and times when he was dispirited by his illness, he lived a happy life. He was a man of work, and his work brought him abundant satisfaction and praise. He was one of the few Czech artists who could say, at the end of his life, that he had remained true to himself. Even in his personal life Čapek was not unhappy. He gained the friendship of any number of genuinely outstanding, distinguished individuals, he maintained an unsurpassed relationship with his brother, and in the end attained even what had previously seemed unattainable to him: marrying the woman he had truly loved and admired for many years, and who, in her own way, loved and respected him as well.

However often he might have complained about being insufficiently appreciated, he received such favor as few authors have ever known, and the love of readers throughout the entire world – and thanks to his journalism, he had more readers than any other modern Czech writer.

While speaking of the interests of readers, I must emphasize that, for several generations in Czechoslovakia, democracy was only a memory from the past. For many readers, therefore, Čapek was a representative and symbol of anti-ideological thought, of tolerance and democratic values, of art that was free and unfettered by any doctrine. Yet I believe that he can be understood anywhere in the world as a man who, in the midst of an insane, chaotic epoch preparing for the bloodiest conflict in history, stood up for the individual against any and all kinds of manipulation. He exhorted us to resist the impending bar-

barization, and he insisted that we can succeed only to the extent that we are cognizant of and honor those values which humankind has already formed. In order for us neither to forfeit those values nor abandon them, Čapek is as valuable and urgently needed today as he was in his own time.

Note for English-Language Readers

When, after World War II, I first began to take an interest in Karel Čapek, he was still among the prohibited authors. At the time of my studies, only some of his works were allowed to be published, primarily those considered "antifascist." Yet he never ceased to belong among those few Czech writers whom everyone in the country knew. Then, in the mid-1950s, his work began to be published once again, and the books disappeared from bookshops within a few hours' time, even though they had been issued in editions of tens of thousands. When early in the 1960s I wrote a small book about Karel Čapek, I could assume that its readers would, or at least could, know most everything he wrote. Therefore it made sense to consider each of these works individually, including those written at the very beginning of his career, even though his early writing differed considerably from the later works that brought him world renown. I am not certain whether Czech readers today are still familiar with those first literary efforts, and since, understandably, English-language readers are unlikely to know them, there might seem little purpose in examining them. But even excluding all that he wrote before and during World War I (most of which were written with his older brother, Josef), a remarkable amount of work remains – all the more remarkable in that Čapek died at the relatively young age of forty-eight.

I am not among those who consider the object of literary study to be the interpretation of what authors are actually trying to communicate in their work. If I occasionally attempt to do so in this book, it will be purely to acknowledge Čapek's own stated intent in the brief explanations that accompanied most of his significant works.

The greater part of Čapek's writing was done for newspapers, and even many of his novels first appeared in serial form in the progressive, highly respected newspaper for which he worked. While taking away nothing from the quality of his writing, this nonetheless suggests that a considerable portion of it was of a topical nature, written in response to the political issues and societal problems of his time. This political portion of Čapek's work is almost entirely unknown to English-language readers (for the most part, it has never been translated) and so, occasionally, I have quoted from it more extensively than is usually the case, so that the reader can become acquainted with at least a few of Čapek's splendid stands on timeless issues as well as the issues of his time.

Since every great literary work is an authentic expression of its creator, one should seek to discover all that determines the creator's journey through life and defines the creator's values. In other words, to search for the primary sources of the author's inspiration. This I have tried to do, and I believe that this approach to Čapek's life and work will appeal equally to Czech- and English-language readers alike.

1. A Trio of Geniuses

Over the past two centuries, the fortunes of the Czech nation have been volatile, full of ups and downs and events that often end tragically. As late as the beginning of the nineteenth century, it seemed that the Czechs' distinctive identity was nearing its end. The Czech state was merely a part of the Austro-Hungarian Empire. Though the Austrian emperors also had themselves crowned as Czech kings, this was just a formality: Vienna was the seat of each and every government, and the last of the powerful emperors, Franz Josef I, who ruled from 1848 to 1916, never did have himself crowned as king of the Czechs. Since the aristocracy, the urban middle class, and the majority of the intelligentsia spoke only German, it appeared that the Czech language, which for all practical purposes was spoken only in the villages, would be incapable of a revival that would allow for the expression of complex thoughts, much less the writing of literary works.

Yet during the age of romanticism and the awakening of European nationalism, something almost unbelievable happened. A few dozen enthusiasts, who felt their Czech identity strongly, took it upon themselves to revive their native language, and with it the Czech people. They directed all their efforts to these great, suprapersonal goals, and within a short period of time they had succeeded in resurrecting deadened national sentiments and winning over to their cause at least some of the influential strata of society.

The first literary works in Czech to appear at the beginning of the nineteenth century were written by these enthusiasts, the majority of whom abounded more in good will than in talent. Their writing was intended primarily for a rural audience, but when on occasion it was directed toward a more educated stratum, the intention was often no more than to demonstrate that the Czech language was capable of expressing anything, and that it was possible to translate into Czech Greek and modern classics (in 1812, for instance, Milton's *Paradise Lost* was published in a Czech translation), including such giants of contemporary literature as Byron, Goethe, and Pushkin. This situation changed relatively quickly, to the extent that, by the mid-1830s, one of the most remarkable works of Czech poetry had appeared: Karel Hynek Mácha's *May*, but the gifted poet died tragically at the age of twenty-six. Some twenty years later, Božena Němcová wrote the first significant work of Czech prose, *The Grandmother*, and at that same time there also appeared works by the distinguished journalist Karel Havlíček Borovský, the man who laid the foundations for a tradition of democratic, combative journalism (as well as a less fortunate tradition of Czechs who, in the course of their journalistic and political activities, were persecuted and imprisoned). Nonetheless, in the first half of the nineteenth century the majority of Czech-language books do not compare well with what was being published at that time in other languages whose cultural and linguistic traditions were not severed as they had been in the Czech Lands.

Nineteenth-century economic and political development in Austria-Hungary, however, benefited Czech national life. For some sixty years, the monarchy had adapted to Western European laissez-faire development. Though the monarchy did not grant rights of national self-determination, it did on the whole make possible, for the majority of its subject peoples, an independent linguistic and cultural life. Industrially, the Czech Lands became the most highly developed part of the empire, and this gave rise to a great flow of country people into the expanding towns and cities. The Czech portion of the urban population grew rapidly, and by the last quarter of the century Czechs had become predominant in Prague and in the other cities. Numerous Czech political parties, clubs, theaters, newspapers, and dozens of periodicals sprang up, and a Czech university had already begun offering lectures by leading scholars.

This rich cultural life began to bring forth its first results, above all in music, as Bedřich Smetana, Antonín Dvořák and, somewhat later, Leoš Janáček achieved world fame. Nearly all works of consequence in world literature were translated into Czech, and some from Czech literature also had been translated, primarily into German, but also into Russian and other languages.

At the same time, within a space of fewer than seven years, three writers were born in the small Czech Lands, all of whom belong among the greatest figures of modern world literature. Born in Prague in April 1883, the author of *The Good Soldier Švejk*, Jaroslav Hašek; in the same city, some three months later, Franz Kafka; and lastly, on January 9, 1890, in the mining town of Malé Svatoňovice, northeast of Prague, Karel Čapek.

Surely one could cast around for some sort of rule that applies to this coincidence, especially if we consider the fact that in the region three more major prose writers were born during this same ten-year period: Stefan Zweig and Hermann Broch in nearby Vienna, and Robert Musil, who spent his youth in still-nearer Brno. We can speculate about the extent to which the end of the monarchy might have inspired these great authors, or the extent to which the shattering ordeal of war influenced their works, but we should not ignore the almost startling differences in the works of the three first-mentioned authors. Despite the fact that Hašek, Kafka, and Čapek came from similar middle-class backgrounds and in so many ways experienced similar lives and generational circumstances, we could hardly find any three individuals so dissimilar as individuals or as writers.

Kafka – decent, inwardly oriented, odd, a loner who only rarely moved out of his circle of Prague Jewish friends. His broken health excused him from military duty during the war, which, but for a few jottings in his diary, went unrecorded in his writings. His two-sentence entry on the day hostilities broke out reveals more about his attitude than an entire essay: "Germany declared war on Russia. Went swimming all afternoon."[1] His life seems drearily uniform, lacking in external events of any kind. He wrote his austere, largely unfinished but always poetic, metaphorical stories (which originated in the experiences of his inner world) in perfect "Prague German," although he had a practically faultless knowledge of Czech.

Hašek – eccentric, irresponsible, a bohemian anarchist and rowdy surrounded by a pack of equally irresponsible drunks and buddies, a soldier in the world war who deserted any number of times and even, at one point during his madcap sprint through life, served as a red commissar, just like in his story of that name. He churned out hundreds of often sloppily written humorous sketches, and not until *The Good Soldier Švejk* did he step out from the shadows and change his language into a gifted, artistic depiction of the way people actually spoke, including their vulgarisms.

And lastly Karel Čapek – an outstanding student who with his brother Josef, a painter, quickly became part and parcel of the vibrant cultural life. His writing was provocative, he dressed eccentrically, he was full of a zest for life. When the unexpected war broke out, like Kafka he was not conscripted due to the state of his health. But the war broke his spirit, and it was during the war that his direction and his writing were completely transformed. He was the only one of the three who lived through all twenty years of the first, free Czechoslovak Republic, and it was thanks to his writing and his commitment to the struggle to preserve the nation's democracy that he, like President Masaryk, became a symbol of both democracy and the First Republic. He wrote his newspaper columns, his essays, his lesser and greater prose in Czech, and he had an exceptional feeling for linguistic communication, more precisely for the spoken language of his time. It is thanks to Čapek that the written Czech language drew closer to the language people actually spoke. It drew closer, but it lost none of its richness, and to this day his written language still astounds by its utter everydayness.

When I consider what these three had in common, I find only an extraordinary fragility, which denied them the experience of living to a ripe old age and of spending their adulthood by the side of a woman and, accordingly, raising a family. (Hašek, although homosexually oriented, it seems, was the only one who had a child, although he fled from both wife and son and in no time returned to his bohemian life.) Čapek did not make up his mind to marry until his forty-fifth year, not long before his death.

2. Mama's Boy

The region where Karel Čapek was born had already produced one remarkable though tragic literary personality – Božena Němcová. This region of foothills is picturesque. "No matter which hill you climb," Čapek wrote of it, "you look north and see Mt. Sněžka (Snow Mountain), the highest mountain in the country, which used to be snow-covered the greater part of the year, even long after the fruit trees had lost their blossoms." Čapek was born in the health-spa and mining town of Malé Svatoňovice, where his father had been practicing for seven years as a spa and mining physician. Čapek wrote:

> Malé Svatoňovice, my birthplace, is known for its Shrine of the Holy Virgin, admittedly not as powerful as her shrine at Wambierzyce, but nonetheless just as miraculous. My mama would walk there with me to make an offering of a small wax model of a human torso, so that my lungs would be strengthened; those wax torsos, however, always had a woman's breasts, which gave rise to the peculiar notion that we boys didn't have any lungs, and to the futile expectation that, under the influence of my mother's prayers, they would grow on me. Scattered about the region are old farms and estates where peasant rebellions were born, but today there are government factories, and kilometers of hand towels and worsted unfold from Úpice to the world. I remember the Australian and Chinese postage stamps, the stamps from India and the Cape Colony, which I collected in baskets from the factory mail room.[1]

And elsewhere he wrote about his native region:

> In the valley between the Metuje and Úpa rivers are peaceful, rolling hills of black sandstone intermingled with silver groves of birches and dark groves of spruce and bogs of peat. The hills are strewn with cottages where, even in the years of our childhood, you could still hear, banging away from morning to night, the

> hand-built looms of mountain chroniclers, spiritualists, and members of unusual sects...
>
> Up a bit higher runs a meandering linguistic borderline, which beyond Náchod curves toward Prusk and Kladsek. This neigborhood of two nationalities used to be quiet and peaceful. The Germans, in their Teuton-style caps and their waistcoats sprinkled with shiny buttons, spoke a dialect that not even the Austrian authorities understood. They had little contact with us or we with them; that linguistic border was like the edge of the world, beyond which there was nothing.[2]

Úpice, where he spent his childhood, was a typical small town that was expanding rapidly at the turn of the century, especially due to the building of textile factories, yet the traditional, small-town world of artisans and shopkeepers still survived. In the Čapeks' neighborhood alone stood the workshops of a wheelwright, a smith, a stonemason, and a cobbler. Karel often recalled how he would peep inside them, trying to grasp something of the mystery of crafts.

The world of childhood accompanies every author throughout his life. For Čapek what mattered more was that for his entire adult life he moved in a very dissimilar environment. The ordinary, everyday people were gone, and his friends came to include presidents, ministers of state, fellow writers, actors, directors, and journalists. Yet in his work, the ordinary, everyday people obstinately lived on. We come across them time and time again in his feuilletons and in *Tales from Two Pockets*; and in the novel *Krakatit* we come across the idyllic home of a country doctor. One set of Čapek's grandparents were peasant farmers, and his mother grew up at a rural mill, where the grandchildren spent their holidays; surely these childhood experiences in the country gave him confidence in writing the novel *Hordubal*, situated in a remote Subcarpathian village. In the novel *An Ordinary Life*, the hero, a railway official, writes about his childhood, how his mother "used to take me by the hand to a miraculous place of pilgrimage to pray for my health; she sacrificed to the Virgin Mary a little wax bust for me, because she said my lungs were weak. I was deeply ashamed that for me she had sacrificed a woman's bust, it humiliated me, it affected my pride in being a man..."[3]

Perhaps Čapek's childhood environment is evoked most directly in his fairy tales, into which he frequently inserted the names of real people, and the region of his childhood is recalled in its place-names. He even set his water sprites in its fishponds and rivers, and quartered his magicians, *hejkals*, and nymphs in its forests. "If you think, children," begins "The Water Sprite's Tale" in his *Nine Fairy Tales,* "that there aren't any water sprites, then let me tell you that there are, and all sorts of different kinds! Just to take a few of our own, near the place where we were born, one lived in the Úpa River, just below the weir, and one lived up there by the wooden bridge at Havlovice, and one hung around the brook near Radeč. That one was German, and he couldn't speak a word of Czech, but he came to see my papa once, to have a tooth pulled, and to pay for it he brought a little basket filled with pink and silver trout neatly tucked into a bed of nettles so they'd stay fresh. And you could tell he was a water sprite, because he left a wet mark on the chair. And one lived near grandfather's mill in Hronov, and he kept sixteen horses under the water below the weir, and that's why the engineers say that, at that spot, the Metuje River has sixteen horsepower."

His wife, Olga Scheinpflugová, recalled:

> I saw how Karel Čapek's entire life stayed with him, as if there were no distance between the world in which he later lived and his previous world, the one in which for the first time he had looked about him with a newborn's eyes. "That's how it was for us in the foothills," and "That's how we did it back home, my girl," he said as often as he could."[4] *and:* "That's like it was at our house," he would remember in Norway, in the Alps, in the Dolomites. Everything in the world was a continuation of the panorama first revealed to him in his distant natal nest. And outside our home, he would often look around and compare: "That's the way the water was at grandfather's mill – hemlock,

> my grandma used to gather it on foot – owls, listen to them, I haven't heard them hoot that monotonically since childhood."[5]

I mention this because those admonitory and appalling visions of the destruction of civilization and all humanity, of a time of great murders, were written not only by a highly educated intellectual who worked out in his mind all possible consequences of the contemporary world's sinister tendencies, but also by a somewhat conservative countryman alarmed by the direction in which humanity was racing. But the era of appalling visions was still far off. In the meantime, very much to the contrary, it seemed that the world was taking on a better, more pleasing form.

In everyone's life, relationships with those who are nearest play a defining role – above all, relationships with one's parents and siblings. And the amorous relationships of one's adult years usually are based on the relationship one had as a child with one's parents.

With respect to Karel Čapek's childhood and the relationships within his family, one can find much in Čapek's own works and correspondence, as well as in the work of his brother Josef, and above all in the reminiscences of his sister Helena's books. We can also learn a great deal from several characteristics of Čapek's personality. What is often seen in creative artists, and especially visual artists, is the significant role played by a mother's love in the creation of their characters. In the case of the Čapek family, it's quite possible to conclude that his mother's love for Karel was nearly pathological. To all appearances, in her relationship with her youngest child she was compensating for the absence of romantic love, and this, it may at least be supposed, she could not obtain from her husband.

In the recollection of all three siblings, the papa appears to have been an unequivocal figure: a powerful man thoroughly devoted to his medical calling, which in a small town at the turn of the twentieth century had something of a National-Revivalist aspect. "At our house everyone went in for books," Karel's older brother Josef recalled. "Sometimes we surprised father in his consulting room when, in those rarest of moments, he had spare time, he would write a lecture or occasional verse, or "paint" – that is, copy reproductions from magazines in pencil or in chalk."[6]

And from their sister Helena:

> Papa was large and powerful. He would take us along with him, whenever the thought struck him, to workshops whirring with fearsome, evil-smelling machines, or to the opulent homes of millionaires. And he would take us down quite different roads to the most wretched of huts, where he had to stoop way down to get through the very low door and, after that, bend still lower over the bed of a wheezing invalid.
>
> He knew all sorts of springs and called them all by their ancient names, and he also knew the names of the forests and mountains, as if he were christening them himself that very moment.[7]

According to the children, he was a man fully dedicated to his work, who almost never had a free moment. "Medical practice, house, garden – not even these were enough for this strong, athletic man; he was immoderately fond of the entire region, bestowing on it a generous and compassionate affection. That shy, quiet little town's day had come, and Papa, without even realizing it, became its soul."[8]

For the children, Papa was a paragon of work and relationships with people.

> He wanted us to be first in everything, in physical labors, helping at home, and completing our assignments; he instilled in us such self-discipline that we couldn't manage to idle away a second. He trusted us, and it wasn't possible to fool him; that's why we all did our honest best when it came to using our intellect. He loved us beyond measure, but so unostentatiously that we didn't even suspect it, nor did he ever cuddle us gawky scamps. And still less was he easy on himself; comforts and coddling aroused horror and shame in him, for they were 'unseemly.' The one proper rule for all things in life was disciplined work.[9]

Another person who recalled Dr. Čapek was the proprietor of At the Golden Cross, the tavern where he was a regular patron: "He had a straightforward nature, he was ambitious, and he held the position of both municipal and factory doctor. He was head of the town council the whole time he was in Úpice, and many things that were accomplished in the town were his doing. Čapek's favorite place was his garden, where he sweated away at his work, his wooden pipe in his mouth, and every now and then he'd come here to the tavern for a glass of beer. He'd do that several times a day."[10]

We might mention at this point the idyllic picture of the doctor's home in *Krakatit*, perhaps the most idyllic setting in all of Čapek's work, with its grumbling, good-natured doctor. Also living in the house are a beautiful daughter, a maid, and a dog; only a mother is missing from the scene.

Čapek's mother was obviously a contrary woman. Her father, a miller, baker, and trader in grain in Hronov, would have welcomed his only daughter marrying a rich miller, or someone else who would take over the family business. The daughter, however, succumbed to the insistence of a young doctor and married him, although she was "secretly in love with a handsome assistant teacher in Hronov."[11] In quick succession she gave birth to three children: daughter Helen in January 1886, son Josef in March of the following year, and lastly, in January 1890, Karel. She was obviously unhappy in her marriage, and she took no satisfaction in her wifely role, where her primary and sole concerns were to manage the household and raise the children. She suffered from bouts of depression which gave way to fits of hysteria. During some of these periods, she refused to communicate with members of her family, with one exception: her youngest, her darling, on whom she bestowed all her unstable feelings. "Mama spoke only to the maid and to Karel, and he passed her words on to all of us, even to Papa. Poor Papa, spartan by nature, did what he could; he built a nice white house for his family and didn't even notice how impossible life was in it. Two big, fancy rooms to fulfill

Mama's dreams, and occasional social gatherings; we were forbidden even to set foot in these rooms. Our parents made do with a small bedroom, and between them, in the middle of the bed, slept Karel. Things went badly if he snuggled closer to his father than to his mother."[12] The mother subsequently separated the two beds that had been pushed together to form the marriage bed, and this was not, according to the daughter, merely a symbolic act. Her love for her youngest always had pathological aspects; she lived in incessant fear for his health, and whenever Karel fell ill she became hysterical. "And Karel, too, might contract inflammation of the kidneys or rheumatism, just as she had! Her hypochondria grew in regard to both of them and she no longer believed anyone, no less Papa, and not even his colleagues from around the region. The only one of us she tolerated near her, and would have preferred to imprison within her body once again, was Karel."[13] She went to great lengths to tear him away from the rest of the family, so that she might have him all to herself.

"The hysteria of her immoderate love for him made us shudder, and all our lives long we used a self-invented, restrained but at the same time wholesomely racy secret language only the three of us understood. We loved our mother wholeheartedly, but there emanated from her a certain unhealthiness, a hidden world of good permeated by evil, an instinctual propensity for believing more in evil than in good, in the worse of any two things. It was no wonder that in our childish way we searched ruthlessly for a countermeasure and tore Karel away from her querulous, unreasonable love."[14]

On a conscious level Karel Čapek managed to free himself from this unhealthy love.

On a conscious level he respected and loved his father and became, like him, a workaholic, loving to boast that a single day was sufficient to accomplish anything. Whenever a father appears in his writing, he is strong, optimistic, and grumpily good-hearted, be it the old doctor in *Krakatit* or the protagonist's father in *An Ordinary Life*, the novel with the most autobiographical snippets, such as: "I loved my father because he was strong and straightforward. Touching him gave me a feeling like leaning against a wall or a strong pillar."[15] This characterization is close to that of old Dr. Čapek in his daughter's memoirs. The novel's portrait of the mother, too, wholly corresponds to her portrait in her daughter's book, an important key to understanding much of what seems odd, puzzling, or even inexplicable in Čapek's later life.

> Mother was not so straightforward a person as Father; she was far more emotional, irritable, and overflowing with love for me; there were moments when she pressed me to her and sighed: My only one, I would die for you! Later on, when I was a boy, these outbursts of love would bother me; I would have been ashamed if my friends saw my mother kissing me so passionately. But when I was quite small, her fervent love placed me in a state of subjugation, a state of serfdom, and my love for her was full of fear. When I whimpered and she took me in her arms, I felt as if I were dissolving; I liked terribly much to sob on her soft neck, wet with tears and a child's dribbling ... I connected my mother with my need to cry and be soothed, and with my morbid need to enjoy my pain. I did not feel an aversion to such feminine manifestations of emotion until I became a five-year-old little man. Then, I turned my head away when she pressed me to her bosom and I wondered what she got from it. Papa was better, he smelt of tobacco and strength. ... She cherished the idea that I was a weak child, that some misfortune might happen to me, or that I might die ... That's why she was always rushing out to see where I was and what I was doing ... And she kept asking: Are you all right? Do you have a tummy ache? ... This notion has remained with me all my life: that my mother had to do with illness and with pain.

Interesting and telling also is the conclusion of this obviously autobiographical passage about the protagonist's parents.

> They made a decent man out of me, they made me in their image. I wasn't as strong as Father nor as great at loving as

> Mother, but at least I was industrious and honest, sensitive and, to a certain extent, ambitious – that ambition is certainly a heritage of my mother's vitality; what in me used to feel wounded most likely came from my mother. And you see, even that had its place, its role; and along with the man who tries his best, there is in me a man who dreams.[16]

We would be hard pressed to find better words to let us grasp the roots of Čapek's personality. And in this same novel we find yet another indication of his mother's influence on the protagonist's personality, one which almost too closely corresponds to Čapek's personal experience: "[I]t was Mother who fostered in me my lifelong timidity and lack of self-confidence, that physical feeling of inferiority I grew up with. It was Mother's pathological love that led me to regard myself as the object of endless nursing and coddling, an inclination I nestled up to, practically indulged, whenever the first tap of a real illness gave me the opportunity."[17]

Josef Čapek's wife, Jarmila, also left a succinct account of the damage the mother did to the family: "Her lack of emotional fulfillment and her excitability often caused the mother to lash out at and hurt the family members in their routine, everyday life, and perhaps she was to blame for certain biases, phobias, and misogyny in both brothers. She was immensely gifted and perceptive, and I heard the doctor say that 'women like her often have sons who are geniuses.'"[18]

As so many pathologically loving mothers do, Karel's mother encouraged his awareness of his own exceptionality and intensified his extraordinary sensitivity, while at the same time fostering his lifelong hypochondria by doing her best to gain the favor and sympathy of others by emphasizing her own suffering.

In an effort to escape from his mother's overemotionality, Karel clung more tightly to the rest of his family. He often recalled, above all, his grandmother, the one on his mother's side. Most singular, however, was the relationship between the two brothers. With a few exceptions, in the early days of their careers they jointly composed all their literary works – or at least they jointly signed them.

According to the accounts of their contemporaries, they broke into artistic circles as an inseparable duo.

> The Brothers Čapek's dual appearance immediately attracted attention, but their true legitimacy, of course, lay in their writing of sensationally brilliant little grotesques in all sorts of veins, which they published in such journals as *Stopa* (Footprint). To date, the signature under these pieces had been 'Brothers Čapek,' assumed by readers to be the enigmatic pseudonym of some brilliant big-city writer. Now we had him here before us, in his twofold form. It was an even greater surprise that the appearance of both brothers contrasted utterly with the dandified, worldly, metropolitan posturing of their prose. For the two of them stepped into the Café Union in the same sort of studenty, milk-chocolate-brown outfits, with identical middle-class bowler hats and neckties, with healthily rosy complexions, and with their dark hair painstakingly combed flat against their heads, so that, taken all in all, they were very nearly the embodiment of freshness and health, and above all unpretentiousness, maybe even rusticity. From their first day at the Union they emphasized that they wrote in unison, an indivisible duo. They walked through the door together, sat next to one another, and simultaneously consumed black coffee and crescent rolls. It seemed that even out on the street it was impossible to encounter one without the other.[19]

Karel worked with his brother on the editorial staff of *Národní listy* (National Pages), and when Josef was let go, Karel decided to leave with him. He accepted a new position at *Lidové noviny* (The People's Newspaper) on the condition that his brother would work there as well. Even after Josef had married, the two lived together in Říční Street, in the Malá Strana quarter. Not until October 1923, when their parents moved into the apartment, was Josef severed from his brother, albeit for a short time only. Not quite two years later, the two of them built a two-family house in the garden suburb of

Vinohrady, on Úzký ulice (Narrow Street), which in 1947 became ulice Bratří Čapků (Street of the Brothers Čapek). It is unquestionable that Josef, contemplative and in his own way deeper or more authentic, had a lifelong influence on his brother, and that it was he who encouraged Karel's interest in the visual arts. Nevertheless, on a subconscious or unconscious level, Karel never broke free from his mother's influence, and I am convinced that it was his mother who fatally influenced Karel's relationships with women, and that she contributed to his anxiety regarding conjugal life, even though he tried to explain it away on all other possible grounds.

3. Visual Artist or Writer?

A comprehensive volume entitled *Karel Čapek in Photographs* was published in Prague in 1991. In one of the photos, taken on the last day of 1911, Karel Čapek is a young man, a student of literature, esthetics, and philosophy, standing with his brother and several painters and architects, all members of the avant-garde Group of Visual Artists. To the uninitiated, the photograph shows no more than thirteen youthful faces, but they are those of the foremost figures in modern Czech art: the painter Emil Filla, the sculptor Otto Gutfreund, and the architects Pavel Janák, Josef Gočár, Josef Chochol, and Vlatislav Hofman, all of whom had a considerable hand in shaping twentieth-century Prague and, during the interwar period, made it one of the centers of modern architecture. But among them can be found two very young writers, Čapek and his lifelong friend František Langer, thus confirming that both these writers were deeply interested in the visual arts (Karel Čapek was skilled at making witty drawings as well as photographs, and he illustrated a number of his books, in particular his travel books). Their appearance in this photo also confirmed the fact that at that time the visual arts and architecture were the most rapidly evolving and revolutionary of all the arts. Anyone not wishing to seem conservative and well outside contemporary trends, had to take a position on the efforts of such giants as Picasso, Braque, Ernst, Arp, Zadkin, and Le Corbusier.

Karel Čapek, surely under the influence of his brother, professed the same beliefs as the other young artists, and in a succession of articles he advocated modern art – above all cubism – and explained its principles. "But one day the art lover will come to understand the new art, and at that moment something better and more valuable will fall into his lap: the new art will appeal to him as naturally and inevitably as what he holds dear today. For modern art is not here to be understood, but to be appealing, to be beautiful. Never was art capable of so many nuances and kinds of beauty as now, when the most robust, refined beauty fits into the frame of a single point of view. It is as if we were deciphering a system of signs: suddenly what till now were letters turns out to be a personal confession, points of view, an experience..."[1]

To the objection that modern art is estranged from reality, that it defiles reality and merely transforms it into geometric shapes, he countered: "But reality, at least in art, is always what is made of it; every art finds its own solution and will go on solving. Its model isn't external, in the nature of things, but what is in man himself, a spiritual and poetic creature who gives things his own form and measure..."[2]

Certainly his interest in the visual arts deepened during his stay in Paris, where he had followed his brother in the spring of 1911 and where, at the Sorbonne, he took courses in German Studies for the remainder of the semester. The greatest Czech Čapek expert, Miroslav Halík, quotes from an undated manuscript containing Čapek's reminiscences of Paris, which testify to his enchantment with the city, at that time as much a promised land for painters as for writers:

> Like so many of our young people, before the war I traveled to Paris as if to the Holy See of artists, formally as a student at the Sorbonne, but in reality as an unknown, intoxicated pilgrim knocking about between the Louvre and the shop of Ambroise Vollard, between the second-hand bookstalls along the Seine and the bohemian cafés and brasseries on the Rive Gauche ... As a result, the enchantment was deeper still; I think I'll not be rid of it as long as I live. Enchantment with the people, the life, the art...[3]

It stands to reason that, after returning from the "global metropolis" of Paris, the young men must have looked upon Prague as a provincial town. What was famed and acclaimed at home seemed poor and trifling in comparison with what was happening out in the world. Both of them joined the Group of Visual Artists; no literary review served as a platform for the younger generation except for *Umělecký měsíčník* (Arts Monthly), which the young artists launched as their organ.

Modernity became the most important criterion for artistic and even spiritual efforts. Karel Čapek expressed his allegiance to the visual artists shortly before the outbreak of the First World War, in one of his numerous letters to the older, hot-headed poet S. K. Neumann:

> It is possible that young people will not be able to exhibit or be reproduced, that they will be completely suppressed by the makers of kitsch ... these battles will probably be grim and the young people's cause is uncertain, so you can understand that our most pressing interest now is this, even for me; you know that I belong more to a generation of visual artists than of writers.[4]

While there were outstanding cubist works in the Czech visual arts and architecture, in literature there were few successes. If the Čapeks had not written the works that later made them famous, their first collaborative play, the comedy *The Fateful Game of Love*, would likely be forgotten today. But before Karel Čapek or his contemporaries could create what for them, in theory at least, embodied modernism, the modern age showed its Janus face. (Surprisingly, the one who at that time was filling the Czech demand for poetry with new subject matter was Neumann himself, a member of the older generation; with inordinate fervor Neumann celebrated the achievements of a technological civilization in his *New Songs*). The war began on St. Anna's Day, 1914, a war then unprecedented in its bloodiness and brutality.

4. Civilized Optimism Swept Away

Airplanes – symbols of the modern age, they took off into traditional skies and dropped nontraditional, thoroughly modern bombs. The neon lights so loved by modern artists were extinguished, and the machines so praised by poets were now running at top speed to produce tanks, machine guns, mines, and ammunition. Magazines and journals which not that long before had been published in the Czech Lands by the dozens, ceased to exist, their place taken by news from the front. "In the morning darkness, hysteria, weeping, souls in purgatory. In the afternoon disgust, numbness ... Life of former times, when will you return?" asked Josef Čapek, and he continued: "One hour is wound around another like the strands of a long rope, a great noose from which I hang, from which we all hang..."[1]

And Karel, devotee of modern life and technology, the dandy who loved his walking stick, hat, padded shoulders, and charm, who sneered at everything that seemed old-fashioned and conservative, confided to the poet S. K. Neumann: "Much melancholy has devolved upon mankind, and it is detestable to me that might will triumph in the end ... Art must not serve might ... I think that I am slowly becoming an anarchist, that this is only another label for my privateness, and I think that you will understand this in the sense of being against collectivity." And in the same letter: "Art alone is brave, and no other bravery or might impresses me."[2] Later, in a 1932 series of articles for the journal *Přítomnost* (The Present Day), in which he attempted to characterize his attitudes before and during the war, Čapek wrote: "Shipwrecked and swept away was the world of the young, prewar Europeans, swept away was trust, civilized optimism, naïve activism, the joyful feeling of cooperation and being part of a community."[3]

Posturing disappeared, and only the solitary man remained. It was as if nothing remained from all that used to be. Older friends disappeared on the battlefields, only his brother Josef remained – he was in the barracks, saved by his poor eyesight. Both brothers eluded the front, Karel because of a condition in which his spine was slowly becoming immobilized. He was spared the battlefield, but death searched for him in other places. His malady was later diagnosed as rheumatism of the vertebrae, and he had painful gout in nearly his entire spinal column.

In these disconsolate times, Čapek found refuge in his work. In October 1915, he completed his studies, and his dissertation, entitled "The Objective Method in Esthetics in Relation to the Creative Arts," was considered excellent, as were the results of both his rigorous doctoral examinations. (Karel, unlike his brother Josef, had been an "exemplary" student since primary school.) As soon as his studies were completed, he endeavored to dedicate himself to what, from that moment, became the substance of his life's work. There was no hint in his writing of anything that had preceded it in prewar days, but at the same time it did not even begin to suggest what he would write after the war ended. First of all, true to his love of France, he began translating modern French poetry. In his own words, he felt this to be a "literary expression of solidarity and of a spiritual connection with the nation that lost so much blood at Verdun, for a cause that was also a cause in our own hearts."[4] It is worth noting that, not counting several youthful poems and some political – often polemical – remarks in verse for his newspaper, Čapek practically never wrote poetry. Yet at the outset of this world-famous playwright and prose writer's career stands a book of translated poems, translations moreover so outstanding that they became the foundation for modern Czech poetry. Vitĕslav Nezval, one of the founders of Czech surrealism and without doubt one of the great modern poets, wrote of the translations, "Never before Čapek's encroachment into poetry was such a tone heard in the Czech language. None of his literary predecessors gave us poetry in which iambs and dactyls would lose their numerical pathos so completely as they do in Čapek's ... Never before 1920 did poetry speak to me with such a unique and intensive voice as in Čapek's Apollinaire, Vildrac, Fort, Birot, Jammes..."[5]

Another of the foremost Czech poets of the younger generation, František Hrubín, wrote in the afterword to his own translations of Verlaine: "Most especially are we grateful to Karel Čapek. Newborn Czech poetry was rocked to the rhythms of his translations..."[6]

Čapek was not only translating, of course. During this same time, his first prose written without the collaboration of his older brother appeared in various journals. In the fall of 1917, his first book of short stories was published, *Wayside Crosses*. These stories are witness to the change in his outlook on life: they are filled with speculation about the meaning of what people do, and they repeatedly introduce situations in which their protagonists encounter something irrational. One example is a single human footprint in a pristine, snow-covered field. Another is the strange encounter between two brothers who, after many years apart, unexpectedly meet in a tavern; one of them inexplicably disappears, yet no one has seen him leave. A third time, it is the mysterious word, "Return," written on a wall by one of the characters, a man who is not aware that he himself has written it or when he might have done so.

At the outset of these stories, Čapek sets up a conflict between one character who seeks a rational explanation and another who believes that irrationality is a part of life. "Well, according to mechanistics, that atrocious doctrine, the only truly natural thing would be: a miracle. The only thing that would answer man's deepest questions ... If things came to pass in a way that was natural for our souls, miracles would happen."[7] And in the story about the single footprint: "But I too want to be saved, and I'm ready for a miracle – – for something to come and turn my life around."[8] And in "The Mountain": "Only when confronted with something enigmatic does one become conscious of one's spirit – and tremble and feel awe."[9] Man never attains certainty, of course. "Everything is equally no good. It's just as bad to beat as not to beat someone," the police detective in the same story paraphrases the famous quotation from *Hamlet.* "Everything has its dark side and its faults ... What's most reasonable is to obey. To comply with orders."[10] In "The Lost Way," the nameless hero ponders: "Your logic is woven from routine, and the roads you travel from thousands of bygone footsteps; and that is why you leave everything behind and begin to stray off course, so that you can search in the unknown. That is where you find what is most strange and what is furthest from routine."[11]

Čapek himself asserted that in these stories he was interested in no more than the evocation of experiences and impressions – of landscape, snow, speed, drunkenness, a sunny day, water. But we can never completely believe authors whose calling, after all, is to dream up stories, when they speak about their own work (and this especially applies to Čapek). At any rate, in the closing of the letter to Neumann where he characterized his prose works in that way, Čapek added:

> But the ideas that are in the book, for example man's deliverance in moments of freedom – even though I wasn't concerned about them – apparently reflect an obsession or personal crisis and, primarily, the war-time atmosphere. The war hurled man horribly into his own internal world, and when he was at his most miserable, he felt inside himself something nonheroic, of course, terrified and sad, but nevertheless free and unenslavable, his own soul. There is neither philosophy nor religiosity in this, but rather blind, dogged feeling."[12]

It's a wonder how Čapek, who in later years was perhaps the most direct of all Czech writers in his reaction to political events, could write during the war years a book impervious to any mention of war, of suffering, of hunger, of everything that was consuming the lives of the people amongst whom he was living. His stories dealt more with metaphysical questions than with people.

In these stories there is plenty of unsophistication, preaching, abstract pondering, exaltation, and sentiment. Often, the stories and their characters simply demonstrate the author's theses; this was noted in contemporary criticism, and its most important representative, F. X. Šalda, considered Čapek's writing to be merely at the margins of philosophy, denying him any capacity for poetic vision. (Only on the rare occasion did Šalda praise Čapek's literary ability, and then mostly from other motives which had nothing to do with Čapek. The young Čapek, in turn, attacked Šalda several times, unscrupulously.)

Čapek had not yet mastered either the brilliant storytelling or the natural command of language with which he astounded people in his later works, and he was still unable to avoid a degree of bookishness in the dialogue of his characters. On the other hand, *Wayside Crosses* is in its own way more authentic than his later books. In these stories, Čapek did not attempt to separate his characters from himself, nor their questions and problems from his own questions and problems. Nor did he try to connect them to large societal issues. The wonder he felt concerning the mysteries and peculiarities of life, which he was later able to express splendidly in thoroughly concrete observations, he still expressed in universal formulations. In literature these formulations are not very impressive, but they do make it possible for a writer to express his thoughts and feelings precisely and without any possibility of hiding.

In addition to stories whose main theme is seeking for answers to primarily philosophical questions, we also find stories in *Wayside Crosses* with more plot to them, and even an attempt at a love story ("Love Song"). In his relationship with a woman, Čapek's protagonist in this story is clearly shy and inexperienced (and this will remain true in the majority of Čapek's later works). A few platonic infatuations aside, at age twenty-six Čapek had obviously not had experience with women, and his strongest emotional relationship, as is also obvious from the stories, was still his connection to his brother Josef.

Wayside Crosses anticipates Čapek's future work in the way it poses uncomfortable questions and seeks answers about the nature of truth: what are the limits of our knowledge and experience, and what should be each person's mission in life? Čapek's lifelong theme is suggested most forcefully in the story "Help!" This very short story tells of a man who, in the middle of the night, is awakened from a dream by "a woman's trembling voice from outside, pleading, 'Please, come at once and help us!'" The sleeper does not want to get up out of bed, and he convinces himself that he cannot in fact help anyone. "For that matter, how could I be of any help at all? ... Do I know anything that might be useful? My God, I can't even offer advice or consolation; I wouldn't know the words to ease even a portion of someone's burden, nor could I give sympathetic support to anyone. All I want is to be left in peace, to be rid of people..." After all, he realizes, he is not even able to help himself. But he cannot bear to do nothing, and so he first turns on a light so that it can be seen through the window, indicating that he's awake and is prepared to help in some way. Then he sets out into the darkness to look for whoever is in need of help. During his journey through the night he realizes that, up to this moment, his life has had no goal, no direction, that it resembles a prison in which the days cannot be distinguished one from the other.

> Lord, Brož whispered ... I was waiting for your help, for miraculous deliverance, for a great event to occur, a sudden light through the cracks, a forceful knock on the door with a strong voice commanding: Lazarus, rise! I've waited so many years for the strong voice of the conqueror; you never came, and I no longer count on it.
>
> But to the extent that I am still waiting, then it is for help and deliverance. For a voice that will summon me from my prison. Perhaps it won't be strong, but so weak that I must back

> it up with my own voice. Perhaps it won't be a commanding but a beseeching voice: Lazarus, rise, so that you can help us! ...
>
> Perhaps you've been waiting for an earthquake; listen rather for a soft, beseeching cry. Perhaps the day you await will come not as a holiday, but as an ordinary day, one of life's Mondays, a new day.[13]

In his pre-war study of Čapek, the eminent structuralist critic Jan Mukařovský claimed that in *Wayside Crosses* Čapek discovered a narrative method in which "the event we suspect to be the main topic of the narrative remains hidden to us. Even though we have an epic work before us which is not lacking in plot tension, the fact that should be the subject of the narrative is hidden. This very clearly indicates the distance between event as 'reality' and narrative as a report on that reality..." According to Mukařovský, Čapek "tried in *Wayside Crosses* for the first time (later he was to do this many times in other ways) to separate narrative as meaningful totality from event as fact; he then proceeded in such a manner that he disengaged the narrative from the event as an insoluble mystery. He succeeded in evoking epic tension without a subject, a tension so strong that it is able to set in motion even a static description."[14]

It is possible to agree with this explanation of the narrative style in *Wayside Crosses* – and in the last-mentioned story, Čapek abandoned entirely the original motif of calling for help and substituted instead philosophical reflection. Equally, in the much longer story "The Mountain," the author paid more attention to the Hamlet-like reflections of a police detective than to the question of the dead man's or the murderer's identities. Even though Čapek sometimes moves on to a completely different event from the one with which he opens a story (we see it in *The Makropulos Secret*, for instance) or turns from the principal event to a completely different one (as in *Krakatit*), he usually wanders away from the basic event for short periods of time only; in his later works, however, he develops his plots epically and brings his basic plot line to a conclusion.

5. Not Two Sheaves, But Rather Thousands of Stalks

Čapek's doctoral work at Charles University in Prague was in philosophy and esthetics, but in truth he had been studying philosophy his entire life, and during his youth he published well-informed analyses of philosophical works. Shortly before the beginning of the war he attended a series of lectures on American pragmatism. The lecturer was the future president of the republic Dr. Edvard Beneš, and it was he who awakened Čapek's interest in this philosophical approach. Čapek prepared a well-grounded paper on pragmatism, which was published in 1918 as "Pragmatism, or a Philosophy for a Practical Life." It was not a very long essay, but we cannot pass it by for one very simple reason: Čapek accepted the basic tenets of this philosophy, and for nearly his entire life deduced from them a way of solving the fundamental social and human problems about which he wrote so urgently. It will be useful at this point to mention at least briefly this almost forgotten philosophical school of the Anglo-Saxon world.

To properly consider pragmatism, we must return to the beginning of the twentieth century, a time of sharply accelerating scientific and technological development. Many thoughtful people felt that the explanations of the world found in traditional religions could not satisfactorily respond to questions that had been disturbing people for centuries. Nor could philosophy, which was increasingly becoming an academic discipline far removed from life and its problems. People thus found themselves in a spiritual vacuum, without intellectual or moral support. The "great ideologies" of nationalism and the Marxist theory of so-called dialectic materialism attempted to fill this vacuum. Marxism in particular proclaimed that it knew the truth about all societal (and scientific) problems, and it offered its radical and singularly correct dialectical method, which was allegedly capable of exploring the most complex processes in society and nature, and finding solutions. Marxism was accepted by the social democratic parties organized at the Second International as a theory which offered a revolutionary remedy to the societal problems of its time.

Like Marxism, pragmatism also responded to the contemporary societal and spiritual situation through its focus on the practical problems of people's lives. However, the similarity between Marxism and pragmatism ends there. Pragmatism had much more modest ambitions and most assuredly did not attempt to change the societal order by revolutionary means. According to William James, one of its main proponents, pragmatism was not supposed to serve any particular purpose; rather, it was intended to be "a method of settling metaphysical disputes which otherwise might be interminable ... The pragmatic method ... is to try to interpret each notion by tracing its respective practical consequences. What difference would it practically make to anyone if this notion rather than that notion were true?" Such an approach also, understandably, had consequences for a conception of truth: "If no practical difference whatever can be traced, then the alternatives mean practically the same thing, and all dispute is idle."[1] Whether the Earth was created by God or evolved the way materialists say is not important, simply because no practical consequences for the life of humankind follow from it. Useful argument should concern only questions which have some practical meaning. A man can be a materialist, just as he can believe in God – let him follow what he is more comfortable with; what will bring him more delight or be more useful will be more truthful for him than anything else. It is important, however, that he not force his truth upon others. Moreover, what we recognize as truth should not be in conflict with sound reasoning, and it should stand up to close scrutiny. The pragmatists' attitude toward truth was relativistic. "The practical value of true ideas," James reasoned, "is thus primarily derived from the practical importance of their objects to us[2] ... 'The true,' to put it very briefly, is only the expedient in the way of our thinking, just as 'the right' is only the expedient in the way of our behaving."[3]

Pragmatists responded to the dominant philosophers of their time by reproaching them for being too remote from life, for holding real human problems in contempt. According to James, "[t]he more absolutistic philosophers dwell on so high a level of abstraction that they never even try to come down. The absolute mind which they offer us, the mind that makes our universe by thinking it, might, for aught they show us to the contrary, have made any one of a million other universes just as well as this. You can deduce no single actual particular from the notion of it ... What you want," he told his American audiences, "is a philosophy that will not only exercise your powers of intellectual abstraction, but that will make some positive connexion with this actual world of finite human lives."[4]

People need a philosophy that is be able to connect them with the real world of finite human life. In a world ruled by an absolute spirit or Creator, everything is given, truth as well as evil. But in the real world in which we live, nothing is given in advance; it is a world of possibilities, it is an open space for our actions.

While academic philosophers, in an attempt to answer the great questions of the world and existence, were offering such abstract concepts as God, Reason, Law, Spirit, Nature, Polarity, Dialectical Progress, and Idea, the pragmatists avoided abstractions altogether. In opposition to abstract concepts they placed the actual experiences of each individual. They emphasized that abstract concepts can result only from human experience; however, human experiences are variable, because they are subject to new experiences and newly discovered facts. This is how people advance beyond concepts that for centuries have been considered valid, such as the Ptolemaic system, Euclidian space, and Aristotelian logic.

The world that surrounds us is understandably independent of us; but at the same time, what we assert about the world is a human construct. We fashion and alter the world with our knowledge and our actions. Thus did the pragmatists arrive at another important question: what does it mean if we are aware that reality actually depends on us, on our actions? The answer was again practical: we are as creative in the sphere of knowledge as we are in the world of action. The world is waiting to be fashioned by our activity. People create their own truths in the world, and this task increases their dignity and responsibility. It was the emphasis on each person accepting responsibility for his actions that attracted Čapek, who wrote in his treatise on pragmatism:

> In his theory of conflict, Dewey attempts to explain the individuality of truth. Where it is a matter of truth or error, it is up to us to assume the closest, most direct relationship to the object of our thought; it is from this relationship that we must create our own life crisis. Only conflict gives birth to an unequivocal, definitive, and consequential decision, guaranteed by our taking complete responsibility. We are responsible for truth obtained in this manner, and this truth is for us the only fixed and binding truth; if it is personal, it is at least responsibly personal. Truth would then be that content of our thought which we guarantee by taking responsibility ... This theme of responsibility pervades Dewey's philosophy, and it is also the moral authority he placed above all the labors of our intellect. Better for philosophy to wander in search of human good than to be infallible and without any value for a moral life."[5]

The views of the proponents of this philosophy certainly reflected the atmosphere of a dominant America at the beginning of the twentieth century, an intoxication with the results of production. The spirit of the New World manifested itself in the emphasis on success as the criterion of truth, as well as intolerance for others' criteria, and in the emphasis on sound reasoning as an important criterion for knowledge and understanding. Not even in America, however, did pragmatism find many adherents, and even some of its proponents parted company with it, including John Dewey.

Čapek's original interest in pragmatism involved its American lineage. He wrote later:

> And when Wilson gave Germany an ultimatum, the young intellectual was turning in a book about Anglo-American pragmatism. Friends, it was not 'the philosophy of a generation,' it was politics, an intellectual connection to Wilson's America; it was in its own way a small crumb of what is called 'internal resistance.' Not that it would have any weight, but it was experienced more deeply than you think. It was the creed of democracy and freedom, it was the democratic spirit of the republican and civil West, which – in the simplified wartime ideology – stood against the caesarism and militarism of the Central Powers.[6]

It is entirely possible that the first impulse which led Čapek to pragmatism was political. The young writer-philosopher wanted to express defiance toward the powers that had unleashed the war and that for the majority of Czechs embodied national and social oppression. Nevertheless, Čapek remained true to this philosophy throughout his life, and it was in its spirit that he sought a way out of the great conflicts that often formed the content of his work, and this surely cannot be explained by a wartime preoccupation.

As I have already said, this period of Čapek's life was also a time of great ideologies that proclaimed unquestionable, all-encompassing truths and solutions. Čapek, however, refused to accept any simplified, ideological view of the world. In 1920, he published in a journal a philosophical piece in which he had Pilate talk with Jesus's follower Joseph of Arimathea about truth (this piece was later collected with similar stories in the book *Apocryphal Tales*).

> "You are a strange sort of people and you talk a great deal," Pilate says to Joseph. "You have all sorts of pharisees, prophets, saviors and other sectarians. Each of you makes his own truth

> and forbids all other truths. As if a carpenter who makes a new chair were to forbid people sitting on any other chair that someone else had made before him. As if the making of a new chair canceled out all the old chairs. It's entirely possible that the new chair is better, more beautiful, and more comfortable than the others, but why in heaven's name shouldn't a tired man be able to sit on whatever wretched, worm-eaten, or rock-hard chair he likes?"

When Joseph refuses this comparison of truth to a chair (which is, of course, simplifying) and asserts that truth is like an order to be obeyed and is the only valid order, Pilate asks which truth for everyone he means. Joseph answers: "The one in which I believe."

> "There you have it," Pilate says slowly. "It is only *your* truth after all. You people are like little children who believe that the whole world ends at their horizon and that nothing lies beyond it. The world is a larger place, Joseph, and there is room in it for many things. I think that there is actually room for many truths ... I believe, I believe passionately that truth exists and that we recognize it. We recognize it, yes, but which of us? I, or you, or perhaps all of us? I believe that each of us has his share of it, both he who says yes and he who says no. If those two joined together and understood each other, the whole of truth would be known. Of course, yes and no can't join together, but people always can; there is more truth in people than in words."[7]

Another aspect of pragmatism that suited Čapek was its very active and at the same time responsible approach to life. From the English philosopher Ferdinand C. S. Schiller he singled out the assertion that in every regard the world can be made better than it is, because it is boundlessly improvable. We cooperate in such efforts, and we take collective responsibility for the results. This position was considerably closer to Čapek's own beliefs than the radical positions and revolutionary views asserting that the world can be made better only by a violent change in social relations.

For Čapek, the world was always filled with possibilities for action. In a 1924 essay entitled "Why Am I Not a Communist?" he wrote an extensive answer to the question, ending it: "Today's world does not need hatred, but good will, acceptance, harmony, and cooperation; it needs a moral, kinder climate. I think that, with a bit of ordinary love and kindness, miracles can still be accomplished."[8]

At the end of that same year he published the article "Ignoramus and Ignorabimus," in which, with impassioned articulation, he restates his lifelong relativistic creed. In contrast to the man who believes that he knows the single, correct truth, "whose active participation is expressed mainly in the form of rage against other opinions and also in the constant repetition of certain cardinal words," Čapek constructs his ideal:

> Worse and more difficult is the other, 'indifferent' road. You never know beforehand on which side you will find good or bad. Never do you finish with comparisons, never are you immune to disappointment, and no hope is foreign to you. You see not two sheaves, but rather thousands of stalks, and this multiplies your possibilities for choice a thousand times over. Stalk by stalk you gather what is good and useful in the human world, stalk by stalk you sort the wheat from the weeds, and no Ant King comes to your aid; you yourself must complete the entire task. You don't call for the oppression of thousands, but for the oppression of one at a time; you must invalidate one truth in order to find thousands. You cannot see the world just because you want to help it. You cannot fight for truth, because he who fights cannot see ... Your certainty is not in principles, but in facts; undecided in the face of principles, skeptical of words, you trust only what you see; but you are not like doubting Thomas, because the wounds you encounter cannot be probed by fingers. And when all is said and done, for want of anything more perfect, you simply believe in people.[9]

Similar thoughts, variously expressed in stories, parables, and the like appear repeatedly in Čapek's work.

6. From Tutor to Editor

Čapek's life, despite the eventfulness of the wartime years, on the whole passed rather smoothly. He did not have to go to war, and because his family was still living in the countryside, he did not suffer from the hunger that so cruelly afflicted most people in Prague. He finished his studies and, even though he had already been a regular contributor to several journals prior to the war and, during the war, together with his brother, had published his first book, *Luminous Depths* (1916), and even though he and his brother were receiving a small annuity secured for them by their father, he felt the need to find steady work. A letter has been preserved which in the summer of 1916 he sent to the writer František Kohl, librarian at the National Museum in Prague:

> I am looking for some sort of position, some steady source of income, even if the amount is small, but so far without success. I do not know if it would be possible to find a position in the Museum library or the State Archives. My preparation is only a doctorate in the field of art history and esthetics; I myself don't know what this degree makes me suited for, or if there is any place in the world where I might be needed. Would you please kindly advise me, or possibly send me some information as to whether I would have any hope at all for a position at one of these great institutions...[1]

The tone of the letter speaks to Čapek's modesty, but even more to his not particularly great desire to hide himself from the world in the cloistered environment of a library or archive. In any case, his application for a position as librarian was not answered. Instead, in the spring of 1917 he accepted the post of tutor at the castle of a patriotic Czech, Count Lažanský, in the town of Chyše in western Bohemia.

In a letter to S. K. Neumann, Čapek described his stay at the castle in the darkest possible colors: "I am still in the service of the nobility, this time at a castle; and as you can imagine, in such circumstances so much bitterness and humiliation build up in a person that if I were to begin to write, there would just be lamentations..."[2]

Čapek's grievances are not to be taken literally, because he always liked to give the impression that he was suffering. In a letter in which he was trying to recruit a friend for a similar post at the castle, he was very generous with his praise in regard to the natural beauty, the food, and the Czechness of the count's staff. Years later, he wrote about the old count with admiration and praise. But whether he was satisfied or not, his stay at the castle made it possible for him to learn about an environment which otherwise would have been closed to him, and he made use of this knowledge many times in his work, in the castle passages of *Krakatit*[3], in *An Ordinary Life*, and in *Nine Fairy Tales*. His experience as tutor also served as a source the longest and, in my opinion, the most successful of the stories in *Painful Tales,* "At the Castle."

He soon left his position as a tutor and returned to Prague. When, many years later, he recalled leaving the employ of the patriotic count, he wrote: "I left him in the fall of 1917; I told him that I was going to work at a newspaper."[4] This decision was very important. Newspapers were uniquely meaningful to Karel Čapek's life and work. *Národní listy* (National Pages), the newspaper which offered him employment, was one of the oldest and most important dailies in the country. Founded in 1861, it became the voice of such prominent Czech politicians as František Palacký, Ladislav Rieger, and the Grégrs, and nearly all of the prominent Czech writers contributed to it. At one time, one of its editors was Jan Neruda, one of the most remarkable Czech writers and journalists, whose skillfully written columns were unquestionably a primary influence on Čapek.

In the penultimate year of the war, *Narodní listy* was practically the only Czech daily given permission to be published. (This benevolence on the part of the Austrian bureaucracy had been preceded by a purge of the editorial staff, whose leading personalities – who were at the same time the leading personalities of the Austro-Hungarian resistance – were imprisoned, sentenced to death, and escaped execution only thanks to the fatal illness of Emperor Franz Josef.) The paper became even more the voice of the Czech intelligentsia. *Narodní listy* had always had a strong nationalist streak, most understandable at a time when Czechs were attempting to acquire a greater measure of independence, and especially understandable when Austro-Hungarian politics, which the Czechs never considered theirs, drew them into a war whose goals could in no way be identified with their own.

Some who write about Čapek say that he hesitated for some time between careers as an academic (that is, a philosopher or art critic) or as an artist (that is, a journalist and author). I don't think that Čapek did hesitate. He was a man who felt an intrinsic need to express his opinions on social and political questions, and on current events, as directly as possible. For this he needed contact with everyday life as well as a platform from which to speak. At a time when neither radio nor television existed, what medium other than the newspaper could meet his requirements?

In "Newspapers and Science," one of his first articles to be published in *Národní listy*, Čapek put forward the concept of the socially responsible newspaper:

> In times of peace people have often called for the cultural level of newspapers to be raised, and rightly so ... But is *this* the time and place to launch a new cultural agenda? Every thought today must be directed to the freedom of the nation and only to that! To the freedom of the nation, yes, but add to that also the freedom of an educated, free-spirited nation. And in this respect we are not fully prepared.
>
> The struggle for nationhood is not ours alone, it is a worldwide struggle. It is not about us alone, but about all mankind, about all of life ... If we want the world to be with us, then we must be with the world, at its side, at least whenever in

> history and in the present the world has striven for freedom and the ideal human condition.[5]

In the fall of 1918, the war ended with the defeat of Germany and Austria-Hungary. On October 28, the creation of a new state was declared: the Czechoslovak Republic. The first days of the new republic understandably roused great enthusiasm, but also great illusions about life in a free country. The editors of *Národní listy* welcomed independence with the impassioned, utopian declaration: “Let us all be aware that no longer are there any governments, friendly or unfriendly, above us, that we govern ourselves and that with any animosity, be it class, be it professional, be it partisan, we diminish ourselves, and thus our republic and our freedom as well. Nation, nation, we would like to teach you only love, great love...”

After the war and after the explosion of enthusiasm over independence, however, the nationalism of the politicians involved with this newspaper became more clear-cut, as did the political situation. The newly-free nation expressed not the least inclination for mutual love. The war, the poverty, and the international situation – above all the new Soviet Union, which demagogically declared itself the state of workers and peasants – radicalized all of Europe. In 1919, right in the backyard of the newly-created Czechoslovakia, there even sprang into existence (though only for a few months) a Hungarian Socialist Republic, whose army invaded Slovakia, forcing Czechoslovak soldiers to defend the territorial integrity of their new state by fighting bloody battles.

The domestic political situation in Czechoslovakia also became increasingly tense: not only did the pro-Soviet faction in the governing social democratic party grow stronger, but there were also mass demonstrations against the high prices of basic goods. Revolutionized workers joined these demonstrations and demanded the socialization of large industrial enterprises – mines, iron and steel mills – in accordance with the example set by the Soviet revolution. As rapidly as possible, the social democratic government strove to institute compromise social policies such as extensive land reform and the maintenance of economic controls, such as the regulation of the cost of living and of basic foodstuffs. Without a doubt, these socialist policies led to a constant worsening of the economic situation. In his excellent, multi-volume study of postwar Czechoslovakia, the prominent Czech journalist Ferdinand Peroutka wrote:

> Worries about supplies weighed particularly heavily in governmental thinking throughout all of 1920. Agricultural production was 30-40% below peacetime levels, which, if foodstuffs could not be imported from abroad, often meant famine. Speakers in parliament compared the republic, with reason, to a fortress under seige, where food is running out ... And thus was life lived, with imported food moving directly from railway cars to mouths, and every delay in transportation – every irregularity in the railway system (a frequent occurrence at that time), a frozen river or a delay at some reloading point – could cause a severe food crisis...[6]

The revolutionary faction in the social democratic party grew stronger during this time and attempted to overthrow the democratically elected government. In December 1920 it declared a general strike. The strike was not entirely successful, even though some two hundred thousand industrial and agricultural workers participated in it (figures differ as to the exact number of strikers, within a range of a hundred thousand). In some places outside of Prague, revolutionary workers tried to occupy factories and organize units of a Red Army. The government, however, proved to be sufficiently decisive, even at the cost of using force. In suppressing such revolutionary actions, dozens of people lost their lives (in the mining region of Mostec alone, five people died and twenty-two were wounded). The revolutionaries tried to assert their demands through negotiation, but both the government and the president rejected these demands. The revolution was squelched, and the majority of its leaders were imprisoned for a short time. "Never before," wrote Peroutka, "was the state so sharply split into two camps, into two worlds."[7]

Čapek had no sympathy for the revolutionaries. Without hesitation, he placed himself among those who stood up for democracy. As is evident from the satirical poem below, he blamed the irresponsible communist leaders for the bloodshed. He published these lines – none too successful even rhyming in the original Czech – in the humorous weekly *Nebojsa* ("Fear Not," the name of a brave little man in fairy tales):

> They played with fire, they played with the crowd,
> they played with people's pain.
> They stirred up hatred and bloodied poverty.
> Now, or never. The right moment has come.
> The world is so tired. Just a bit of terror.
> Just a bit of courage to play the leader.
> Now or never we climb.
> Now or never we wash our hands of it all.
> The state is so young, barely established.
> To arms, comrades! People, you're being duped!
> Away with the bourgeoisie! Long live the revolution!
> We've sowed incendiary words.
> Soon the street will meet its master.
> Not even violence will make our hearts beat faster.[8]

Still and all, the conservative, belligerently nationalistic environment of *Narodní listy* could not have suited him. In the spring of 1921 he and his brother left and joined the Prague office of the Brno newspaper *Lidový noviny* (People's Newspaper), where Karel remained until his death. The paper was essentially the only liberal, non-partisan daily in the country; it is unquestionably due to Čapek that *Lidový noviny* became the best Czech daily, as well. When we consider that during this period he also worked as a literary adviser and artistic director of the Vinohrady Theater, we might well say that in his professional life as a writer and journalist, he no longer experienced any big, disturbing changes. But no such thing can be said about his personal life.

7. The Shy Boy as Robber

In a letter to Olga Scheinpflugová, Karel Čapek mentions working on the novel *Krakatit*: "I'm looking forward to tomorrow; I'll be writing an erotic scene between Prokop and the princess, and I haven't written anything erotic for quite a while. Unfortunately, it seems I'm no longer able to take it very seriously."[1]

The amorous scenes between Prokop and the princess are indeed something unique in Čapek's oeuvre. He didn't take erotica seriously, but not just erotica. Love was the main if not the only theme of the theatrical comedy *The Robber*, yet after *Krakatit* he avoided love affairs with striking consistency. And the mutual relations between his male and female characters were mostly, in one way or another, unusual or even abnormal. Women might be passionate, but their passion would cast men into a subordinate, nonmasculine role. Even early on, in *Painful Tales*, we find a story about a husband who passively accepts his wife's infidelity but wants at least to make some money out of it.[2] The protagonist in another story from the same collection, finding himself actually having to touch a woman who has come to him unexpectedly to declare her love, hisses with disgust and can think of only one thing: how to get rid of her decently, but as fast as possible and forever.[3] In Čapek's play *The Makropulos Secret*, Emilia tersely responds to Gregor's declaration of love with "Well, go kill yourself then, you fool. And that will be it. That 'love' of yours is just a lot of fuss. Oh, if you only knew ... if you only knew how ridiculous you people are!"[4]

In the novel *Hordubal*, the protagonist returns from America to his farm and finds his wife in an adulterous relationship with a young farmhand. He refuses to acknowledge her infidelity, however, and in the end, despite the scorn of the entire village, he betroths his daughter to the farmhand, even though she has not yet outgrown her childhood. The protagonist of *An Ordinary Life*, who later has an "ordinary marriage," speaks anxiously about his relationship with his future wife: "[G]reat and difficult is love, and even the happiest love is horrible and its excessiveness overwhelming. We cannot love without pain, if only we would die of love, if only we could measure its vastness with suffering, for no joy can reach its bottom."[5] His later novel *The First Rescue Party* depicts a miner's unusual relationship with a romantic woman who loathes him and refuses to live with him from the outset. The husband bears this with unbelievable humility and repays her hatred with doglike love and admiration.

Why did Čapek, who possessed such masterly gifts of observation, portray human life in all its ordinary, everyday manifestations while avoiding one of the most basic human relationships – and when he did describe it, do so in the most unusual forms? I'm convinced that authors are most authentic precisely in this most intimate of realms, even though they often, like Franz Kafka, for instance, hide behind magnificent metaphors or stories which seemingly bear no resemblance whatsoever to their own stories. Čapek's stories seem to say that physical love is not what is most fundamental between loving people; something else exists, something higher, something more ideal, something more sublime. We can accept his stories as portrayals of his ideal of love – or, equally, as a distinctive portrayal of his own behavior, of his own lot in life.

When he was fifteen and still a student in Hradec Králové (he was forced to leave this school due to his activities with a students' secret society), Čapek fell in love for the first time with fourteen-year-old Anna Nepeřená. The letters to "Anielka" that remain reveal an adolescent infatuation, but they also foreshadow much of what would become symptomatic in Čapek's romantic relationships, namely, a strange mixture of sensing his own importance yet simultaneously being self-deprecatory in his relations with the one he loved and adored.

> True, I am laughable, I am not handsome nor am I interesting. And I, ugly boy and crazy poet, decadent, cripple, a jester and a fool – I, I am looking for love. It's paradoxical and comical, but absolutely tragic and horrible ... You are healthy in your soul and your heart, I am a cripple, unsuited for life ... You're young and you know how to be young ... You know how to use youth beautifully and well, and I might never have been young and never will be, because I am a cripple and a fool and a wretched human being.

It's worth noting the repetition of the word "cripple" three times by a boy who, at that time, knew nothing about the future ailment that would complicate his life.

In the same letter he defines his conception of love. Again, we have to consider the idealism of a fifteen-year-old boy, but the future will show that this conception persisted into adulthood:

> I have an odd conception of love: it is boundless sincerity which does not conceal even the slightest vibration of the mind; it is mutual adoration, so that one would dare only to kiss the other's hand; it is more than flirting, it is more than passion, more than anything else it is reaching the summit.[6]

Love, in the conception of the young Čapek, is close to an enfeebling disease and, like a patient, he longs for an understanding human being in whose lap he can repose in tears.

> I am such an odd person, overly sensitive like a sick child, a wretched, neurotic boy who might go mad after mental exertion, who has weak, sickly nerves, who has feelings reason cannot regulate ... I am terribly enfeebled, beaten down by everything. My strength has reached its summit in that I have gathered the courage to tell you that I love you beyond measure. That has enfeebled me, and I have only strength enough left to keep from dying. I am lonely and, like a sick child, I would love to lay my feverish head in someone's lap and weep away.[7]

This image of a sick child longing for maternal love, which obviously expresses the young Čapek's feelings with such candor, would hardly have impressed the girl whose favors he sought. And though I don't want to minimize Čapek's illness, I'm convinced that it was not the only reason why he was later so hesitant in his relationships with women, above all with his long-time friend, the actress Olga Scheinpflugová. Clearly, he had been marked by his mother's unhealthy love. He tossed back and forth between his longing to be accepted and his fear of being devoured, between begging for love and refusing it, between his need for intimacy and his fear of it; fear seems to have been predominant.

During the fifteen years after his emotional letters to Anielka, Karel Čapek led a very active social and artistic life. He finished his studies and was rapidly gaining a reputation for being an exceptionally gifted writer. Nothing, however, indicates that he had any meaningful love affairs. Yet early in his career as a dramatist there is a play about love: *The Robber*.

This, the second of the plays Karel wrote alone rather than in collaboration with his brother, was produced in the spring of 1920. It stands out from all his other plays, in that the rest of them have primary motifs that are either fantastical or openly political. In the first category are *R.U.R.: Rossum's Universal Robots* and *The Makropulos Secret*; the second category would include his last play, *The Mother*, and (excluding their earliest effort) two plays he wrote with his brother, *From the Life of the Insects* and *Adam the Creator*. Unlike the other major plays, *The Robber* not only appears to be light comedy, but in addition has something quite extraordinary for a work by Čapek: a theme involving the male conquest of a woman.

The story, again unlike the majority of his subsequent plays, takes place, classically, within a twenty-four-hour period. It takes place in the midst of a forest, in front of the country house of an old-world professor and his wife. After their older daughter runs away to join her lover, they transform their house into a prison, complete with iron bars, where they rigorously keep guard over Mimi, their younger daughter. The protagonist, who has no name but is referred to by the others as the Robber, is dragged onto the stage by the actor playing Prologue and is immediately characterized as a brash intruder, a thief, a dangerous man capable of anything. As soon as the Robber catches a glimpse of Mimi, he determines that he will win her, and with his cocky, swaggering behavior he does indeed charm the young woman. The night scene between the lovers is among the most emotional scenes Čapek ever wrote.

The play is full of reversals and an abundance of fast action. At one point, the Robber is shot and carried away, but not to a hospital: after a night of revelry he returns, charms Mimi again, and succeeds in getting into the house, where he barricades himself and bravely faces all those besieged in there. At the conclusion of the play, the professor's older daughter unexpectedly returns with a child; she has been abandoned, and she wants to warn her sister against reckless love. The play ends with the Robber's flight from the beseiged house. Love disappears just as abruptly as it appeared.

I have said that this play seems entirely different from the other Čapek plays, as if it had not been written by the author of the contemplative and rather depressing *Wayside Crosses* and *Painful Tales*. Nothing of either the war or the postwar atmosphere appears in the play, but this could be explained by the fact that a first draft of the play had already been done before the war, a joint effort by the brothers. Karel wrote about it:

> The idea and the first version of this play were done in Paris in 1911; it was born of a longing for home ... it grew out of memories of youth and freedom, of my native region, my friends, in short of home. But it was not only memories, it was also a farewell.
>
> Friends from those days tell the author that his 'Robber' is at least in part a portrait of himself, 'you,' they say, 'who used to dance at the Zátiší tavern, grabbed every girl, plucked every rose, all while raising a revolt against the current taste in art.'[8]

But even references to the year of the play's first draft do not explain why Čapek reached for his old topic again later, at a time of such political radicalism, a time when, as is obvious from his other work, he was yeasty with new approaches that would make it possible for him to express himself on the substantial problems of the age and of civilization itself, on the themes, that is, which obviously enticed and excited him.

Yet we should not be misled by Čapek's later work, which, among other things, was preceded by new personal experiences. There was clearly one more theme, a very personal one, which he needed to express: the theme of love or, more precisely, masculinity. The "odd, oversensitive, wretched boy with weak, sickly nerves" wrote out his dream about a rebellious hero, not an intellectual but a man of action, a man who does not doubt that he will attain anything he chooses to attain. "I will win her, mistake me not," the Robber says to provoke the Gamekeeper who also is in love with Mimi. "I will get her – just like this, see? In the wink of an eye! And I will get her today, today – she will be mine, today – and she will laugh at you – "[9]

It's a play in which the author apparently tried to remove himself from his dependence on his mother, and also to overcome his shyness and oversensitivity. Only ostensibly, only thematically does *The Robber* stand apart from the rest of Čapek's plays. Otherwise, it has most of the characteristics that are typical of Čapek's plays and, for that matter, of Čapek's work in general. In my comments on *Wayside Crosses*, I mentioned Čapek's tendency to turn ideas into works of art. Indeed, one of the most characteristic elements of Čapek's work is the one-dimensionality of his characters. They move not according to impulses flowing from their nature, but according to their author's need to demonstrate a particular truth, a certain point of view, or even for the sole purpose of moving the plot forward. We can easily follow this tendency in his novel *The Absolute at Large*, the plays *R.U.R.* and *The Makropulos Secret*, as well as in the plays he wrote with his brother, and later in the novel *The First Rescue Party* and throughout his *Apocryphal Tales*.

Aware that his characters could have been lifeless and therefore unconvincing, Čapek, like no one else in Czech literature, concentrated on their language. He stylized it so brilliantly that it served as an authentic record of contemporary speech. He was also successful in capturing so many of the external aspects of human behavior, brilliantly observing details, gestures, predilections, and deportment, thus enlivening his characters and giving them not only credibility but also the appearance of multidimensionality. In *The Robber*, he even used the dialect of his native region in order to make his characters more lifelike. The audience thus has the feeling that they have been transported to somewhere in the eastern Bohemian countryside, that they are watching a realistic play about an athletic ladykiller and his boyish charm. In reality, the play is more a meeting of various views of love: on the one hand, the Robber embodies the author's dream of conquering masculinity; on the other hand, the Robber's character sets up scenes in which the other characters can express their own opinions about love and, at least in several sentences, add their own often long-past experiences, longings, and unfulfilled expectations. At the same time, the Robber himself seems to be the personification of exactly those never-realized longings.

Another element typical of Čapek's works, as I've already mentioned, is his relativistic approach to truth, which, when staging a meeting of opposing views, led him not to stand fully behind any of them. Just before the end of *The Robber* he brings on the professor's unhappy elder daughter, who appears to negate all dreams and illusions about romantic love. And in the end, the Robber, who seemed to be the hero on whose side Čapek stood in the battle with the besiegers, simply flees, abandoning both Mimi and his heroic posturing. In his theater program notes to *The Robber*, Čapek wrote that the comedy of youth "became a comedy of love, where everyone loves, where all are in the right; thus the spectator loses the well-deserved pleasure of sympathizing with one side against the other. But might it not be permissible – at least in a comedy – to wish all of them well?"[10] We can also ask, however, whether the Robber's unexpected flight is not largely a personal confession that Čapek's dream of all-conquering masculinity remained nothing but a dream.

It's worth mentioning one more of the principal motifs of Čapek's plays, the motif of the siege, of being surrounded, and Čapek's sympathy for characters who resist a siege. An unknown man is surrounded in the story "The Mountain" in *Wayside Crosses*, as are all the humans in *R.U.R.* and Prokop in *Krakatit*, who in a magnificent nighttime scene fights against the numerical superiority of his captors, like the murderer against two police officers in one of the *Tales from Two Pockets*. The Čapek expert František Černý presented the interesting reminiscences of Mathesius, a translator and contemporary of Čapek, about the author's curious sympathy for people under siege.

> Suddenly Čapek came to a halt, brandished his walking stick, and began to relate with an enthusiasm that was unusual for him the story of a police siege of a thieves' hideout, which at the time – April 1912 – was filling the columns of the world's newspapers. Unless my notes from the time fail me, it involved the besieging of two Parisian apaches ... in a garage in Choisy-le-Roi, near Paris, where they held out for a good two-and-a-half hours against superior numbers of policemen. Čapek knew all the details from the French press and even drew a map of the garage and the surrounding area for me.
>
> *Čapek and Mathesius later researched similar sieges in the library.*
>
> Čapek found information about the January 1911 siege in Sidney Street, in London's Whitechapel, of some murderer who held out for an entire night against a thousand policemen and soldiers, and I triumphantly ... hauled up from somewhere or other the story of Fort Chabrol, the bunker in a Parisian street in which a certain Dumont, accused of conspiring against French president

> Loubet, set himself up and held out against the police, the army, and the gendarmerie for thirty-eight days ... That report hit the nail on the head, and Čapek copied it out with a blissful smile.

When, years after the besieging scenes in *The Robber*, *R.U.R.*, and *Krakatit*, Mathesius recalled their long-ago search in Čapek's presence, Čapek supposedly burst out laughing: "You know, what you study hard in your youth...," an old Czech saying that ends, "comes easily in your old age."[11]

Most contemporary Czech critics did not understand Čapek's early play and explained it too realistically. To them, *The Robber* seemed amoral, anarchistic, and ruthless. Yet some, his new friend Neumann for instance, saw how idea-oriented the author was, as well as how uneasy he was about taking any character's side – which contradicts the rules of drama. According to the accounts of those who remember seeing the play, however, it enjoyed great popularity with audiences. And today it is not only the most performed of all Čapek's plays, but also the most performable, probably because it has fewer contemporaneous political references and less philosophizing. Speculating about love, or dreaming about masculinity, has more lasting validity than speculating about the future of humankind.

8. Olga: Love with a Secret

Just before opening night of *The Robber*, the thirty-year-old writer met Olga Scheinpflugová, a fledgling actress thirteen years his junior. It was the beginning of a fateful relationship that, with complex twists and turns, lasted until the end of Čapek's life.[1]

> Come, come, come! I don't know whether from heaven or from hell, but there came over me today a craziness such as I've never known before. I must see you; it would be terrible if you didn't come today, I don't know what I would do ... Olga, dear girl, you little urchin, come, for everything in the world, come, and come soon! Olga, Olga, Olga, yesterday you said that I am no longer mad; today I had a serious attack of madness. Dearest, it would be too cruel if you didn't come today.[2]

Somewhat abridged, this is one of the first letters from Karel Čapek to Olga Scheinpflugová, at least of the ones that have been preserved.

When they first met, she read for Čapek from *The Robber*, and as she reported later, she was enchanted by the play as much as by the author, even though, or so she insisted, some instinct told her that her love for him would bring her many difficult times.

> For a moment she looked at his face with wide-open eyes, as everyone had to look at him – and she saw everything all at once. She noticed his suit, how poorly made it is, my goodness, how it softens the slender lines of his body with the diffidence of its cut! How different he is, entirely different from all the people she has known since childhood, whose faces she has seen in pictures and whose characters she has read about in books. Different from all the men in the theaters where she had worked and studied. So different from the images that surrounded the half-child's bed at night. The mix of naïveté and deep wisdom

> sparkling in his eyes induced a strange confusion in her. And yet everything in and about him was familiar, as if she had known him all her life, in image and in concept, in every contact with the world; she knew him in her nerves ... She breathed heavily in blissful, trembling awareness that it was him, him alone, to whom her youth, her wild and vivid thoughts were drawn, all her feverish wanting, sensing, and seeking. The powerful and outright religious joy that came with this realization changed instantly into another feeling, a merciless, violent feeling, a fear of something grave and unfamiliar, which her instinct told her was like a ghost with neither voice nor face.[3]

Dozens of Čapek's letters from the fall of 1920 confirm that the young actress's relationship to him was not at all clear. Čapek repeatedly begged for meetings at which Olga never showed, nor would she apologize or make excuses – sometimes her behavior brought him happiness, but more often it caused disappointment and despair.

> Olga, please realize that this disgrace, which a *gymnasium* student might bear, is a little too much for me. I beg you to take care as best you can to spare me this disgrace; I cannot rid myself of the feeling that you could do this ... When you are thirty, dear child, you wait differently than you do when you are twenty; please take this seriously ... Perhaps even at eighteen you understand that this anguish is full of despair, that it is a disease in need of a healing hand, an unusually delicate one ... Understand that this is not a matter of a few minutes or half an hour walking out on the street, but rather a matter of extremely delicate, extremely important internal events which are terribly, brutally ripped apart by the sort of moments you have bestowed on me. Olga, Olenka, I am writing you an angry letter; I am writing with tears in my eyes.[4]

And several days later:

> Perhaps we are mad – or is it necessary to always pay with pain for every happy moment? Come, Olga, don't allow me to suffer any more.[5]

And soon afterwards:

> It isn't good to make a laughingstock of a man – in front of him and in front of others. I merely watch with a frozen heart and count the black pinpricks ... It's horribly sobering, downright icy.[6]

And in the very next letter:

> And now consider the horror of the moment when the waiting man is attacked by the thought that she for whom he is waiting is only making fun of him; that perhaps at that moment she is thinking of the waiting man with amusement at his unmistakable anger. Everything he believed is crumbling into horror and uncertainty ... Self-loathing, self-loathing; at such a moment, a man could thrash himself for the immaturity of his thirty years. He feels rejected, cruelly censured, all his joys laid waste ... Forgive me, I cannot express it well, it's crazier than what I write. A man is crying at his desk out of anger, sorrow, disappointment, I don't know what else; he would like to be lying unconscious, but he can confidently foresee the night, all of which he will spend awake, and the day, all of which he will spend over his untouched work, his mouth full of the mud of bitterness. He would like nothing more than to rip this craziness out of his heart, but he knows that as soon as he hears that dear, lovely voice, he will run on like a madman after an eternal illusion, so he can be a wretched clown, perhaps just as despairing again tomorrow.[7]

The author of *The Robber*, as is obvious, did not shed much of his self-pity. Rather than a robber easily conquering women's hearts, his letters suggest a lovestruck fifteen-year-old student who by describing his suffering hopes to move the heart of his beloved. "But it's impossible not to find five minutes in three days' time in which to write a few words and toss them into a mailbox. Only a few words, and one man would be spared terrible days and nights. This is no longer indolence, this is derision. Whoever he may be, he is, after all, only a man with great weaknesses and unfortunate sensitivity ... And now the man is sitting and trying to face the thought that all is lost. Apparently, he is younger than is written in the birth registry and dumber than anyone in the world would believe; he would most obligingly die. If he does get out of this hell, he will not be as he used to be. No one faces without consequences the thought that all is lost."[8] And the author of the letter goes directly into a long litany in which he makes up his mind not to beg, not to be laughable, not to impose himself on her, and then ends by begging once again for a bit of news, for her to take note that he is waiting for a reply.

In Olga's version, things were somewhat different. From the beginning she was struck by Čapek's personality.

> Art, life, time, the world, all these are Karel, him and only him, with his soul gifted with such marvelous vitality, with his listening mouth and sparkling eyes. She crossed into his world with its different kind of perception, discrimination, and expression, and she could never return to her former world. Love was just a bridge between two planets, a bridge that brought them together. And even if she hadn't loved him, she would have had to stay near him, he was someone impossible to abandon.[9]

She learns, however, about his diseased spine and realizes that Karel "has been living alone with his relatives like an old bachelor, even though others of his age have long been married." And her father, who works with Čapek at the newspaper, reveals to her what Čapek had told him some time ago, "that he must live alone." She knows that she would love him "be he lame and legless, so much already she knows regarding her entire future, that the more fate does him damage, the more devoted she will be to him ... Something tells her in a sweet, tearful voice that there are other great things that, as much as happiness, belong to love: sacrifice, humility, suffering ... She tries to avoid him, to let him decide whether he wants to take the path of mutual torment, which she sees as the only possibility. And so she refuses to meet with him."[10]

Thus, from the beginning, Olga Scheinpflugová speaks about Čapek's illness as the only obstacle to a relationship filled with love. It is of course necessary to take into consideration not only her attempt to depict herself as an understanding wife prepared to sacrifice and seeking how to be most helpful to her beloved husband, or at least to harm him as little as possible, but also the fact that her account appeared many years later, during which time her relationship with Čapek had undergone much peripeteia, many reversals of circumstance and fortune.

Whether those first months were marked by her hesitation or indeed by an attempt to save Čapek from a dilemma which might have been too brutal, their relationship nevertheless intensified, and it seemed that neither Čapek's spinal disease (about which there can be no doubt) nor his oversensitivity, which he sometimes considered a disease, would stand in the way of their life together. They traveled to Čapek's native Krkonoš Mountains for a pre-wedding trip of sorts. In Scheinpflugová's version, Čapek proposed to her on that trip and she enthusiastically accepted. She wished "to go hand in hand with him and not ask where, for his destinations are grand and beautiful..."[11]

Then they both went in different directions, she back home and he to visit his parents at a health spa in Slovakia, where his father was practicing and where Karel hoped to get treatment for his spine. The description of the events of the following months are quite different in Scheinpflugová's novel than in their correspondence. In her version, Čapek inexplicably fell silent, then wrote a letter to her father (Olga was still a minor) about his illness. The father related Čapek's decision to his daughter: "You are never to see each other again. Your relationship is over, you would be sacrificing your youth for him ... The doctors supposedly forbid him everything that would allow him to be infinitely happy with you. This, unfortunately, is called love, my child."[12] Čapek, Scheinpflugová asserts, continued his silence and did not turn up even after his return to Prague. In despair, Olga had a nervous breakdown.

> A second week of waiting in vain, waiting for some merciful scrap of paper containing his handwriting, hoping in vain that she had only dreamed that her father had told her she had lost

> him ... Suffering has its signs which she, in her inexperience, does not know how to deal with. The heart becomes calm only after taking sedatives, the hands and feet are paralyzed with weakness, the malevolent hand of spasms plays with the mouth.[13]

This account is untrue in at least one essential point: the preserved letters testify to the fact that Čapek wrote to his lover daily, moreover letters full of love. Still, on August 11, 1921, he wrote her that he had informed his mother that he was to be married and that she had received the news with understanding. He also wrote about how the two of them would arrange their life together. From his letters, it also is obvous that Olga had received his letters and answered them. But then something significant happened, something not mentioned in any letter and which apparently changed or at least influenced their relationship.

This incident suddenly appears in his letter of August 15:

> And as to your worries, be at peace; I have considered everything, and come what may, I am at peace and this will please you. I ask only that you be without worries and not ruin your days, or even a minute, until I return. I ask you to do this and I insist on it. Don't worry about a thing till I return. Be completely, completely content.[14]

And the following day:

> ...your two little letters arrived together. Sad little letters, like little white moths with torn wings. My child, I repeat once and for all, be cheerful, trust; 'everything works out in the end,' there's nothing to fear. Be at peace! ... Ola, my dear little girl, I'm going through so much, but your suffering is a thousand times more tormenting to me, because your suffering could not withstand the strict test of autumn's ripe beauty and cold skies. Everything seems to be telling me something, and I faithfully report to you: 'Let happen what must happen, and be at peace with it. What is inevitable is good. Bear what has been given you to bear. There is a useful, deeper meaning to all you cannot escape.' Dear one, believe in the wisdom of the powers of autumn and of the skies; I too came to believe and to learn two

> things: accept dutifully what must be and carry out bravely what it is good and beautiful to do … Dear one, be strong … You see at least how *my* autumn put me back on my feet; if you are afraid that for *you* it means summer came after too short a spring, then good: be strong and content – autumn awaits you as well, and if you are wise, it will be beautiful, more beautiful than anything that came before…

The letter concludes with an important statement. "My health has improved considerably."[15] On August 18, Čapek was quite disturbed or even frightened by something. He wrote:

> Dear little girl, your two express letters from August 15 and 17 just came. I do not agree that you should do anything, do you hear? I – if it matters to you at all! – forbid any such attempt, and you will cause me terrible pain if you do not obey me. I had hoped you'd understand it when I wrote: be at peace, be content. It meant that I take this entire business on myself and that you should trust me completely. Live as if nothing had happened. Everything is well, I gladly accept everything, with hope and, yes, with pleasure. I am pleased, my dear girl, and I ask that you be pleased with me. I'm looking forward to the responsibility and the worries I will be taking on myself. I'm terribly looking forward to what I've not been naming in my letters. I have thought about the enormous obstacles in the road ahead, and I know how to surmount them. Rely on me alone. I would run right to Prague to tell you everything, but at this stage it is dangerous to interrupt my cure, things could get worse, and I am afraid of that for myself and for you. Therefore I ask you: please wait patiently. I see and even feel a completely seamless solution: my only request is that you trust me … It's dreadful nonsense for you to torment yourself; on the contrary, be happy. My present happiness, which is spoiled only by this terrible sympathy for you, has been based primarily on an image I see before me. And so, dear Olga, be at peace. Above all, don't do anything! Don't meddle with your fate! … I'm immensely afraid that you have done something already, which I would very much regret.[16]

The following day, Čapek repeats even more insistently his request that his beloved do nothing.

> Perhaps you received my express letter before you did anything horrible or senseless ... When I think about your doing something, I feel terrible. I don't want, I do not want you to act, I cannot write you everything, but do not move a single finger, do not take even one bad, unhappy step. God, when will I have news from you?[17]

And finally, on August 20, resigned and crushed:

> Dear girl, I had in mind another sense of 'courage' and 'strength' – but let it be, it's done. I don't want to scold you now, as perhaps you deserve. I keep looking for something good in all that has happened, but it's as if I were surrounded by emptiness. I'm afraid to think about it, to blame myself too much. Oh God, if I could undo it. You don't know how bitter I feel. That's why, above all, that is why I wanted everything done differently, so that I would bear the weight of matters, the responsibility, so that I would force fate to turn the grave mistake into something good. Now the good has escaped me. I did nothing more than suffer a bit. It's horrible. Now I stand above the ruins of good intentions, by which I wanted to make amends for my guilt. And now, only you have paid. As for me, nothing, absolutely nothing. I just feel terribly bitter toward myself. What have you done! What have I done! ... I would like to bring upon myself some sort of severe pain, in order to know what it is like.[18]

Exactly what it was his not yet nineteen-year-old beloved did, we can only guess. Perhaps she was expecting a child, and because she was at the very beginning of her theatrical career, decided to terminate the pregnancy. The father could have been Čapek, likewise it could have been someone else. Perhaps Čapek began to express doubts about the planned wedding in a letter we don't know about, which perhaps he sent to her father, and Olga threatened suicide. But it doesn't seem that what she did was a suicide attempt – even if, according to her autobiographical novel *Český román*, she did attempt suicide a number of years later.

There are no longer any witnesses who could tell us what happened, and Čapek's delicacy did not allow him to be explicit about intimate matters. We only know that what Scheinpflugová wrote in her novel as her own recollection, years later, does not correspond to reality. Nevertheless, we can see that something changed in the relationship between them. Passion and infatuation have disappeared from Čapek's subsequent, still-frequent letters, and though the theme of a possible life together did not disappear, it was at least postponed.

Love, like pain, is often a deep source of inspiration. Those four years, in which Čapek experienced both loves and painful disappointment (his second love, about which more later, ended in a wedding at which Čapek obviously was not the groom) mark the most important creative period in his life. In addition to his work at the newspaper *Lidové noviny*, he became literary adviser and then artistic director of Prague's Vinohrady Theater. During this period, in the years 1920 through 1923, he completed and published his *Painful Tales*, wrote the play *R.U.R.*, wrote *The Absolute at Large*, a witty, satirical political novel with a philosophical ending, collaborated with his brother on *From the Life of the Insects*, and also wrote, on his own, the play *The Makropulos Secret*, the script for the film *Little Golden Key*, outlines for other screenplays, his travelogue *Letters from Italy*, and lastly, in August 1923, he completed his most substantial novel, *Krakatit*. In addition he wrote roughly two hundred short and long articles, critiques, and feuilletons. The first anthology of some of these articles, entitled *A Criticism of Words*, was also published during this time.

The immense strain of work, combined with the suffering that came from his love affairs, must have had an effect on his physical health and his mental state.

9. The First Report on the End of Civilization: R.U.R.

When I said that Čapek's succession of powerful emotional experiences obviously resulted in creative inspiration, I did not mean that the problems of his personal life were directly projected onto his work or that they were the main inspiration for his work. With the exception of *Krakatit*, it did not happen that way at all. Throughout his entire life he was drawn by the big societal issues of the day, the moral questions facing contemporary civilization, and philosophical problems, above all questions about knowledge, the nature of truth. He succeeded in embodying these big issues in plays, works with fantastical premises, and parables.

The first work to bring Čapek world renown was *R.U.R.: Rossum's Universal Robots*, a "collective drama" about artificial people, the robots of the title. This original play quickly circled the world, became the basis for film adaptations and, thanks to the play's success, the word "robot" (invented for Čapek by his brother) entered the world's languages. It's often considered a utopian work, but in fact Čapek merely used a utopian theme for a much more serious purpose.

The basic idea (and for that matter the plot) we find in abbreviated form in the Čapek Brothers' story "The System," which had been published in the autumn of 1908. In that story, factory owner John Andrew Ripraton explains his vision for a solution to the workers' question and the organization of large-scale production:

> Exploit the entire world! The world is nothing but raw material. The world is no more than unexploited matter. The sky and the earth, people, time and space and infinity, everything is just raw material. Gentlemen, the task of industry is to exploit the entire world ... Everything must be speeded up. The workers' question

> is holding us back ... The worker must become a machine, so that he can simply rotate like a wheel. Every thought is insubordination! Gentlemen! Taylorism is systematically incorrect, because it disregards the question of a soul. A worker's soul is not a machine, therefore it must be removed. This is my system ... I have sterilized the worker, purified him; I have destroyed in him all feelings of altruism and camaraderie, all familial, poetic, and transcendental feelings...[1]

Čapek liked to exploit themes he or others had already used. He twice exploited the motif of mysterious footprints in snow, first in *Wayside Crosses*,[2] and the second time in *Tales from Two Pockets*.[3] He elaborated on a similar motif in one of his newspaper columns, where he substituted for mysterious footprints a more concrete but equally incomprehensible half-liter of beer perched on an asphalt roof, from whence it just as mysteriously disappears. We can find in Čapek's columns and stories, and even in his philosophical essays, many motifs that he later fleshed out in his longer works. In the novel *An Ordinary Life*, he developed the idea that in every life there is material for many other lives we are not able to live. He more succinctly expressed this same idea earlier in two of the *Tales from Two Pockets*.[4] These tales, in fact, form the basis for many parts of Čapek's novel trilogy, *Three Novels*.

Other times, he exploited someone else's motifs. In his own personal genre of apocryphal tales, he presented familiar biblical, literary, and historical incidents in new and often controversial versions.

The theme for *R.U.R.* can be found in the story "The System." By its consistent development of a utilitarian relationship with employees, capitalistic rationalism achieves the ideal of a dehumanized worker, leading to a fantastic increase in production. But this dehumanization can be taken only so far. The moment workers understand their position within the system, they rebel and destroy it.

The first part of the play *R.U.R.* is an extensive prologue. Helena, daughter of the president, arrives on the island where the firm Rossum's Universal Robots is manufacturing robots. She is given a thorough account of robot history, and she also meets all the human characters: Domin, the factory director; Fabry, engineer and general director of technology; Dr. Gall, chairman of the physiological and research divisions; Dr. Hallemeier, head of the Institute for Robot Psychology and Education; Busman, general marketing director and chief counsel; and the builder Alquist, chief of construction. (As is usual in Čapek's world, all the male characters are apparently old bachelors.)

In addition to the account of how robots were invented, Helena is introduced to the artificial people, who, although indistinguishable from real people, are nonetheless dehumanized, merely obeying orders. Also in the prologue, Čapek gives each human character a brief opportunity to explain his perspective on life. Factory director Domin labels the current age, following the age of knowledge, "the age of production." The ideal worker is the one with fewest needs. "Robots," Čapek repeats his old idea through Domin's mouth, "are mechanically more perfect than we are, they have an astounding intellectual capacity, but they have no soul ... an engineer's product is technically more refined than one of nature's creations."[5]

Similarly, the author puts the technocratic point of view in engineer Fabry's mouth: "It's great progress to give birth by machine. It's faster and more convenient. Any acceleration constitutes progress, Miss Glory. Nature had no concept of the modern tempo of work. From a technical standpoint, the whole of childhood is pure nonsense. Simply wasted time..."[6]

Marketing director Busman is proud of the fact that robots are becoming cheaper to manufacture, since the cheaper their cost, the cheaper the price of the goods they make. The psychologist Hallemeier emphasizes the advantages of robots over human workers: they have no particular needs, no sense of taste – they can be fed anything – they have no free will, no interests, no passions, no need to laugh.

Čapek assigned traditional cultural values to only three characters. Two of these are women, Helena and the servant Nana; the third is the builder Alquist. In the prologue, the entire problem of rationalization merely serves as a basis for witty conversation. Alquist's remark that robots will deprive all workers of work only gives Domin a reason to further develop his utopian vision. The workers will be out of work, "but in ten years Rossum's Universal Robots will be producing so much wheat, so much cloth, so much of everything, that things will no longer have any value. Everyone will be able to take as much as he needs. There'll be no more poverty. Yes, people will be out of work, but by then there'll be no work left to be done. Everything will be done by living machines. People will do only what they enjoy. They will live only to perfect themselves."[7] Nothing in the prologue hints that these statements mark the beginning of a catastrophe. Moreover, the ending of the prologue is almost theater of the absurd: Domin asks his unexpected visitor for her hand.

Ten years pass between the prologue and the first act, which takes place on the anniversary of Helena's arrival. Helena has indeed married Domin, whose technocratic vision has been fulfilled during this period. But as with the realization of all utopian visions, people did not foresee the consequences. The servant Nana, more or less representative of folk wisdom, speaks of God's punishment. As God drove man from paradise, so will he drive people from the world. The builder Alquist also passionately condemns the vision of a technocratic paradise. To Helena's question about why women have stopped having children, he answers: "Because it's not necessary. Because we're in paradise, understand? ... Because human labor has become unnecessary, because suffering has become unnecessary, because man needs nothing, nothing, nothing but to enjoy – Oh, cursèd paradise, this. ... Helena, there is nothing more terrible than giving people paradise on earth! Why have women stopped giving birth? Because the whole world has become Domin's Sodom! ... The whole world, all the lands, all mankind, everything's become one big beastly orgy! People don't even stretch out their hands for food anymore; it's stuffed right in their mouths for them so they don't even have to get up..."[8]

Enter Radius, one of the robots which, in accordance with Helena's wishes, Dr. Gall has begun to produce differently (apparently he has given them feelings and a consciousness of their own "ego," that is, a soul). Radius declares that robots no longer need people, people only order them around, people create nothing but useless words. Helena, who from the very beginning of the play has considered the plight of the robots evidence of man's inhumanity, in a highly emotional moment takes the secret formula for their production out of the safe and burns it. It appears, however, that in the meantime, several of the experimental robots who were manufactured "differently" have incited all the other robots in the world to rebellion and have issued a proclamation that humankind is to be wiped off the face of the earth.

In the second and most dramatic act, the entire top management team involved in robot production is besieged. In an attempt to save themselves, they want to offer the robots the formula for their production in exchange for their own freedom. When they learn that the formula has been burned, they decide to put up a courageous defense. This situation, in which the human characters are facing death, gives Čapek a pretext for allowing most of them to evaluate their lives, intentions, and deeds with a pathos worthy of the moment. While Alquist accuses the others of working for no other purpose than to assure the stockholders of their dividends, Domin once more defends his technocratic dream:

> To hell with their dividends! Do you think I'd have worked even one hour for them? ... I did this for myself, do you hear? For my own satisfaction! I wanted man to become a master! So he wouldn't have to live from hand to mouth! I didn't want to see another soul grow numb slaving over someone else's machine! I wanted there to be nothing, nothing, nothing of that damned social mess! ... I wanted a new mankind![9]

Alquist opposes him:

> I blame science! I blame technology! Domin! Myself! All of us! We, we are at fault! For the sake of our megalomania, for the sake of somebody's profits, for the sake of progress, I don't know, for the sake of some tremendous something, we have murdered humanity! So now you can crash under the weight of all your greatness! No Genghis Khan has ever erected such an enormous tomb from human bones![10]

In the closing act, which takes place after an indeterminate period of time, humankind has been slaughtered. The robots have spared only Alquist, because they appreciate his ability to work with his hands; but in return they ask that he tell them the formula for their production, without which they are doomed to extinction. Broken-hearted, Alquist cannot and does not even want to do anything of the sort. "Oh, just go away! You things, you slaves, just how on earth do you expect to multiply? If you want to live, then mate like animals!"[11] He finds out, however, that two of the robots who were formed "differently" have fallen in love, which means that they are capable of love. Rational, intelligent life is preserved, and Alquist can deliver the painful closing monologue about life beginning anew from love:

> [I]t will start out naked and tiny, it will take root in the wilderness, and to it all that we did and built will mean nothing – our towns and factories, our art, our ideas will all mean nothing, and yet life will not perish! Only we have perished. Our houses and machines will be in ruins, our systems will collapse, and the names of our great will be shed like autumn leaves. Only you, love, will blossom on this rubbish heap and commit the seed of life to the winds.[12]

R.U.R. was written at the beginning of 1920, a time when the battles in Russia between the defenders of the legitimate government and the red army were ending, when Europe was only with difficulty recovering from the war, and circumstances seemed conducive to utopian visions: societal as well as technocratic. Both sorts of vision intrigued Čapek his entire life, but ideas for revolutionary change struck him as dubious and dangerous.

Critics around the world offered countless interpretations of the play's message and of what exactly the robots symbolized. For no other of his works did Čapek write so many comments. Perhaps the most precise characterization of the play's aim appears in his 1923 article for *The Saturday Review* (London), in which he reacted to a debate, with George Bernard Shaw and G. K. Chesterton as participants, that had taken place following the play's London premiere.

> ... I wished to write a comedy, partly of science, partly of truth. The old inventor, Mr. Rossum (whose name means Mr. Intellect or Mr. Brain), is no more or less than a typical representative of the scientific materialism of the last century. His desire to create an artificial man – in the chemical and biological, not the mechanical sense – is inspired by a foolish and obstinate wish to prove God unnecessary and meaningless. Young Rossum is the modern scientist, untroubled by metaphysical ideas; for him scientific experiment is the road to industrial production; he is not concerned about proving, but rather manufacturing. To create a homunculus is a mediæval idea; to bring it in line with the present century, this creation must be undertaken on the principle of mass production. We are in the grip of industrialism; this terrible machinery must not stop, for if it does it would destroy the lives of thousands. It must, on the contrary, go on faster and faster, even though in the process it destroys thousands and thousands of other lives ... A product of the human brain has at last escaped from the control of human hands. This is the comedy of science.
>
> Now for my other idea, the comedy of truth. In the play, the factory director Domin establishes that technical progress emancipates man from hard manual labour, and he is quite right. The Tolstoyan Alquist, to the contrary, believes that technological progress demoralizes him, and I think he is right, too.

Čapek continues by enumerating the truths of the individual characters. Helena is right, Busman, even the robots are right.

All are right, in the moral sense of the word, and they advocate their truths on the basis of ideals.

> I ask whether it is not possible to see in the present societal conflict an analogous struggle between two, three, five equally serious truths and equally noble ideals? I think it is possible, and this is the most dramatic element of modern civilization, that one human truth is opposed to another truth no less human, ideal against ideal, positive value against value no less positive, instead of the struggle being, as we are so often told it is, one between exalted truth and vile selfish wickedness. These are the things I should like to have said in my comedy of truth, but it seems that I failed, for none of the distinguished speakers who took part in the discussion have discovered this simple aspect in *R.U.R.*[13]

Thus did the author himself explain the play's message (or at least one of its messages) in the spirit of his relativist philosophy. For that matter, he explained the majority of his writing from this period in the same way, and in some of his works he succeeded in embodying his theory of truth more organically. In *R.U.R.*, however, as he says with disappointment, he did not succeed very well: the ending of the play speaks against all truths being of equal weight, and the author himself obviously sided with Alquist, who resisted Domin's technocratic vision. And after all, it was the realization of this vision that, in the end, brought the world to the catastrophe in which all people, without exception, perished. That all of them could have been guided to their truths by equally sincere beliefs is, at the moment of total catastrophe, of little significance – and the author proved himself to be aware of this by the way in which he constructed his characters, by the time on stage he gave Alquist in comparison with the others. I would say that, as should be in a work of art, a vision triumphed over a thesis. A vision of the destruction of the world, brought on by the terrible machinery of production, eclipsed the thesis that each has his own noble idealism.

In its external features, *R.U.R.*, like *The Absolute at Large*, *Krakatit*, and later *War with the Newts* or *The White Plague*, belongs to the genre of science fiction. This genre, still seeking a place in serious literature, usually tries to create an image of another world – another civilization, whether in the future or on some other planet.

The time of *R.U.R.* is clearly in the future, a very near future, some time at the end of the twentieth century or, as a poster for the world premiere announced, circa 2000 (the world premiere was performed by an amateur group in the city of Hradec Králové on January 3, 1921).

The fundamental dramatic element was a revolutionary invention that changed people's way of life. Čapek exhibited his great technical foresight in this play. Robots have a phenomenal memory. "If one read to them the *Encyclopedia Britannica* they could repeat everything in order, but they never think up anything that's original."[14] This is wonderfully applicable to today's computers, about which no one knew anything, of course, when *R.U.R.* first appeared.

On the other hand, if we consider the play as a picture of the human world of the future (even as a picture of the world of Čapek's time), it is in many respects inconsistent, if not naïve. At the time of this revolutionary invention, it's still in many ways the beginning of the twentieth century. The besieged have no weapons other than pistols to defend themselves with. The factories that underpin the economic operation of the contemporary world are not protected by security services. The managers of the most important plant on the planet have neither an airplane nor a helicopter at their disposal to allow them to escape, and the Robot uprising takes humanity completely by surprise. Within a very short time, all are exterminated, that is, they appear to have neither the ability nor the technical resources to defend themselves. The entire business of robot production is dependent upon a formula, the only copy of which, placed in a room next to Helena's sitting room, is easily accessible. There are too many inconsistencies for us not to suspect that the author was aware of them. Rather, they simply didn't make any difference to his working through his vision of the world of the future.

The construction of the play also seems odd. Even though it was rather fashionable at that time for the protagonists of plays actually to be a collective (probably fighting for their rights), the term "collective drama" does not correspond to the content of the play. The robots, after all, are not the protagonists, and the directors of the Rossum firm could hardly be termed a "collective." Rather, the play's protagonists being less individualized and more representative of humanity as a whole, and their fate being the fate of all humanity, Čapek felt the need to speak of it as a collective drama.[15]

Although it was a time when the contemporary stage was depicting either social conflict or character-based drama, when passions were on display, Čapek was interested in none of that. For a love scene he provided just a few sentences parodying a love scene. Considerably more space was devoted to chemical formulas, to the production and sale of robots and, above all, to problems connected with the consequences of mass production. Čapek also treated the play's time span untraditionally. Ten years pass between the prologue and the first act (it was necessary to give the human characters new make-up), and an unspecified period of time passes between the second and third acts, as well.

At a time when plays were expected to lead up to a dénouement (be it tragic or comic), after a tragic climax and the extermination of the protagonists, Čapek left one entire act to be played out, and it bore no relationship whatsoever to the fate of the protagonists (who were, with one exception, dead), but rather to the fate of other characters, which of course were merely there to symbolize the continuation of rational, intelligent life. Yes, there are too many transgressions for us to consider them unintentional. Rather, the entire structure of the play referred to rules other than those professed by the theater of that time.

Even the protagonists' names are worth considering, because Čapek sometimes chose names with symbolic meanings, and he did so most consistently in *R.U.R.* As Čapek himself stated, at the source of the whole idea of robot production was reason. Reason propelled man farther and farther in his rebellion against the natural order, and as the play demonstrated, in the end it brought destruction to humankind. Many critics deduced from this an entirely anti-rationalist, romantic point of view on Čapek's part. But not only was the inventor of the robots (who never even appears in the play) symbolically named "Reason," but all the characters were given symbolic names, derived from various languages. Domin came from the Latin *dominus*; Hallemeier, the one who administered and took action, from the German for "steward of a market hall;" Busman, the financial genius who died with half a billion next to his heart, was derived from the English word "businessman." Nana came from the Russian *njanji* ("nurse"), and Dr. Gall from the famous Greek doctor Galen. The name of the builder Alquist was derived either from the Latin *aliquis*, "someone," or from the Spanish *el quisto*, "most favored," since he was the character closest to Čapek in philosophy of life, as can be seen from lines such as "I think it's better to lay a single brick than to draw up plans that are too great,"[16] which can be found many times over in Čapek's works. Sometimes names merely represent the functions or professions of their bearers, in other cases the names have a more evaluative meaning. Certainly, the variety of linguistic origins has its own symbolic value. Not only individual human beings perished on that unnamed island, but whole nations, the whole of humankind was destroyed.

We must not forget one last incident in the play. Man goes too far in his rationality, and his creation turns against him. The conflict between man and his creation ends in catastrophe for human beings and for all of human civilization. But then atonement follows. Rational, intelligent life, which man in his arrogant pride threatened, is reborn.

The fundamental message of the play is: estrangement between people and the products they create ends in catastrophe. The characters are lacking in psychological development, and their actions are quite simply characterized in or defined by their names – and these actions arise only out of their relationship to the fundamental or, one could say, fateful conflict.

Contemporary reviewers concentrated either on the social message of the play, seeing it as critical of capitalistic attitudes toward workers, a warning with respect to the dangerous differences between humanism and cold rationalism, or, focused on the play's conclusion, they saw the play as the embodiment of a romantic longing for "the primitive, the spontaneous, the vital," as F. X. Šalda wrote. Formally, the play was considered simply a dramatic utopia. Some thought it original, others "an impotent experiment, dry construction on paper" (the Norwegian newspaper *Morgenbladet*).[17]

Should we wish to understand and explain all the inconsistencies and peculiarities of the play, we would need to turn to the very beginning of dramatic creation, to the great, fateful conflicts of the ancient myths. In these too, man is usually only a representative of his tribe, engaging as such in conflicts about the meaning of existence, of justice, of truth. In these too, conflict does not derive from the clash of characters, but from the clash of principles, of man against fate, or man against supernatural forces, and the outcome of these clashes depends on the favor or disfavor of the gods.

In Aeschylus's *Oresteia*, between Agamemnon's murder and the arrival of his son, a period of time passes in which Orestes matures, yet this does not disturb the rhythm or unity of the drama. Drama was always about acts of murder and revenge, never about the character of the murderer or the avenger. And in these dramas, after revenge has been taken, after the protagonists have died, there is still a long epilogue involving the reconciliation of the Furies, the assessment of guilt, and the weighing of both deeds and their causes, an epilogue in which new characters, new protagonists appear. In mythical drama, people fight not only with each other but with a higher, fateful force, with destiny, which can be resisted but never changed. The point is to succumb with dignity.

The destruction which befell the representatives of the human "tribe" in *R.U.R.* in the end is not an expression of the will of the gods, but a consequence of human will. It is, however, equally absolute, equally irreversible, equally fatal. The destruction flows from the very essence of our civilization.

Čapek's penchant for the drama of antiquity was expressed in an article written in 1911, when he was twenty-one. In it, he praised the dramatic arrangement of Plautus's *Menaechmi*, which, ten years later, he would use in constructing his own play about robots. "After plays for all sensitivities and moral tastes, after Ibsen, after Intimate Theater ... we find in Plautus, in comparison, a simple, calm, direct classical farce ... Every character is assigned from the outset a single interest which he pursues one-dimensionally throughout the play; in the characters there are no turning points, no changes, no psychological development at all. The characters are sketched broadly, they are understood to be types, general, consistent, and simple..."[18]

R.U.R. was a remarkable attempt to give back, to an atomized world, a story of humankind as an entity, to depict fundamental contention in both its magnitude and its simplicity, something realistic drama is unable to do. To accomplish this, it was necessary to elevate individual characters to the level of representatives of humankind and of the power with which it wrestled – to elevate humankind to the level of its fate.

Considering all the above, Čapek's play seems to me, even after many decades, as effective and stimulating as when it first reached the stage.

10. The Second Report on the End of Civilization: The Absolute at Large

In September of 1921, *Lidové noviny* began publishing, each Monday, a chapter of Čapek's novel *The Absolute at Large*. "When the book came out," the author wrote some years later in a foreword to one of its many editions, "I read various well-deserved reproaches concerning it: that it was no match for Balzac's *In Search of the Absolute*, that it ends with the undignified consumption of sausages, and mainly that it is not truly a novel. That hit the nail on the head. I admit that it's not a novel at all..."[1]

The premise of Čapek's new work was within the realm of science fiction. A Czech inventor, Marek, discovers how to obtain an incredible amount of energy by splitting the atom. Čapek precisely describes this (for his time) audacious concept, and foresees humankind on the threshold of a new era that offers abundance in all areas of consumption. However, when Marek's invention is in operation, it produces a singular side effect; also present in the atom-smashing process is a non-material and therefore indestructible substance which, when unleashed, affects people's behavior in unexpected ways. This substance might be given the name God, or the Absolute, and its effect on people seems to be positive, without exception. That is to say, people who come into contact with the Absolute turn into saints dedicated to doing good deeds, and they lose interest in their ordinary activities. At the same time, the Absolute reaffirms people's belief that their individual convictions and faith are uniquely true.

The premise develops quickly. An industrial tycoon, Bondy, visits the inventor. At first he expresses understandable incredulity regarding the revolutionary invention, but he nevertheless agrees to examine the Karburator, as the atom-splitting machine is called. While doing so, he is contaminated by the Absolute, which induces in this cynical industrialist a sensation of floating, as if overcome with holy exaltation. He also envisions that, as a source of energy, Karburators are the invention of the future and a splendid prospect for a highly lucrative business, and so he immediately starts producing them.

The consequences of an abundance of inexpensive energy are overwhelming. The manufacture of all goods rises sharply, their price falls sharply and at the same time, of course, there is an increase in the numbers of those who have been contaminated by the Absolute.

Čapek skillfully made use of this science-fiction premise for the purpose of contemporary satire. Modern society cannot function well when people are driven to do nothing but good works. Says the Karburator's inventor:

> I suffered through some horrifying phenomena. I read people's thoughts, light emanated from me, I had to struggle desperately not to sink into prayer and begin preaching about faith in God. I wanted to clog the Karburator with sand, but suddenly I began to levitate ... There have even been several serious cases of workers in the factory seeing the light. I don't know where to turn, Bondy. Yes, I've tried all isolating materials that might possibly prevent the Absolute from getting out of the cellar: ashes, sand, metal walls, but nothing can stop it. I've even tried lining the cellar walls with the works of Professors Krejči, Spencer, and Haeckel, all the Positivists you can think of; if you can believe it, the Absolute penetrates even things like that.[2]

More and more, people become possessed by religious fervor. "At the Petřín telegraph station, religion broke out like an epidemic. For no earthly reason, all the telegraph operators on duty were sending out ecstatic messages to the whole world, a sort of new gospel saying that God is coming back down to earth to redeem it..." The Minister of Defense "suddenly saw the light at his villa in Dejvice. The following morning, he assembled the Prague garrison, spoke to them about eternal peace, and exhorted the troops to become martyrs..."[3]

Is it possible to eliminate the Karburator from the world? It is not. The moment some begin to protest against it, their adversaries begin to defend it. The Roman Catholic Church at first repudiates the Absolute, then declares it to be nothing other than the God to whom we have clasped our hands in prayer since childhood.

It appears that modern society cannot exist unless people turn into saints. Čapek describes the religious delirium of the Karburator factory's board of directors with sarcasm, and even moreso when saintliness overcomes bank employees: "They opened the vaults and handed out the money to anyone who came in. They finished by burning bundles of banknotes on a bonfire in the main lobby."[4]

The plot develops episodically. At times it seems as if the author simply wanted an excuse to write a satire about the behavior of the Agrarian Party and its supporters, at other times about freemasons, journalists, scientists (or pseudoscientists, rather), bureaucrats, politicians, and diplomats, so that he might put to good use his flair for aphorisms and paradox: "Thus there came into the world an unlimited abundance of everything people need. But people need everything except unlimited abundance."[5] … "You can have a revolution wherever you like, except in a government office; even were the world to come to an end, you'd have to destroy the universe first and then government offices."[6]

The story of the revolutionary invention and its consequences continues. On the one hand, the world is flooded with a multitude of products; on the other hand, there is an outbreak of mass unemployment. As the number of Karburators increases, so does the number of men and women who, having seen the light, profess the most disparate faiths, and become followers of holy leaders – a merry-go-round owner named Binder proves to be one of them, and another is the swimmer Kuzenda, who levitates and preaches from a dredge on a river. If people stand in opposition to each other, convinced that they and they alone have found the one true faith, they must, in Čapek's world, necessarily come into conflict.

The first clash seems utterly insignificant, no different from any other ordinary village brawl; it takes place between the adherents of the merry-go-ground owner and the followers of the swimmer Kuzenda. After the first clash, however, others ensue, with bigger consequences, until finally the world is caught up in "the so-called Greatest War," in which the majority of people perish. Bondy, the messenger of the author's warning, later explains the causes of the catastrophe to a sea captain with whom he has landed on an atoll in the Pacific Ocean. What was the war about? About borders, colonies, trade agreements? No, nothing that important.

> "About truth, that's all."
>
> "What sort of truth?"
>
> "The absolute truth. You know, every nation insists that it has the absolute truth."
>
> "Hm," said the captain. "What is it exactly?"
>
> "Nothing. A human passion of sorts. You've heard, haven't you, that over there in Europe, and everywhere else in fact, there came into the world ... well, you know ... God."
>
> "I did hear that."
>
> "Well, that's what it's all about, understand?"
>
> "No, I don't understand, old man. If you ask me, a true God would, you know, put things right in the world. The one they've got can't be the true and proper God."
>
> "On the contrary," said G. H. Bondy ... "I tell you, it *is* the true God. But I'll tell you something else: He's far too big ... Yes. He's infinite. That's the problem. You see, everyone measures off a few meters of Him and thinks that's the whole God..."[7]

The story actually ends at a village tavern where some of lesser participants in the great catastrophe are eating sausages with sauerkraut and chatting, as is usual at dinnertime, about the food as well as about the recent war.

"People always get back to where they used to be," observed Mr. Binder. "That's what Mr. Kuzenda always says. 'Binder,' he says, 'no truth is won by fighting. You know, Binder,' he says, 'that God of ours on the dredge wasn't so bad, and that one of yours on the merry-go-round wasn't either, and yet they're both of them disappeared. Everyone believes in his own excellent God, but he doesn't believe that somebody else might believe in something good, too. People should believe in other people, first of all, and then the rest will take care of itself.' That's what Mr. Kuzenda always says."

"You bet," Mr. Brych agreed. "You might think some other religion is a bad one, but you shouldn't think that a person who follows it is bad or nasty or deceived. Same thing in politics and in everything else."

"That's what so many people have hated and killed each other for," said Father Jošt. "You know, the bigger the things a man believes in, the more fiercely he despises those who don't. And yet the greatest of all beliefs would be to believe in people."

"Everybody thinks the best of people in general, but when it comes to the individual, not by a long shot. I'll save mankind, but I'll kill you. And that's not right, Father. The world will be an evil place until people begin believing in people."[8]

Such was the explanation of the destructive war, both the invented war (Čapek placed the novel at the beginning of the 1950s) and the real, recently ended war. Behind the genially formulated sentences of a tavern get-together, we hear the views of Čapek the philosopher. He rejected absolute truths, especially insofar as they were intended to stand above people's lives and practical concerns. He found the cause of societal conflict to be above all intolerance – in this his polemics were directed indirectly against fashionable Marxism, which sought the cause of all conflict in the disparate relationships between individuals or entire groups ("classes") and the means of production, that is, in the areas of economics and property ownership.

As I have already mentioned in the introduction to this chapter, Czech critics received *The Absolute at Large* with considerable reservations. They felt that the author had lowered himself to a substandard level, that the author's humanism was only theoretical, that real people were missing from the novel (which had merely schemata), and that the work was not sufficiently poetic.[9] It was said that Čapek had only superficially accepted pragmatism, because it conflicted with his sphere of experience, that he raised petit-bourgeois seclusion to an ideal, that his modernity was evident only in the theme, the book being conservative in composition, that he was unable to master the composition because he neglected the creative aspects, and so on.[10]

In general, Czech critics understood Čapek much less than did critics abroad, and they were far less favorable in their reception of his work than were Czech readers. They did not care for his lightness of tone, and they censured him for the impurity in his use of genres, for his strange mix of thrilling plot, satire, parody, science fiction, philosophical generalization, moralizing, and journalism, even for superficiality. *The Absolute at Large* certainly had these attributes, but alternatively we can appreciate the way Čapek integrated his literary and journalistic talents, and his goal of engaging his readers, entertaining them, making them laugh, and at the same time giving them moral lessons, alarming them about the direction in which civilization might be headed. He showed himself to be topical in his analytical observations and universal in his philosophical conclusions. Čapek was original also in his ability to write about highly serious events with an ironical smile, to create the most fantastical of situations with a Chaplinesque believability and persuasiveness. His aim was not, as we have already said in regard to *The Robber*, to attain a psychological thoroughness in his protagonists, because for him they were chiefly conveyors of certain ideas. He succeeded nonetheless in giving them a lifelike nature in a way few of his contemporaries were able to do. He succeeded as well in constructing a plot so convincingly that the philosophical conclusion which was to flow from it seemed like the only logical conclusion. The fact that he put his explanation of the nature of societal conflict, his formulation of humanism, into the mouths of folksy characters, people whom he allowed to philosophize over their plates of sausages with sauerkraut, was certainly more intellectual provocation than idealization of the "little man" or the kind of pub-philosophizing Jaroslav Hašek so brilliantly portrayed. The choice both of these folksy characters and of their milieu contributes to the fact that author's message took the form of common sense, that is, views with which it would be preposterous to disagree.

In responding to the critics' reproofs, Čapek asserted that the book was serious in intent: "I am, in my opinion, a rather dull and tireless moralist, perhaps unsuccessful, as moralists usually are. If I must tell the truth, the entire utopian plot of the book, all the joking, all the 'lowering to a substandard level' is only an excuse, a means of expressing several ideas I take very seriously."[11] I would add that, in both form and content, *The Absolute at Large* contains the last traces of the recent experience of wartime.[12]

Every literary work that attempts to react to some contemporary situation, every satire of a period risks losing its topical relevance, and therefore its effectiveness, after so many years. Such passages can be found in many of Čapek's works, and it is true that, in an attempt to entertain, Čapek at times could not resist the occasional cheap joke. But the majority of his works continue to enchant, due to their extraordinary inventiveness and wealth of ideas. As for *The Absolute at Large*, it is remarkable how many of his satirical observations and comments can even today not only entertain readers but invite comparisons with the contemporary state of affairs, even though it will soon be a hundred years since the book was written.

In *The Absolute at Large*, Čapek attempted for the first time a sprawling epic form, and he wisely chose the form of roman-feuilleton. Up to that time he had published only shorter works of prose, but the feuilleton was the genre he mastered best, and feuilletons remained his favorite form all the way to the end of his life (the majority of his later books consisted of selections from his newspaper columns). After having had a go at "how to write a novel," he could now try a "real" novel. Shortly after *Absolute* was published, he started work on *Krakatit*. But of course he still had to finish the comedy *From the Life of the The Insects*, the next-to-last work to be written with his brother Josef.

11. A Morality Play about Insects and People

The majority of writers in the first quarter of the twentieth century were influenced by two important events: the First World War and the Russian Revolution. The war shook people's faith in the prewar societal order, and exposed dangerous tendencies in contemporary civilization. Technological development could bring people affluence, but it could also bring about mass slaughter. The war revealed just how fragile a system democracy is, because in a moment of military madness the will of the people means nothing, and a human being becomes merely an object to be manipulated by ruling powers. It was as if the war had laid bare the inequality inherent in everyone's social position, deepening the misery of the poor and helping the nouveaux riches. Ordinary citizens lost all their rights in wartime, including the most important one – the right to live. Whereas official propaganda proclaimed that citizens could redeem this right through heroism, people were more likely to rely on their own shrewdness, their ability to deceive the apparently almighty government machinery. This is what Jaroslav Hašek tried to demonstrate in his brilliant novel about the Good Soldier Švejk, and he succeeded. (The book's first volume appeared in bookstores in March 1921.)

It was this shaken faith in traditional values, in divine and human justice, and in democracy as defender of citizen interests, that helped so many people believe so blindly in the ideals of the Russian Revolution. The Čapek brothers' friend S. K. Neumann wrote enthusiastically about the revolution[1]; later he would become one of the most dogmatic and most pugnacious of Czech Stalinists. Ivan Olbracht, a gifted writer and contemporary of Hašek, was one of the first Czech intellectuals to visit revolutionary Russia, in January 1920, and the articles he wrote from there in celebration of the new political system, while naïve, were filled with ardor.[2] Hašek himself became a red commissar for a period of time during his stay in the Soviet Union.

To many young writers and artists it seemed axiomatic to profess the ideals of the October Revolution, to show solidarity with the poor and the proletariat, to accept socialism as a higher and more just societal order than the system in which they lived. A whole new movement of proletarian Czech poetry came into being, the avant-garde group Devětsil, with which not only poets but a majority of other talented, creative people of the time were associated. One of the most gifted, the communist poet Jiří Wolker (who died of tuberculosis at the age of twenty-three), in one of his polemical essays, defended hatred as the feeling on which human dignity is contingent.

> As long as there are classes, there will be class hatred amongst them. As long as there are classes, there will be hearts filled with mustiness ... Let us suppose that class hatred could be eliminated while classes continued to exist! Nothing could harm the proletarian more than this. He would become an ox under an everlasting yoke, for it is hatred alone that sustains his human dignity ... Let proletarian art be like proletarian life: militant, antihumanist, dogmatic. Belief and inner verity will be its only adornment.[3]

The young poet also embodied his theories in his poetry. In one of his last poems, "The X-Ray," he placed a worker behind an x-ray shield, that machine "with the magical beauty of the XXth century." The worker complains of a heavy feeling, "as if I had lead and vipers in my chest." The doctor discovers that the man's lungs have been eaten away by want and tuberculosis, but the worker asks for a deeper x-ray. What the doctor then finds is the heaviness of a heart longing for love. The end of the poem is impassioned:

> And this heaviness, doctor, I know.
> Deeper, deeper, to the depths of my body!
> There you'll find the heaviest of burdens.

I can hardly bear it. And I'm certain
that when it emerges, it will rock the earth.
Deep as you can go, poor man, I see hatred.[4]

In his response to a survey done by the journal *Most* (Bridge) in April 1922, Čapek argued against the thesis that the new art must be class-conscious, proletarian, and communist.

> The point is not that this youthful thesis is debatable, but that a very bad habit has lodged itself in some of the younger generation, the bad habit of judging works of art according to whether they contain 'bourgeois ideology' or 'class consciousness.' My God, if certain works really do contain bourgeois ideology, it's not very nice of them; not because they're bourgeois, but because they contain any kind of ideology at all, because they have a doctrine inserted in them instead of constituting their own search for truth in the world or in some inner experience. Just because the new art has a communist ideology doesn't make it better or freer or more modern.

To understand the motivations of these artists passionate in their advocacy for revolution and revolutionary art, we must take into consideration not only the shattering experience of the war, not only the fact that all the horrors of the Russian Revolution were no match for the horrors of the war that had preceded it, but also the fact that the Bolsheviks were still proclaiming noble ideals of social justice, freedom, and equality – and that the dogmatic theory of socialist realism, enforced by threat of violence, did not yet exist. On the contrary, art was pushing in nontraditional, avant-garde directions: futurism, for instance, or the new, magnificently staged collective drama. Modern architecture and abstract painting also seemed to gain favor in the first years of their post-revolution development. Bolshevik ideologues offered artists, whose support they were still courting, not only new creative possibilities but also a new, broader public that would understand them better than the cursed, conservative bourgeoisie. Art was supposed to be for the masses. The eminent leftist literary theoretician Bedřich Václavek wrote:

> It is clear to us that art as a part of human life has no purpose in and of itself, that its purpose is to advance, to surmount human life ... The socialist way of looking at the world will be not a label, but the artist's most inner experience and basic orientation of thought, which rather than thwart true art, will deepen, strengthen it ... It is certain that this will be an art for the people, that it must not be the aristocratic privilege of a few individuals of a particular class ... There are other questions, as well. Will this art make full use of the people's artistic creativity? Or will it utilize only the people's lives? To what degree will it cultivate social themes? What stand will it take on cubism, on futurism, which some consider to be the new art of the proletariat? Further, it is necessary to clarify the concept of collectivism in art. Does it mean that the collective will be a subject for artistic creation? Does it mean that the collective will participate directly in artistic creation? Above all, does it mean that the poet is the voice of the collective?[5]

Although Čapek shared neither the ideals nor the illusions of the leftist artists, this does not mean that he had no reaction to similar experiences, that he would not try to answer similar questions. Like Václavek and the leftist writers, he too was convinced that art has no purpose in and of itself, that "literature should shape people, it should strive to have an influence upon reality itself." He added, however: "I do not so much believe in slow educational influence as in the magical, creative influence that directly generates new realities ... every literature, every grand fabulation elicits corresponding events from the fullness of life. In this I see a great moral responsibility for writers, not because they can hurt or improve people by their writing, but because they directly generate people in the image and likeness of what they write about."[6]

Čapek did not differ from leftist or communist writers by refusing to write for ordinary people – on the contrary, he wrote in a far more popular vein than most of them. He differed in his opinions on revolution and democracy. He was convinced that societal development is an important moral responsibility for each individual, and not for some sort of collective conscience ensconced by a revolution. Even writers cannot avoid their individual responsibilities, and therefore they should not support the dark forces in man, but guide their readers so that each might make his own, perhaps imperceptible contribution toward the betterment of the world and toward his own "salvation." In a journal article entitled "Save Yourself Who Can," he wrote:

> Well, I can readily understand that man expects salvation to come from the outside, simply because salvation is bound to be something different from oneself. Because he cannot believe in himself, he believes in 'something' and 'from somewhere.' If there is an error in this, it is that man wants to be completely and instantly saved.
>
> Let's suppose that 'to be saved' is just like 'to lift oneself up.' Perhaps each of us as a child tried to pick himself up ... Unfortunately (to mankind's great disadvantage), it's not possible. Man cannot lift himself up to any height. Man cannot save himself. Either he has to be let down on some sort of rope from above, or he has to be given some sort of hoisting power. Apparently it's the same with salvation.
>
> And yet man can indeed 'lift himself up.' If it's not possible to go straight up, he can go at an angle. If he can't grab his pants and pull himself up, he can build a ladder and climb that. He 'lifts himself' with every step taken under his own power. And so perhaps it is possible to save ourselves by our own power. If not straight up, then at an angle; if not instantly, then step by step, gradually, in small, everyday, partial acts of salvation. Perhaps it's possible to substitute for absolute redemption a relative salvation of thousands of steps. Perhaps it's even possible to save oneself a little bit each day. Wherever we are. In our ordinary everydayness. Perhaps the error in our view of salvation is that we are used to saying 'to be saved' instead of 'to save oneself.' ... All I'm saying is: of course salvation is possible, because we need it. So save yourself who can. Save yourself.[7]

For Čapek, as we shall see, the revolutionary stance was an expression of negativism which presupposed that, for the creation of a better world and better relations, it was first necessary to eliminate the old world and its relations by force. For the majority of its proponents, that meant expropriation, the deprivation of rights and, if need be, the wholesale slaughter of all whom the revolutionary leaders consider their enemies. Revolution, which for leftist writers meant the purification and renewal of humankind, was for him no more than an expression of an immoral, corrupting force that let off steam above all by destroying values.

Čapek responded to Wolker's praise of hatred in his 1924 article, "Why Am I Not a Communist?" "In one of his ballads Jiří Wolker says: 'Deep as you can go, poor man, I see hatred.' This is a terrible word, particularly because it is entirely the wrong one. For deep in the hearts of the poor is a remarkable, beautiful cheerfulness. The worker at his machine likes making jokes far more than does the owner or director of the factory ... and if someone in a household is singing, it's far more likely to be the maid, scrubbing floors, than her mistress..."[8]

In 1921, the Čapek brothers responded to the socially tempestuous time with the allegorical comedy *From the Life of the Insects*. It was the most critical and moralizing depiction of human behavior ever written by Karel, with or without his brother. This insect morality play consists of three different sections – the Butterflies, the Predators, and the Ants – linked by the character of the Tramp, the only human in the play. The Tramp (often in overlong monologues) comments on what the audience is seeing on stage.

Of course the play has a unity of purpose: to caricature, through the lives of several species of insects, such base human traits as snobbery, superficiality, stinginess, selfishness, cruelty, envy, the herd mentality, and deceit. The first, Butterfly part – the section most conspicuously bearing the earmarks of the younger Čapek's hand – is full of witty Shavian or Wildian conversation. Here is a satire on sex, with eager women, an old philanderer, and a shy poet, all within a small space. The butterflies can be understood as critical portraits of decaying morals, primarily in the upper circles of contemporary society.

In the second section, the conversational lightness has disappeared, undoubtedly owing to the change in theme. Instead of love, the satire here is about the rapacity, heartlessness, and cruelty that govern society. One species hunts another, the hunters accompanying their merciless activity with high-flown words about their own goodness and family affection – soon, however, they themselves will become the prey of still other predators. The death of one improves the odds for another in the fight for one's life. This section of the comedy is composed of small scenes "from life," with parodic declarations that aim to capture in simplified form the "ideals" of contemporary bourgeois society.

Mr. Cricket brings his pregnant wife to their new apartment and happily explains that it previously belonged to another cricket who, only the day before, had been impaled on a thorn by a butcherbird.

> Mr. Cricket: I swear it, Honey, spiked him all through and through. Just imagine! He's up there wriggling his legs like this, see? Hihihi! He's still alive. And I thought right away, there's something in this for us! We'll move into his apartment. Bang! What luck! Hihi! What do you say?
>
> Mrs. Cricket: And he's still alive? Ugh! What a horror!
>
> Mr. Cricket: Isn't it? Oh, we're so lucky! Tralala, tralala...[9]

A Dung Beetle rolling around a stolen ball of dung comments: "Well, I say it's nice to own things. My treasure! My beautiful little fortune! My jewel! My everything! To have my own! To put away a little something..."[10]

When Mrs. Dung Beetle declares: "A ball ... that means family. That means the future. That's what life is all about...," Mrs. Cricket objects: "Oh, no. Life is having one's own house, one's nest, one's shop. And pretty curtains. And children. And one's own Cricket. One's own household. And that's it."[11]

The Parasite's views are meant to caricature revolutionary slogans:

> Parasite: There's no equality. For example, I don't kill anybody. My mandibles are too soft for the job. What I mean is, my conscience is too soft. I don't have the necessary tools of production. All I have is hunger. And this is supposed to be right?
>
> Tramp: No ... no ... one should not kill.
>
> Parasite: My words, my friend. Or at least one shouldn't hoard. You stuff yourself and you've had enough. Hoarding is robbing those who don't know how to hoard. Stuff yourself and then stop. Then there would be enough of everything for everybody, isn't that right?[12]

In the third section, about an ant nation and its great war, the authors elaborate on the idea that all the goals of war, any war, in comparison with the cosmic dimensions of time and space, is futile and vain. In an echo from the recent war, they have the ants prattle on about world peace, national will, and historic rights, about longstanding rivalries and lebensraum, their own territory consisting of a small scrap of a path between two blades of grass. It is over this terrain that the ants will fight a life-or-death battle.

Another type of futility and vanity – this time of life in general – is represented by the character of the Chrysalis. From this will emerge a mayfly, who declares in ecstacy its paradoxical message:

> Chrysalis/Mayfly: Oh - oh - oh! (Stops) I proclaim the era of life. I command all creation: Live, for the kingdom of life has come. (Whirling) Oh - oh - oh!
>
> A few last mayflies: Eternal, eternal is life. (They fall dead.)
>
> Chrysalis/Mayfly (stops): The entire world swelled up to bring me forth, / and cracked in pain. Hear, oh hear, / I bring a tremendous message; I bring you tidings / of immense things! Silence! Silence! / I bring great words. (Falls dead)[13]

This dismal picture of futility, this dark picture of a society in which everyone lies in wait to deprive someone else of property or even life, seems to be far outside the usual Čapekian view of the world, in which each has a mission to add his imperceptible contribution to the common good. This departure may certainly be explained by the influence of his co-author; the older of the brothers had decidedly less lightness and lenience than did Karel, nor did he have any philosophical barriers against speaking with considerable overstatement about what he found most oppressive and disturbing in the contemporary world. Many critics accused the play of cynicism, negativism (which Karel rejected outright), pessimism, and also, of course, of formal dispersion, an inability to give the work a unified shape. But since Karel agreed to co-write this bitter allegory, he must have had a reason. I think that, in those stirred-up postwar times, when most artists prided themselves on their opposition to bourgeois society and declared the working man their sole life-affirming hero, the younger brother too felt a need to demonstrate his understanding and condemnation of what was repellent in contemporary society. The brothers exaggerated human attributes to the point of stereotype, with stinginess exemplified by dung beetles, lethal insatiability by ichneumon flies, brainless flirting by butterflies, the poverty of the bourgeois ideal by crickets, and the vileness of revolutionary slogans by parasites – and with a society in which some are manipulators and the others merely an obedient mass, symbolized by ants. And when they were criticized for presenting so dark a picture of society, the brothers pointed out that behavior in the insect kingdom could never be transferred in its entirety to human society. What appears to people to be brutal murder in the realm of the insects is matter of course, is necessity, in fact.

The insect allegory – quite unusual for that time – allowed for all kinds of interesting production possibilities. The play was successful at home as well as abroad. One of the communist critics of the time was puzzled by the paradox that those sitting and enjoying themselves in the audience were precisely the same bourgeoisie being ridiculed and attacked. Another critic predicted that the play would one day serve as valuable evidence of postwar psychosis in Czech society. Yet when I recently saw a new production of the comedy, it seemed to me that its simplified symbols had lost much of their potency – in particular the ants' militaristic, totalitarian state, an allegory which, after the experiences of the twentieth century, seemed almost too riddled with slogans to be effective. But of course, *From the Life of the Insects* was only a small digression for Čapek.

12. To Live Briefly, But Fully

Not long after *The Robber*, *R.U.R.*, and his collaboration on *From the Life of the Insects*, Čapek wrote another drama, *The Makropulos Secret*. This play, too, had a fantastical theme, but it opens realistically, in the law office of the attorney representing Albert Gregor in a property dispute with Jaroslav Prus. The lawsuit concerns a piece of real estate valued in the millions, it has been going on for nearly one hundred years, the High Court is about to pass final judgment, and it is obvious that the decision will favor Prus, the property's owner. At that moment a famous singer, Emilia Marty, appears. She has learned of the trial, and she informs the attorney and his client that there are some hundred-year-old documents, hidden in a cupboard at Prus's house, which will provide evidence in Gregor's favor. The most important of these, in a sealed yellow envelope, is a will bequeathing the disputed estate and its lands to one of Gregor's ancestors.

The attorney considers this news to be an inept joke, because no one can know the contents of an envelope that has been sealed for a hundred years. In defiance of any reasonable explanation, it so happens that the envelope has in fact been lying forgotten in that exact spot and, further, it contains a last will and testament that indeed provides evidence in Gregor's favor.

In declaring her detailed knowledge of various events that took place centuries ago, the character of Emilia Marty becomes even more puzzling. It also happens that a certain elderly nobleman appears and finds that Emilia looks incredibly like his Spanish lover of long ago, a dancer named Eugenia Montez. Emilia is famous, beautiful, mysterious, and at the same time cold and cynical – which may be what makes her so attractive to men that they lose their heads over her. The young Janek

Prus, upon discovering that his father has spent the night with her, even commits suicide.

The thriller, essentially a realistic story with a secret, develops over three acts. The playwright gradually transfers the audience's interest from the introductory property dispute to the character of Emilia. Who might this enigmatic woman be? Why has she turned up to help Gregor, whom she does not know at all? At the conclusion of the play, the puzzle is solved. Emilia is the daughter of the famous Greek alchemist Makropulos, who served at the Prague court of Holy Roman Emperor Rudolf II and who discovered the elixir of eternal youth, guaranteed to halt the ageing process for three hundred years. The emperor was afraid to drink the elixir, so he ordered his alchemist to test it first on the alchemist's own daughter. Thus it happened that Emilia has lived on, under many different names, for another three hundred years. Now, however, the elixir has run its course and is no longer effective, and Emilia has come because the formula for the elixir is among the old documents hidden in Prus's house. She obtains the formula by spending the night with Prus. When the others discover the revolutionary information contained in the old parchment, they drug Emilia and, while she sleeps, begin to discuss whether they shouldn't take the formula away from her. Their discussion soon turns toward another question: what would it mean to own the key to longevity, or even to immortality? To whom should they allow access to the formula?

Vitek, the law clerk, advocates the possibility of a prolonged life: "We die like animals. What is life after death? Immortality of the soul? Only a desperate protest against the shortness of life. Man has never accepted this animal part of life. He cannot accept it because it is too unjust to live for such a short time. A man should be a little more than a turtle or a raven. A man needs more time to live."[1]

Prus objects that even the time allotted is unnecessarily long for ordinary human riffraff. "But, if I may: the ordinary, small, stupid human being never dies. A small person is everlasting, even without your help. Smallness multiplies without rest, like flies or mice. Only greatness dies."[2] He proposes that the formula be made available only to the strong and capable, so that a new aristocracy may be established.

Emilia wakes up and enters into this passionate dispute. She describes the horrors of longevity. Life loses its tension, freshness, unexpectedness, and turns into endless tedium. "No one can love for three hundred years. Nor hope, nor create, nor look on. Everything is tiresome. It is tiresome to be good, it is tiresome to be bad. Heaven and earth are tiresome. And then you find out that there is nothing at all: no sin, no pain, neither heaven nor earth, nothing. The only thing that exists is a thing with meaning. For you, all things have meaning ... You live, but in us all life has stopped..." In her despair she cries: "Idiots! You are so happy! ... And all because of this silly accident, you will soon die!"[3]

The play ends with Emilia offering the formula to the others, but they have become so frightened by her dispirited testimony that they refuse it. Finally, the youngest of them, Vitek's daughter Krista, accepts the old parchment and, just as in *R.U.R.* Helena had burned the formula for the production of robots, before everyone's eyes Krista burns the formula for longevity. "It's burning out," comments Gregor. "After all, it was a wild idea, to live forever. God, I feel lonely, but a bit lighter, knowing it isn't possible anymore..."[4]

In his foreword to the book edition of the play, Čapek remarked that the idea had come to him three or four years previously, while reading Metchnikoff's theory explaining the ageing process as due to an organism's autointoxication.

For the most part, the creative stimulus for Čapek was an idea rather than a need to depict an individual's fate. Therefore, the entire structure of the play aims not at the revelation of character, but at the revelation of the fundamental idea. He created his characters so as to represent that idea most convincingly, and so that they would arrive at the conclusion to which he wished to bring audiences and readers. The unanimity of the characters refusing longevity is highly improbable, from a psychological point of view, and the characters' behavior, when considered logically, can only be deemed irresponsible. The final lines of the play are among the least convincing, the most contrived of all that Čapek wrote.

What Čapek intended to convey in *The Makropulos Secret* was the idea that people should not yearn for an unreachable longevity whose consequences they cannot begin to foresee, but rather live so that even the brief time allotted to us will have been spent living fully, experiencing things, accomplishing things, and managing to be happy. It should be said that, though Čapek looked for inspiration more in his own ideas than in the fate of individuals, at the same time (as is true of every artist) he wrote about matters that affected him in a personal way. In this regard, *The Makropulos Secret* is characteristic. According to the recollections of those who knew him well, Čapek was very much afraid of death. Jarmila Čapková, the wife of his brother Josef, recalls that when the brothers' father died of stomach cancer, Karel fell into a fit of hypochondria and underwent a meticulous investigation to determine whether his vitals too were threatened by a tumor.[5] His hypochondria, obviously induced by his mother, was intensified by his fragile health, and doctors at that time did not know how to name or diagnose the spinal disease from which he suffered. Their diagnoses differed, and some of them actually predicted a very premature death. The thought that he had only a negligible amount of time to live surely explains his feverish creativity at the beginning of the 1920s, as well as his interest in the idea of longevity, and why and how he resolved the play as he did. In his foreword to the play, he defended himself against those who, because of Emilia's dispirited speeches, found the play pessimistic: "On the contrary, my intention in this comedy was to tell people something consoling and optimistic. I don't know if it's optimistic to maintain that to live sixty years is bad, while to live three hundred years is good. I think that to declare adequate and quite good enough a life of sixty years (on average) is not exactly committing the crime of pessimism."

However much *The Makropulos Secret* might seem a fabricated fantasy, it expressed one of Čapek's essential concerns. It was meant to affirm such life as might be reasonable for the majority of people to expect, and to reject all unrealizable – even though comforting – dreams.

13. Personal Crisis and Flight to Italy

At the same time that Čapek was so urgently courting Olga Scheinpflugová, he met a delicate, intelligent, twenty-year-old beauty named Věra Hrůzová, the daughter of a university professor in Brno. Čapek was dazzled by her. "What exactly should I write to you, Věra?" is the first sentence of the first of many letters he wrote to her.

> It would have to be a lot, things that are very, very odd; or – the rest would scarcely be worth it ... Věra, I'm thinking of one thing: you once said (on December 19, at a quarter to six) that you were a scoundrel. And I said that I was a scoundrel. Now I'm wondering if you're just as great a scoundrel as I. It's a pity you can't write about it; it is, Věra, a burningly urgent theme, and as soon as you return to Prague we'll have to measure our scoundrelosity. I'm living on a knife's edge. I must fall to one side or the other. Enough, enough, we can hardly talk about that.[1]

Whether his reference to a knife's edge and a fall had to do with his relationship with Olga and the beginning of his relationship with Věra, or perhaps to the intensity of his work, we can only guess. Čapek preferred to hint rather than deal directly with personal matters, but he usually wrote quite openly about his work. It's therefore possible that he was considering which of the two women he would prefer. The flame lasted for only a very short time: Věra was engaged to a young nobleman named Dohalský, and Čapek was preparing to marry Olga. Both couples had their plans thwarted, however. The relationship between Karel and Olga changed to friendship, and Dohalský canceled his engagement to Věra. In the middle of June 1922, relations between Karel Čapek and Věra Hrůzová were renewed, although not with particularly serious feelings on Věra's part.

At roughly the same time, Čapek began to consider a new novel with a utopian theme. In a letter dated July 5, 1922, he announced to Olga: "Since I finished with my Elena Makropulos, I've written several short articles and found many nice boletus mushrooms; in addition, I feel pressure in my head from *Krakatit*, you know, that novel about explosives. As soon as I return to Prague, I'll sit down with it in my free moments, because it won't leave me alone anymore."[2]

However abbreviated the reference to "that novel about explosives," it can be assumed that Čapek did indeed intend to write a new utopian work. The basic concept involved the invention of an exceptionally effective explosive and the ensuing peril for humankind. Čapek obviously wanted to develop the idea that those who dream up overly grandiose plans are frequently dangerous to those around them. But what was to become the main theme of the novel was still waiting for its inspiration.

Work on the novel progressed slowly, which was understandable, given Čapek's unusual workload. In a December 16 letter to Věra, he complained about a lack of time. "There is nothing, nothing, nothing new in the world. To date, the novel remains at chapter 11½, I've had to redo much of it: for example, I was studying a scholarly book about explosives, and I discovered that I'd gotten everything about them wrong. God, what a complicated world it is; you can't think laxly even about such a simple thing as chemistry."[3] Not until December 31 did he announce to Olga that he'd finished chapter thirteen. (*Krakatit* has fifty-four of them.)

Although work on the novel was at a standstill, the relationship between Věra and Čapek seemed to be developing, even though Čapek had expressed from the beginning his usual apprehension that the tie might become too binding for him. In one of his first letters in their renewed correspondence, he professes and warns her: "Věra, only one thing in life has value: freedom. And if love and freedom were mutually exclusive, I would choose freedom. Likewise, even to you, who – perhaps from lack of more frivolous amusement – have a preference for love, I say with evangelical earnestness: better black wings than pink handcuffs. 'Serious' love, you know, is love that binds; love must be unserious, immensely unserious."[4]

Soon, however, at least on Čapek's part, the relationship became more intense, tempered only by the distance between the two cities in which they lived. Whenever Čapek traveled to Brno, therefore, he wrote in advance to urgently request a meeting, telling of his sadness and loneliness, and assuring her, even if only in hints, that he loved her and that he was sad precisely because he did love her. Once he ended his letter with "I.K.Y.M.D.V.W.M.W.B. with G.L. etc.," which can be interpreted with the resources of even someone who has little interest in puzzles as: "I kiss you, my dear Věra, with my whole being, with great love." Love can also be heard in his Christmas greeting for the year 1922:

> God, what is beautiful? Beautiful are chrysanthemums, but beautiful also are the stars, the stars in the sky (especially in my Vinohrady neighborhood); beautiful are the nights, love is beautiful, and most beautiful of all is joy; beautiful are memories and longing and meeting together, beautiful is nearness and distance, sometimes even suffering is beautiful. What of all this should I wish you? Beautiful it is to sit at the edge of a field near a factory fence above Královo Pole and not to admit what's real; beautiful it is admit it, beautiful are roses fading on a pillow just abandoned, more beautiful than anything is what was, and what was not and yet can be and will...[5]

Nevertheless, even this relationship did not develop into an intimacy that could end in a matrimonial union. Whether this was because of Čapek's ongoing relationship with Olga or his worsening nervous indisposition, or the fear that none of his romantic relationships could culminate in marriage, cannot be determined. Evidently, a closer union of any sort had never even occurred to Věra.

On March 8, 1923, Čapek reported to Věra that, for reasons of health, he was making preparations for a trip south:

> I'm not well. You see, they've found something wrong inside, and for the most part my nerves are done for; in short, the doctors are sending me south for at least four weeks. So I'm slowly getting ready for the trip; I wanted to go to Spain, but I don't have the courage; therefore to Italy, perhaps all the way to Sicily, I don't yet know, in any case, any place where I can be a mute hermit. I live in solitude, I flee from everyone; I'm not the least bit cheerful, on the contrary bad-tempered, sad. I'm not working, I'm fed up with everything, nothing pleases me.[6]

In April, Čapek actually did leave for Italy, and during his six-week trip he sent back short travel sketches, which were published in *Lidové noviny*. And later that same year (with a few additional sketches thrown in) they appeared as a slim little book entitled *Letters from Italy*.

Letters from Italy may have come as something of a surprise to his readers. It was as if the book's author, who in his latest plays and novels (and often in his journalism) had been dealing with great social themes, who brilliantly linked his utopian stories with satirical depictions of contemporary society, it was if he were suddenly looking at the world differently, more calmly. He wrote again and again about Italian art – and expertly; after all, at the beginning of his literary career he had written dozens of reviews and essays on art. In Padua he praised Giotto and Donatello, in Assisi he reflected on the dissimilarities in the way Giotto and Cimabue painted; he wrote about the great contrast among the classical master painters and among the classical stonemasons, who had produced statues by the hundreds; he viewed Italian baroque with displeasure, just as he did the filth of Naples and the custom of robbing foreigners. With lyrical enthusiasm, at times to the point of exaggeration, he described the beauty of the Italian landscape, the ancient cities, and the sea. And there was in the book an optimism unexpected in so skeptical an author. "Believe me in this: with a bit of simplicity and patience, you could travel the whole world over. By and large – with very few exceptions – you can put your trust in people; nothing strengthens optimism more than this experience."

Certainly it was a most unexpected, limited approach. After all, only a few months had passed since Mussolini's fascist putsch. But Čapek, always so interested in political events, mentioned them only twice, and he did so with a sigh of relief that, thank God, he was not a politician and therefore didn't have to show interest in the fascists. Of course it makes no sense to reproach an author for writing what he wrote about, or for not writing what, for some reason, he didn't want to write about. To mention this sudden limitation in Čapek's outlook makes sense only to the extent that it helps us understand his state of mind, the crisis he apparently was going through. Hidden behind the words and observations of a pilgrim fascinated by art and landscape were the tension and depression from which he was desperately trying to escape, into precisely that world of art and nature where he could set his mind at rest, be calm.

His relationship with Věra, which seemed less full of conflict and which Čapek had as if in reserve (from Italy he sent her only postcards with brief greetings), apparently tortured him less than his still intense yet, as he believed, unfulfillable relationship with Olga Scheinpflugová. At this same time, Olga obviously was pressuring him to seal his association with her in marriage, which only intensified his feeling that he was wronging her with his love.

The letters he sent to Olga from Italy offer a completely different image of the state of his soul from the delightful travel jottings in *Letters from Italy*. "I'm boring deep into my solitude like a worm into cheese," he wrote from Rome. "I have a burning need for some sort of purification."

The thirty-three-year-old writer complained self-pityingly from Palermo:

> I've realized that my greatest passion is being calm; that's why I love the sea and silence. I'm no longer young, so perhaps this entire 'nervous disorder' was merely a transition from an illusory

and somewhat sickly youth into the current state ... Perhaps I'll never again be as exuberant and cheerful as I used to be; I want to be calm and quiet and concentrated. I haven't much enjoyed life, and I suppose I won't be able to anymore, but I don't regret it, I'm not sad or disappointed; it's just as well. If only if I could find a calmness of soul, so that I wouldn't have to torture myself. So I wouldn't be bad-tempered and gloomy.[7]

He asks Olga to believe that, in everything he has done and will do, he thinks more of her than of himself.

Don't beg anymore, my girl, because I find it so painful and shameful that I could cry. But there is something, in regard to me, which I must beg of you. How many times you've told me that you want only to nurse me, to cook porridge for me, put compresses on me and all but change my diapers ... I'm astonished at how little you know me; forgive me, but my approach to life is more masculine and perhaps tougher than you think. The moment I became dependent upon such humiliating attentions, I would simply take my life. My life is discipline, work, a serious search for truth, for love, and other strong and rigorous attitudes. I loathe softness and unmanliness ... And now, to go directly – without detours or weakness – to the main point: you have written me about our marrying, and you're surely waiting for a straightforward answer. Alas, alas, alas! I don't have one. Not yet, I don't yet know what to do, nothing's clear to me yet.[8]

Reminding us of Franz Kafka in his hesitancy, self-accusations, and complaints about his fragility, Čapek claims that the one who has doubts about him is he himself, a broken man suffering from neurasthenia.

[There are days] when a man cannot bear the voice of anyone near, when a man would simply cry out in revulsion if someone came near him. Up to now I've been able to overcome this, but you can't imagine the amount of strain, you can't imagine how I suffer sometimes when you reproach me for having nothing to say to you, for not loving you anymore, and it was perfect torture for me to say anything at all. I don't know if you can imagine these states of mind. Sometimes it's just a need for

> silence, nothing but silence and solitude, other times it's a need for love and quiet conversation, and always, always it's a need for calm. These are not moods, my girl, this is suffering, this is a sickness that needs to be cured ... Perhaps this state I'm in is only a transition to growing old, I don't know; I only know that during this crisis I must live the life of a hermit. Just today, after your letter arrived, I locked myself in, lay down, looked up at the ceiling, and pled my cause to you because my conscience was torturing me again. It will torture me as long as you suffer, and the greatest horror is that I think that you'd suffer more if I were near. Much more and much worse. God, if only these anxieties would stop tormenting me! And don't think that my worries have any bearing on the physical, on what is or is not or cannot be between us. My God, I think about this least of all, especially now, from this distance; I think about it, and it torments me, whenever I'm by your side and I see you so young and so rich in beauty. But here it is somewhat removed from me, I cannot even imagine it; here I listen only to my inner voices and wait to begin breathing more calmly, more like a normal person. I've been awfully irritable today; I'm sick of Naples, with its sun, its clamor, its contented, noisy people. I dream about a sort of frozen solitude in the mountains, where it's immensely quiet ... If there were some kind of monastery without a religion, I would go there immediately.[9]

During the several weeks of separation, however, Čapek was struggling toward a final decision. He begs Olga to believe that he loves her, and he asks that she not feel sorry for him. "I'm a weak man," he declares, "but in my weakness is my strength; my sadness doesn't hurt me; my weariness is, at the same time, my contemplating; my self-denial is at the same time my integrity. I'm a bit different, a bit strange; not a bad fellow, for I love, I love you, people, and the entire world more than myself, and I still hope to do much that is good. I'd like to do something good wherever I look, and you don't know how it tears me apart when I see that I'm causing pain..."[10] This attitude, which couples his weakness with a strength to be provided primarily by the love and understanding of someone near and beloved, reminds us of the poems of the fifteen-year-old student who complained to his beloved Anielka:

> I've grown old too soon and matured in soul and heart ... and so now, though not yet sixteen, my true youth has passed and I am a man without fire, without strength, virtually without a goal, with a soul as sensitive as a mimosa. And yet there was a time when even I myself hoped, and others believed, that something exceptional would come from me, something that would do a great deal, both socially and morally, for humanity and for the nation.[11]

Some twelve years older (although still and always young), Čapek tried to convince Olga that he could offer her only a different sort of relationship from what men generally offered, something different from what she is looking forward to, and he pleaded for her understanding, compassion, and acceptance.

> Understand, finally, this gentle, constant, yet vital bond; for God's sake, this is all that I can give you at this moment with a clean conscience, without feeling anguished and broken, and I beg of you, for God's sake, do not say that this is very little and that it is without value, this would, you see, humiliate me terribly. I give my whole self to you in this union, but without my bad qualities, without my love of solitude, without my instability ... There have been awfully many misunderstandings between us, dear girl, and now I beg you humbly, let there be peace between us! Don't be cruel to me anymore, don't cry, don't suffer, don't complain, don't reproach me; in this respect, I'm returning far more sensitive than when I left, for I've been purified in many things, peeled and covered, in many places, with something like a new, very thin and sensitive skin.[12]

Several days later he adds, with resignation (how can one not be reminded of Franz Kafka's resignation when he gave up on his repeated attempts at love): "Nature drew a circle around me which I cannot cross; I sit within it, and I am learning how to love life, at least for others if not for myself; I work as best I know how, and I am calm."[13]

Six weeks later Čapek returned from his Italian journey, perhaps already having decided how to resolve his relationship with Olga, with whom, after all, he had not that long ago been planning a life together. And as for his other love? Whatever his plans and intentions might have been, they no longer mattered. At the beginning of summer, 1923, Věra communicated to a surprised Čapek that she was to be married. She certainly was not betraying him; more than likely she was saving both herself and him a multitude of troubles.[14]

14. Return of the Robber

Repeatedly invoking his solitary, monkish life, Čapek now felt completely abandoned and, as writers in such situations often do, he fell back on his work. In an imaginary story, he could successfully realize everything that he was unable to do in life, and in his protagonist, who has little in common with him, he could create the man he wished he could be.

His work on *Krakatit* continued with great speed and intensity over the summer of 1923, and at the end of August he wrote to Olga that he had finished the fifty-second chapter and that he was writing with ease, all in one stroke. On September 7 – satisfied with himself in this regard, at least – he announced to Věra that *Krakatit* was finished.

Krakatit really began, and was obviously conceived, as a science-fiction novel about a powerful explosive with a destructive force similar to that of the atomic bomb; in fact, the explosive was founded on the same principle, that of releasing the energy hidden in the atoms of an explosive substance. Since it is capable of destroying entire cities and countries, the explosive – Krakatit – and its inventor – the engineer Prokop – understandably become objects of interest to foreign companies and powers. The greatest threat to Prokop is kidnapping, because he is the only one who knows the formula for producing the explosive, in other words, he holds enormous power in his hands.

The novel opens dramatically with a mysterious explosion of several grains of Krakatit, which Prokop had forgotten to sweep out from under a table (the rest of the substance, in a box, did not explode). Wounded and feverish, Prokop wanders the streets, where he is found by a former classmate, Tomeš, who takes him to his apartment. Delirious, Prokop reveals part of the formula for his revolutionary explosive. His former classmate, about whom the author tells us only that he too is a chemist, that he's in debt, and that he's getting ready to visit his father in the countryside, leaves Prokop lying in his apartment and disappears. Prokop continues to teeter on the borderline between delirium and consciousness. The next morning, a young woman in a veil rings the doorbell, looking for Tomeš. She claims that he is at a very difficult point in his life and might do something to himself unless he receives help. Prokop is so enchanted by the young woman that, in spite of his condition, he promises to find Tomeš. She then brings a small package which Prokop is to hand over to his friend.

In a wretched state, Prokop sets out to find Tomeš's father. But the moment he finds him (the father, just like Čapek's father, is a country doctor), he loses consciousness. When he comes to, some time later, his memory is completely clouded. Fortunately, the seriously ill Prokop is taken care of by the old doctor and his daughter, Anči. What follows is the first love intermezzo – Krakatit is forgotten – in which there is space and time for tender love to grow between Prokop and the doctor's daughter. Yet this simple love, without any conflicts, does not satisfy Prokop (nor the author). His memory returns, and he remembers the small package he was supposed to deliver and the young woman who had so enchanted him. When he opens the package, he finds money and a letter inside. From the letter he discerns that its author, the same young woman about whom he knows nothing, not even her name, is generous and obviously unattached. Suddenly swelled with emotion, Prokop decides that he must find her.

The next scene is a good piece of adventure writing. Prokop is searching for the unknown woman, and some shady people are searching for him. His laboratory has been burglarized and all his notes, the results of twenty years of research, have disappeared. Then a mysterious Mr. Carson turns up at his laboratory, enthusiastic about the destructive power that he surmises Prokop's invention contains, and he tries to entice Prokop into his service, promising him power and wealth.

Prokop refuses, he is obsessed with only one thought: he must find the girl in the veil. Resolute to the end, Prokop sets out for Balttin, an eerie facility for the production of munitions. He believes that he will find Tomeš there, and Tomeš will be able to help him find the young woman he longs for.

He does actually make it to Balttin and there meets up with the mysterious Carson, who welcomes him as someone delivering a revolutionary invention. Prokop has come for an entirely different reason, of course, but he soon realizes that he can no longer leave, that they are holding him there as a highly distinguished prisoner.

In the midst of the Balttin munitions complex is the castle where Prokop is housed and where he is introduced to a group of aristocrats, one of whom he finds himself greatly attracted to: the proud, beautiful princess Wilhelmina.

The "Balttin captivity" is the longest section of the novel, and we can assume that it was not previously planned. Rather, it was Čapek's fictional answer to the situation in which he had suddenly found himself. Just as in *The Robber* – although this time in far more effective scenes – he attempted to create a male character who was a hero of almost mythical power.

Even though he has never ridden a horse, Prokop tames a wild gelding and demonstrates exceptional riding skills. One scene ends with a fall caused by the princess, who tricks him (Prokop is hurt, but he gains her admiration and compassion). In another captivating scene, when challenged by the high-spirited group of nobles, Prokop crushes a thick bottle in his hands. Finally, in two grand scenes he resists an entire army of besiegers. And Prokop's appearance is "roughly" masculine. His face is rugged, his body is covered with scars from all sorts of injuries, he is even missing a little finger.

The new Robber is much more successful than his predecessor. The proud and once indifferent princess gives herself to him entirely and is willing to run away with him, renounce her noble birth, and spend her life with him. What follows is a succession of masterfully written erotic scenes that Čapek will never repeat.

It seems that Čapek embodied in Prokop's character all the qualities life had failed to grant him: physical strength, dexterity, the ability to fight against large numbers of people, and even to gain the physical love of a seemingly unattainable woman.

At the same time, Prokop also gains affection and attention in ways closer to Čapek's own experience and nature: through his physical suffering. Time and again, the hero in *Krakatit* falls deathly ill or is severely wounded – and each time he is tended with affection and love, each time his suffering intensifies the feelings of the women who nurse him.

Love between Prokop and the princess, no matter how passionate, is nonetheless doomed to failure. During the climactic scene, in which their relationship ends, Prokop, in a fit of jealousy, accuses the princess of being nothing but a tool of those who want to acquire Krakatit. In the same speech in which he refuses the princess, he again declares his only love to be the mysterious young woman in the veil: "I'm engaged; even though I don't know her, I have betrothed myself to her." The princess is deeply hurt. Afraid that he will lose her, Prokop promises to hand over Krakatit – but their relationship has been irrevocably destroyed. The princess takes Prokop out of the castle and disappears from his life.

This large, love-oriented – we can almost say inserted – section of *Krakatit* ends, and Čapek returns to his original plot. Prokop meets a devilish tempter, Daimon, who takes him to a mountaintop and tells him that he controls a transmitter which can, at a distance of a thousand kilometers, cause Krakatit to explode. In alliance with him, Prokop will have the power to become ruler of the world.

> Do you want to rule the world? Good. Do you want to annihilate the world? So be it. Do you want to make the world happy by forcing upon it eternal peace, God, a new order, revolution, or something of the sort? Why not? Simply begin; it doesn't matter what your agenda is – in the end, you will do

> only what the reality you've created forces you to do ... Stop at nothing in your efforts to achieve your great ideals ... You are the first man in the world who can consider the whole world his laboratory. At the top of a mountain this is the supreme temptation; I am not giving you all that is below you for the enjoyment and delight of power; it is given to you to conquer, to transform, to try and create something better than this cruel, wretched world...

And so Čapek returns to the theme which for years he has repeatedly deployed: his protagonist, by possessing the secret to a destructive explosive, can dictate to the world, can change it to something closer to his ideals. This is the peril that threatens everyone who has power, who desires to somehow change the world.

The plot develops quickly in the next few chapters. Prokop attends a meeting of anarchists; a beautiful anarchist tries to seduce him; Daimon takes him to the place where he transmits the beams that will ignite Krakatit; and Prokop flees from there, searching for Tomeš, who can tell him about the woman in the veil. Tomeš is working at another facility for the manufacture of explosives, and he refuses to see Prokop because he is just now finishing a production run of Krakatit, based on the formula which Prokop, in his delirium, had revealed. Prokop desperately tries to convince the messenger sent by Tomeš to have his friend receive him. In his plea, we hear an exaggerated version of Čapek. "'I – I – ,' stammered Prokop, 'I only want to know the address, you see? That's all I want to know. I'll give you anything if you'll only give it to me. You ... you're married and have children, but I ... I'm alone ... and I only want to find...'" Prokop does not obtain the address of the mysterious love of his dreams. Because he knows that at the moment Tomeš manufactures Krakitit, Daimon's wave transmission will reach it and a disastrous explosion will occur, he prepares to flee. An explosion does occur, and its masterful description seems to foreshadow the horrific image of the atomic bomb.

From the meeting with the mystery woman in the veil, the love scenes with Anči, the doctor's daughter, and the passionate scenes between Prokop and the princess, to the scene of temptation on the mountaintop, *Krakatit* is a brilliant variation on the deep and painful conflict between people's wishes and their non-fulfillment, between the desire to cross boundaries that have never been crossed and the feeling of responsibility.

At the novel's conclusion, the plot becomes calmer, becomes dreamlike once again. Exhausted and abandoned, Prokop encounters a fairy-tale grandfather, and he, in the spirit of Čapek's philosophy, gives Prokop hope for the remainder of his life.

> 'Dear one, dear one,' he said softly, 'you will not achieve the highest and you will not give everything away. You tried to tear yourself apart with your own strength, and yet you have remained whole; you will neither save the world, nor shatter it to bits. Much in you will remain enclosed, like fire in a stove; that is good, it's a sacrifice. You wanted to do too great things, and you will do small things instead. That is good.'
>
> Prokop knelt in front of the fire, not daring to lift his eyes. He knew now that it was God the Father speaking to him.

This was the novel's philosophical message, and so it closed with the conflict between wishes and the limits of their realization. *Krakatit* depicted Čapek's conflicted relationship with women like no other of his works. The women were passionate, compassionate, and proud. They were princesses who lowered themselves to the level of ordinary men, but in essence remained inaccessible. They demanded everything from a man, and so represented a threat to his freedom and independence. Čapek's hero is tossed about between a desire for love and the anguish that accompanies it. In one of the passionate scenes, Prokop completely spurns the princess and indicts her, and then immediately afterwards offers her absolute devotion and a willingness to agree to anything she might ask of him.

Olga Scheinpflugová considered the princess a portrait of her, and Prokop's love for the princess a fictionalized picture of their own unrealized or unrealizable love. But it was not. The description of the princess corresponds more to Věra Hrůzová, and Čapek encoded into his work a key. In one of the amorous passages, the princess takes Prokop to one of her favorite spots near the castle and tells him about her childhood. "I used to pretend, just with myself, that I was a reigning princess. 'What does Her Excellency the Princess wish to command?' 'Harness the coach-and-six, I'm going to Zahur.' Zahur, that was my imaginary place. Zahur, Zahur! My dear, is there somewhere like that in the world? Come, we'll go to Zahur. Find it for me, you who know so much ... You're Prospero, prince of Zahur."

Of course, Zahur does not exist anywhere in the world. One of the most knowledgeable authorities on Čapek, Jiří Opelík, correctly determined that the name Zahur was created by the simple transposition of the letters in the masculine form of Věra's family name, Hrůza.[1]

In the final scene, where Prokop meets the old man who gives him solace, Zahur comes up again. The old man, or God, shows Prokop a box one can look into, through a small glass window, and see pictures of famous places on Earth.

> 'That is the holy river Ganges,' added the old man, with reverence, and he turned the handle. 'And that is Zahur, the most beautiful castle in the world.'
>
> Prokop pressed his eyes to the window. He saw a magnificent castle with graceful cupolas, tall palm trees, and a blue, spurting fountain; a tiny figure with a feather in his turban, wearing a purple jacket, yellow trousers, and a Turkish saber was bowing to the ground as he greeted a lady in a white dress who was leading a prancing horse by its bridle. 'Where ... where is Zahur?' whispered Prokop.
>
> The old man shrugged his shoulders. 'Somewhere over there,' he said uncertainly, 'where it's the most beautiful. Some find it, some do not...'

While reading the castle passages in *Krakatit*, we cannot help but think of Kafka's *The Castle*, which also symbolized the proximity and at the same time the inaccessibility of a beloved woman. Some find love, some do not. Just as Kafka's surveyor enters the village below the castle full of determination and energy, but is unsuccessful at the decisive moment, so too is Čapek's manly hero. Zahur too hid the most beautiful thing the hero could imagine, but it remained in the region of dreams, and its gates never opened to Prokop.

Many readers of *Krakatit* have appreciated the author's scientific foresight. Čapek developed perfectly the hypothesis that, from a minuscule amount of mass, such an enormous amount of energy might be released that it could well destroy the world. But far more than a utopian novel, *Krakatit* was a metaphor for unfulfilled love, for the great and futile wish to exceed one's capabilities.[2] The humble reconciliation at the novel's end was more than the philosophical speculation of one looking for a path out of personal crisis and disappointment. What Čapek did in this novel was to combine, with extreme urgency, a highly personal theme with a fictitious story and his own philosophy. It is precisely because of this combination that *Krakatit* may be considered one of the pinnacles in Čapek's body of work.

15. A Bad Dream

In the summer of 1924, Čapek traveled to Great Britain at the invitation of their PEN Club, and he stayed for almost two months, traversing the island (and nearby islands), meeting with a succession of famous people, visiting a huge British Empire Exhibition, and enjoying considerable goodwill and attention from his hosts. During his visit, he began publishing short travel sketches in *Lidové noviny*, supplemented this time with his own drawings. The sketches came out in book form that same year as *Letters from England.*

The book was very popular, with eight editions in the next five years. It's true, however, that a travel book is like last week's newspaper – it ages, unless it's Marco Polo's account of countries which, except for him, no one has ever visited. Moreover – and this is true of all of Karel Čapek's travelogues – their author was satisfied with run-of-the-mill tourist experiences, and a sizeable portion of *Letters from England* is taken up by lyrical descriptions of the countryside and observations of the people and their behavior, although it cannot be denied that his observations are both witty and perceptive. The most interesting and still stimulating today, I believe, are those passages where Čapek reflects on his own culture in terms of his English experiences, especially those dealing with democracy and freedom, which for him were personified by England.

A confirmed democrat himself, Čapek pays deep tribute to England.

> Wherever in the world you see a parliament, you see a piece of England, for England gave birth to parliamentary government. Wherever you meet with political democracy, you find a piece of English spiritual territory; for England was the first in our world to define the ideals of democracy. And wherever on this planet

> the ideals of personal freedom and dignity, tolerance, respect for the individual, and the inviolability of human rights are valued, that place has the gift of England's cultural heritage ... I would say that the English coastline surrounds any land where the values of freedom are accepted and applied.

Čapek was concerned not only about the fate of democracy, of course. As his play *R.U.R.* and his novels *The Absolute at Large* and *Krakatit* indicate, he repeatedly pondered the fate of civilization and scientific progress; as we have seen, he was notably skeptical in his expectations. In *Letters from England* and in his essays (his two most important essays were written for American and English newspapers), he contemplated the nature of our civilization and very aptly summarized his views on how our modern age overvalues the significance of technological advances. London, the capital of the most industrial of European powers, with its seven-and-a-half million people and overwhelming automobile traffic, induced vertigo and the fear that "human life has no value, that man is only an oversized bacterium swarming by the millions on a moldy potato, that perhaps it's only a bad dream, that humankind will perish in some catastrophe, that man is powerless..."

The magnificent exhibition of the British Empire crushed his spirits even more:

> The sole perfection achieved by modern civilization is mechanical; machines are splendid and flawless, but the life which serves them or is served by them is neither splendid nor brilliant nor more perfect nor more beautiful; nor is the work of the machines perfect, only Them. Machines are like gods ... This perfection of matter, from which the perfection of man does not follow, these superb tools of a difficult and unredeemed life mystify me.

Born in the countryside, an educated philosopher and humanist, Čapek was deeply skeptical about the development of civilization. But his opposition was never facile or superficial. He did not oppose scientific progress, he was simply afraid that in the universal worship of technology and its rhythms, traditional human values were being lost.

Several years later, in his answer to a survey by the London *Daily Express*, he expressed his thoughts precisely:

> We all believe in human progress, but we seem predisposed to visualize this progress in terms of gasoline engines, electricity, and other technological contrivances. We see ourselves living in an enlightened age because we have electric lights; in reality, we are living in a kind of confused and poorly organised primeval age because, for example, we have poverty. If we have some perfect and shining machine before our eyes, we see in it man's triumph; well, to realise man's defeat we only need to set beside that splendid machine the first beggar we meet ... We take as our model America, with its technological achievements, but we forget to ask if America is as advanced on the intellectual and cultural side.
>
> We have made machines, not people, the measure of the human order, but this is not the machines' fault, it is ours ... There is no conflict between man and machine, assuming that you treat said machine properly and that it doesn't run you over. But it is a different matter entirely if we ask ourselves whether the organisation and perfection of human beings is advancing as surely as the organisation and perfection of machines, or whether we are devoting as much imagination and ingenuity to the improvement of human affairs as we do to mechanical contrivances ... Our machines are works of genius, but our social and humanitarian efforts are more or less bungling. If we wish to speak of progress, let's not boast about the number of cars or telephone lines, but boast instead about the value that we and our civilisation place on human life.[1]

For Čapek, the worship of technology was represented above all by America; somewhat simplistically, he opposed the dynamic spirit of the New World against the conservative spirit and traditions of Europe. In an essay written in 1926 for the *New York Times Magazine*, Čapek, who appreciated American democracy and art, but had never set foot on American soil, subjected to very clear-sighted criticism values (or, rather, pseudo-values) he considered central to the American way of life.

> I do not ask whether American ideals are good for America, but whether they are good for Europe. My question is whether Europe should Americanize herself, as many people imagine she should. There are people who wish that America would one day civilize old Europe as Europe once civilized the old empire of the Aztecs. I admit that this prospect terrifies me, as the cultural ideals of the European conquerors terrified the old Aztecs, and in my Aztec tongue I utter a war cry against this threat to our European reservation.

Čapek listed three principal traits of Americanism: the emphasis on speed, success, and quantity. But, he asserted, there are values that cannot be expressed by these categories, let alone measured. Americans cannot stand wasting time, but

> some of the greatest activities of the human mind developed under unheard of squandering of time ... Do you recall how Homer describes Achilles' shield? It took an entire song of the Iliad for the blind poet to portray how this shield was made; in America, you would cast and assemble ten thousand of them per day; granted, shields might be made cheaply and successfully this way, but not Iliads ... To date, things have moved fairly slowly in Europe; it's possible that an American tailor can make three coats in the time it takes our tailor to make one; it's equally possible that an American tailor earns three times as much as ours, but one may well ask whether he also consumes a three-times larger portion of life ... One could say that a European worker is a very inefficient working machine, but this is because he is not a machine at all.

In the same article, Čapek opposed most passionately the argument that success should be measured. "It is really astounding how much this watchword has begun to demoralize Europe." It is fortunate that the greatest minds of Europe were not successful during their lives, because many wonderful deeds would have been left undone had people been thinking of success while doing them. "Foolish Europe found time to interest herself in thousands of things other than success, and those things have survived, while all the successes, no matter how many there were in history, went to hell."[2]

Keep in mind that he made this passionate polemic during what we might term the prehistory of our globalizing civilization, at a time when people could not have begun to imagine the computers that increasingly govern our lives. I myself don't think the fundamental conflict of that time was between American and European values, and it's even less so today. But when we observe the dispute of our own time between proponents of globalization and of unlimited economic growth, and their adversaries, who are horrified by how we wreak our own destruction and who warn us of the pauperization of the entire third world, we find that very little has changed with respect to the substance of Čapek's polemic.

16. A Protest Against Ideologies

In 1923, Čapek published one of his Apocryphal Tales, entitled "Pseudo-Lot, or Concerning Patriotism." In it he retold the biblical story about the only righteous citizen of Sodom, who together with his family is to be led by angels out of the city which the Lord intends to destroy. In Čapek's version, however, Lot refuses to leave his native city. When the angels insist that the people of Sodom are different from him, who is righteous, he answers:

> "I pondered all night long, and I recalled so many things it made me weep. Have you ever heard how the people of Sodom sing? No, you don't know them at all, or you wouldn't have come like this. When the girls walk along the streets, they swing their hips and a song hums through their lips and they laugh as they draw water into their pitchers. No water is more clear than that from the wells of Sodom, and no speech in any tongue sounds more beautiful. When a child speaks, I understand him as if he were my own ... If you judge Sodom, you judge me. I am not righteous. I am like them. I will not go from here."
>
> "You will be destroyed with them," said the angel, frowning.
>
> "Perhaps, but first I'll try to save them from destruction. I don't know what I'll do, but until the last moment I'll think it my duty to help them..."[1]

Čapek's work during these years, like most of his writing, can best be understood within the social and political context of the time in which it was created. He obstinately repeated several fundamental ideas: whoever believes he has found the one truth that will save humanity, will necessarily find himself in conflict with those who refuse to accept his truth, and this leads to dangerous clashes and ultimately to wars. A personal conviction gives no one the right to feel better or more righteous than others. Insofar as we see injustice around us, or whatever else runs contrary to our convictions or morals, we should make every effort to eliminate these wrongdoings, but not condemn the entire societal order. Negativism, like generalization, never results in anything useful.

Today, at the beginning of the twenty-first century, these principles seem somewhat abstract, but at the time Čapek articulated them, they were considered highly political and relevant. The 1920s were the time of the great marshaling of militant Marxist-Leninist ideology, which proclaimed itself to have mastered, for the first time in history, a theory capable of scientifically analyzing and solving social conflicts. The solution was unambiguous. It was necessary to eliminate the existing exploitative society, establish a dictatorship of the proletariat, and build – by force, if need be – a new and more just socialist order. Unlike a number of leftist Czech intellectuals,[2] Čapek unconditionally rejected this revolutionary and, to his way of thinking, negativistic solution. In his view, communists and anarchists were blended together, because he perceived revolutionary negativism as the main attribute of both. He summarized his reasons for this view in the essay "Why Am I Not a Communist?"

> I cannot be a communist, because communism's morality is not a morality of help. Because it preaches elimination of the social order and not elimination of the social vice which is poverty. The most curious and inhuman thing about communism is its bleakness. The worse things are, the better; if a cyclist knocks down a poor, deaf granny, it is proof of the rottenness of today's order; if a worker puts his finger between the cogs of a machine, it is not the cogs that crush his poor finger but the bourgeoisie, and furthermore they do it with bloodthirsty delight. The hearts of all the people who, for these or other personal reasons, are not communists, are bestial and disgusting as a boil; there isn't one good hair on the head of contemporary society; what there is is bad ... I don't think I'm in the habit of painting the world in especially rosy colors, but whenever I stumble across the inhumanly negative and tragic nature of communism, I want to cry out in indignant protest that it's not true, that in spite of

everything things are not at all like that ... It's easy to say that society is bad, but go and try to find fundamentally bad individuals. Try to judge the world without brutal generalizations; before long, not a pinch of your principles will be left ... One of the most immoral gifts of the human mind is the gift of generalization; instead of gathering in experience, it tries simply to replace it ... Hatred, ignorance, fundamental distrust, that is the psychological world of communism; a medical diagnosis would be pathological negativism...

Today's world does not need hate, but good will, acceptance, harmony, and cooperation; it needs a moral, more cordial climate. I think that, with a bit of ordinary love and kindness, miracles can still be accomplished. I am defending today's world, not because it is the world of the rich, but because it is also the world of the poor as well as of those in the middle, those ground between the millstones of capital and of the proletariat, those who today more or less maintain or salvage the greatest part of human values ... I believe to this day that there are certain moral and intellectual properties by which one individual can know another. Communism's method is a broadly based attempt to achieve international misunderstanding, an attempt to shatter our world into pieces that don't fit together and have nothing to say to each other ... Send me the most orthodox communist; if he doesn't slay me on the spot, I expect that he and I could reach an understanding on many things, so long, of course, as they don't have to do with communism. But basically, communism does not come to an understanding with others, not even about things which have nothing to do with communism; talk to him about the function of the spleen, and he will say that this is bourgeois science; similarly, there is bourgeois poetry, bourgeois romanticism, bourgeois humaneness, and so on...[3]

Čapek identified negativism above all with communist ideology. To the extent that he pursued the topic in his creative work, he conceived of it as simply a dangerous human predilection. He returned to "pathological hatred" one more time, in the play *Adam the Creator*, which he wrote with his brother. The play belongs to the fantastic or utopian work of the brothers, and of all Karel's plays up to that time, it is the most philosophizing and also the most polemicizing, taking on the communist vision of a new and better society built on the ruins of the old society, now abolished.

The protagonist, Adam, embodies pathological hatred, and his motto, written on a large sign, states: THE WORLD MUST BE DESTROYED. Adam also has built a cannon, a cannon of negation, with which he intends to destroy the world. The play opens with Adam's manifesto, in which he declares the destruction of the world.

> Reasons: All order is violence. Religion is a sham. Private life is prejudice. Laws are shackles for slaves. All government is tyranny. The only response to this state of affairs is a thundering No! ... We proclaim all order, all customs and institutions to be bad, null and void; we proclaim every effort to improve or reverse the world order to be a cowardly compromise; we proclaim everything bad: life is a bad habit, humaneness is weakness, patience is a crime, and worst of all are compassion and tolerance.

It's not difficult in this manifesto to detect Čapek's characterization of the communist world view.

The authors allow Adam to realize his dream of destroying the world. But they offer him more: God Himself addresses Adam and asks him to remake the world in his own image, granting him the creative powers to do so.

Adam then creates: he creates a superman; he creates an Alter Ego in order to have someone to debate with, to argue with; and he creates a woman to love him. Not only does Adam create, but so does Alter Ego, who adheres to principles that are contrary to those of Adam: Adam creates individuals, intellects; Alter Ego creates man en masse. It appears, however, that neither one of them is able to think of anything original, of anything better than what Adam had previously denounced and destroyed.

The play wanders from topics of substance to farce, from philosophical discussions about truth, government, war, and artistic creation, to parodic dialogues between Adam and his wife, and petty disputes between Adam and his Alter Ego over which of them is the true creator. At the end, they seem to have reached an understanding, but the people they created can't. Everything suggests that their world is just as bad as the one Adam destroyed. No one is satisfied, the two creators are completely forgotten, and the question arises as to whether such a world ought to continue. Alter Ego asks: ADAM, ARE YOU GOING TO LEAVE THE WORLD AS IS? Adam doesn't answer. Then the play ends with the sound of bells cast from the cannon of negation, and again God's voice is heard. The bells fall silent, and God asks: "Adam the Creator! Are you going to leave the world as is?"

With a threefold: "Yes! Yes! Yes!" Adam accepts responsibility for the world he has created.

The last words belong to God: "Me too."

A peal of bells, and the curtain falls.

The play about Adam the Creator is, in essence, a revue, with the protagonists appearing and disappearing, and any number of aphorisms and contemporary political slogans. It was not particularly well received by the public, and even some of the critics were hesitant in their acceptance of it. They faulted the play for excessive pessimism, even if today, with the passage of time and the experience of both communism and nazism, we can hardly fault it for pessimism ourselves. In any event, the play had another goal: not only to show the fallacy of the notion that if the contemporary social order were destroyed, people would be able to create something better, but also to show that someone who takes part in creating something and takes responsibility for it will accept it and refuse to destroy it, even when he sees all of its shortcomings. This view of life and society is inarguably affirmative, and anyone faulting the Čapeks for pessimism could only have misunderstood the message of the play. Others, F.X. Šalda and of course the communist critics among them, reproached the play for its pragmatism, for its endlessly repetitive critique of negativism, and for its too willing acceptance of contemporary societal conditions. "There is something just as cheap as pure negation, and that is the sweeping defense of everything that is. To leave everything as is, and to accept this internally, thus to morally endorse it, is something that is as repugnant to me as one who is fundamentally narrow and lacking in faith, and it inflames me with antipathy."[4] Karel Čapek not only condemned negativism, but just as forcefully, time and time again, he begged people, within their own capabilities and strengths, to better the world. Nothing is supposed to be left as is, but nothing should be destroyed only in the name of a better world. *Adam the Creator* condemned only those revolutionary ideas that require first the elimination of democracy and only then the building of a new and better world (supposedly).

To the extent the play deserves to be faulted, it is primarily for its lack of focus, the way it flits from the serious to the nonserious, from philosophical discussion to the jokiness of a revue; also for being too theoretical and for the brothers' attempt to include in it every significant contemporary social problem. I can well understand this ambition; nevertheless, a desire to see and discuss the world in all its complexity should not lead to superficiality, to slogan-ridden expressions of philosophical and political theses, as is the case with the Capeks' *Adam the Creator*. "There is a difference between the Robber-Professor opposition and that between Adam and Alter Ego," wrote Alexandr Matuška in his extended essay about the works of Karel Čapek. "All are symbolic, but the first two have personal destinies, while the latter two merely debate. There is a similar difference between *R.U.R.* and *Adam the Creator*: the former is a battle of ideas, the latter a dramatized discussion."[5]

17. How to Warn of Destruction?

Some of Čapek's plays and novels were receiving worldwide recognition, for the most part his utopian works, the societal fantasies located in the future, whose plots usually involved a revolutionary invention. This describes *R.U.R.*, *The Absolute at Large*, and *Krakatit*, but even the plays *From the Life of the Insects* and *Adam the Creator* did not take place in a real time or locale, they were attempts at allegory or the ironic paraphrasing of a mythical reality. As I've already mentioned, in the years after First World War, Čapek also wrote several Apocryphal Tales in which his distinctive interpretations of biblical and historical (or pseudo-historical) stories became surprising analogues for modern-day problems or for the way people behave. During this period, he also published the first of his short, inventive fables.

Why did Čapek, who in his newspaper columns responded to current affairs in a way few other writers did, give priority in his literary work to genres which were in his time considered rather marginal?

We might be satisfied with a quite simple, easily understandable explanation: the first utopian play, *R.U.R.*, unexpectedly won worldwide success for its young author, and this seduced Čapek into staying on the path that had made him famous. But the reasons why he continued with a string of similarly fantastic premises were surely more profound, connected to his philosophy and to the way he wanted to expose the causes behind the dangers threatening humankind. Unlike many of his leftist contemporaries, he did not find these in the current social order, nor, like the rightist ideologues, in the weaknesses of democracy – he found the causes for these dangers to lie, above all, in human intolerance and in messianic ideologies that promised people paradise but which, in reality, were preparing the way for catastrophe. He considered equally dangerous people's estrangement from their activities, and their desire to master all natural forces and thereby change the place of human beings within the natural order.

He sought causes for past as well as impending catastrophes, but at the same time he did not want to generalize, to incite one group against another, to awaken passions. Allegorical and utopian stories were well suited for such purposes.[1]

Čapek's allegories were not unambiguous in the style of classic allegories and fables. Rather, they were relativistic, intended, for the most part, to shake up the established opinions, deep-rooted attitudes, and excessive self-assuredness of those who believed that they were in sole possession of the truth.

The classic fable ordinarily featured a humanized animal or inanimate object whose attributes were suggestive of human attributes, and it concluded by warning people about the consequences of bad behavior, enlightening or exhorting how to behave a certain way. Čapek's fables, too, featured animals or plants or things, but ordinarily for the sole purpose of casting a surprising light on a seemingly unshakable attitude or truth, in order to show that it, too, is open to question. Here are a few of them.

> Earthworm: "Brrr! Get underground, fast! Dig quickly into the moist honest soil! Ugh, a man touched me! How disgustingly dry and warm! I can't bear it, it turns my stomach! Yuck!"
>
> Old Pine Tree: "How to reach my age and size? Simple: choose dry, sandy soil, no groundwater, little humus, modest nourishment only. – What, you say the old beech tree recommends the richest soil possible? And the willow recommends the moisture of groundwater? Don't believe it, that's stupid advice; listen to me: the best is just plain sand, and dry, dry, dry!"
>
> Ant: "So! Those idiots have built their house right in the middle of OUR road."

> Centipede: "All I really, really want to know is, are there centipedes on other planets, too."[2]

In his allegorical play *From the Life of the Insects*, Čapek had dung beetles sing a paean to property, their property being a ball of dung; mayflies celebrate the greatness of their missions in life; and ant dictators dream of world rule, their world being a speck of earth between two blades of grass. Thus he conveyed the relativity of most of the "great" goals people themselves pursue.

In all these instances, the effect of the allegory follows from the contradiction between the subjective seriousness of the insects' declarations and the futility of those declarations, as well as from how worthless they look from the human standpoint. But isn't this just as true of declarations people themselves formulate with equal seriousness?

In *R.U.R.*, Domin's rationalistic vision, seemingly attractive and undeniably positive in what it promises humankind, is made suspect by the catastrophic consequences it wreaks upon humanity. In this same way, in *Adam the Creator*, the newly created world casts doubts upon Adam's creation as well as on his previous negativism. What appears in *The Absolute at Large* as unambiguously positive (a surplus of cheap energy and the consequences of the strange radiation that turns people into saints) is also made suspect. In the end, the revolutionary invention brings destruction to humankind. And the miracle-working potion in *The Makropulos Secret* which offers people the immortality they've dreamed about? Čapek's heroine manages to convince everyone that a life lived for centuries is pure horror!

Nothing is so noble, so redeeming, so unambiguous as it seems as first glance – such is the basic message of Čapek's utopias and his allegorical plays.

Of course it would be inaccurate to explain Čapek's fondness for fantastical premises solely on the basis of his relativistic philosophy. It is understandable for an author with such broad talents to seek the polar opposite of his everyday newspaper work.[3] Since journalism bound him to what was workaday and ordinary, in his literary work he turned to a world of pure fiction.

Good authors can usually recognize their strong points and their weak points. Čapek's strong point was his art of fabulation, a talent that combined imagination, the courage to come up with original parables, and the capacity to think through, via these parables, the social as well as technological problems of modern times. He was superb at creating situations capable of carrying a moral, noetic, or even a merely political message. On the other hand, the depiction of subtle psychological nuances was not among his strong points. Surely this is why he was better suited to allegorical and utopian tales than to realistic stories. The true protagonists of his works from this period were not individual people but humankind as a whole,[4] and they were essentially not about conflicts between characters, but about conflicts between concepts or world views. The individual characters who move the story along appear to be mere puppets that help the author present his views on the causes of conflict in the contemporary world.

In times of relative calm in the world and in his own life, Čapek tended to write more realistic works. When he was disturbed by what was happening in the world and felt a pressing need to address himself to contemporary problems, he created fictional worlds where his protagonists moved about on the border between reality and fantasy.

18. Important for the Nation

In April 1921, Čapek left the editorial office of *Národní listy*, whose nationalistic orientation suited him less and less, and moved to the editorial office of *Lidové noviny*, where he worked until his death.

In the late nineteenth century, Czech journalism (like its literature) had neither the tradition nor the quality of newspapers in, for example, England. Yet two journalists living and working in the Czech Lands, excellent writers both, made significant contributions to the field. In the 1840s, it was Karel Havlíček Borovský, an enlightened, indomitable journalist who also wrote wonderful aphorisms, epigrams, and satirical poetry. He was almost alone, after the defeat of the 1848 revolutionary movement, in trying to preserve its democratic achievements with his political writing (and he died at the age of thirty-five, as a consequence of Austrian imprisonment). Twenty years later, the outstanding prose writer and poet Jan Neruda established the tradition of the Czech feuilleton: humorous, often venomous writing about common occurrences and ordinary, everyday matters. (He wrote more than two thousand feuilletons, which were published in book form, in many editions.) Consequently, there was at least a journalistic tradition to continue, and we can say that Čapek, like no one else, combined in himself the gifts of both these remarkable precursors. The author of penetrating and humorous political analyses and commentaries, he was also the author of many hundreds of feuilletons.

Čapek had tremendous admiration and respect for the work of Havlíček and Neruda, and in his declarations of esteem we find echoes of his own journalistic credo.

> It is common enough to say of someone long dead: what would he have to say about today's situation if he could get up out of his grave and spend at least one day with us? – Yes, it's a cliché,

> but it seems to me especially appropriate in regard to two people, Havlíček and Neruda. Havlíček, due to his political clairvoyance, would not be particularly surprised, and he would be more at home here than a good majority of our people. And Neruda would also fit in well, due to his Europeanism. We could say that Neruda was the first European in Bohemia. He exceeded the dimensions of his time. A strong, skeptical, rational intellect, a westernizer, an empiricist, a man of ardent tastes but cool self-control, a man with a world view ... As far as I'm concerned, the finest of Neruda's feuilletons are not those in which he entertained, but those in which he studied people with thoughtful, almost sociological scrutiny, whether in his travels or in his native Prague ... Neruda the poet has been praised enough, and deservedly so; allow me to commemorate Neruda the journalist, observer, ironic judge of what is pertinent ... Observe how astonishingly he embodies the two virtues I cannot imagine a great journalist to be without: a skeptical, nearly brutal intellect, and warm compassion. Intelligence without dogmatism, practical and highly critical; compassion without sentimentality, restrained, temperate ... A fine harvest of spirit, greatness of intellect, education, and critical ability, experience and masculinity, all that made Neruda the second greatest Czech journalist remains an ideal still pertinent to this day.[1]

As for Havlíček, Čapek briefly listed those characteristics he so admired in him:

> An enormously critical intellect, a skeptical knife with at least sixteen blades, a healthy mistrust for clichés, a light touch and assured spirit, humor, sprightliness, worldliness, fifty thousand different interests in life; a tremendous appetite for work, practicality, trenchancy, proficiency in worldly affairs, simplicity in concept, a preference for implementation; in short, an intellect we deem 'French,' and a practical nature we call 'Anglo-Saxon.'[2]

In Čapek's youth, newspapers were owned for the most part by political parties, and they acted first and foremost as platforms for the views of those parties' spokesmen. Reporting was mediocre and sketchy, since politics was most important, along with what were considered matters of national interest.

Lidové noviny was founded in Brno, the largest city in Moravia, the central part of what would become Czechoslovakia, and its main editorial office and printing press remained there even after independence in 1918. It was therefore more of a regional newspaper and, in the beginning, an organ of the Moravian People's Party. Gradually, thanks mainly to the extraordinary journalistic talents of its editor, later editor-in-chief, Arnošt Heinrich, it improved to the point where it became the preeminent Czech newspaper. Heinrich's goal was for the paper to collaborate with as many of the best writers, scientists, and experts as possible. A number of fine writers were already writing for the paper before the war; after the war, that circle widened – thanks in no small part to Čapek's contributions. The newspaper introduced regular columns and sections that no other paper had, but above all it printed what today would be considered a nearly unimaginable amount of belle lettres, including poetry as well as feuilletons, right on the front page.

During the First Czechoslovak Republic (1918-1938), *Lidové noviny* became a leading paper of the Czech non-communist intelligentsia. It defended liberal positions, supported the application of democracy to more institutions, and backed President Tomáš G. Masaryk. (Since the presidential quarters are located in Hradčany, the medieval fortification rising above the city of Prague, *Lidové noviny*'s adversaries referred to it as the "Castle paper.") By the 1930s, most unusually for newspapers of that sort, the press run was large: 44,000 copies for the daily edition and 76,000 on Sunday.

By the beginning of the 1920s, Čapek had become an internationally recognized writer, with his plays, especially *R.U.R.*, being performed all over the world, and this made it possible for him to live off his literary writing alone. In spite of this, he remained true to his newspaper career, and not even when dedicating himself intensively to his longer creative work did he neglect his journalism: his articles, feuilletons, commentaries, essays, and short observations. He published his work not only in *Lidové noviny*, but also in other newspapers and journals, both in Czechoslovakia and abroad. His longest pieces, especially his political commentaries and essays, were published in the weekly journal *Přítomnost* (The Present Day), whose editor-in-chief was Čapek's friend Ferdinand Peroutka. In all, there were several dozen publications to which he contributed during his lifetime. Journalism, therefore, was not a secondary activity for him, but something he considered just as important, if not more important, than his literary work. His later articles, analyzing the causes of the deepening crisis of democracy in Europe in the 1930s, belong to the best of Czech or even European essay writing.

Certainly there is a great array of understandable reasons for Čapek's interest in journalism. He was an extremely efficient man, and his efficiency made him dissatisfied with one profession alone. At the same time, journalism ensured him a connection not only with people, but also with the events of the day.

There was another significant factor that determined his interest in journalism. In the beginning of the 1920s, it was as if Čapek's personal life had come to a close. His relationship with Olga Scheinpflugová changed into a friendship, and while he still saw her every week, he nevertheless would not be starting a family, as he had supposed. The person closest to him, his brother Josef, remained close, but Josef had his own family. It seems as if Karel transferred all his unfulfilled emotion to an entirely different sphere, that is, the newly independent state of Czechoslovakia, its democractic striving, and its head of state. Even though two generations separated them, President Masaryk accepted Čapek as his friend and as one of his advisers in matters of culture.

It was as if the new state served Čapek as a substitute for someone near and dear, someone he needed to care for, a surrogate for the children he would like to have been raising, cultivating, educating. Newspapers, the most important medium of the time, were ideally suited to this activity.

The playwright Edmond Konrád, Čapek's friend (and his least critical admirer), recalled: "Someone asked Čapek: 'And what about some theater again? Or a novel?' He shook his head: 'I must educate the nation now...' A didactic element began to show through his writing more and more, tactful moral teaching and purposeful, essential truths."[3] Konrád then mentioned Čapek's excellent work in the field of international cultural relations, where he was an unofficial cultural ambassador for Czechoslovakia.

Certainly President Masaryk also influenced Čapek's efforts to educate the nation. In her memoirs, Čapek's niece, Helena Koželuhová, even contends that Masaryk made Čapek's acquaintance chiefly for the purpose of enlisting his help with just this goal in mind. "I have the impression that Masaryk was not a good influence on Karel. They were too much alike, both honest, honorable enthusiasts for the good of the nation and humankind, and they fortified each other's opinions. Masaryk also enticed Karel away from Czech literature, toward journalism and writing for instructional purposes."[4]

This statement is too biased. The effort to concentrate on something so far beyond the personal as the education or destiny of a nation came directly from Čapek's character: his feeling of personal responsibility for public affairs, his moral principles, and his need to express his opinion on the fundamental questions facing society. He was doing this even before he came to know Masaryk, and he continued doing it until the end of his days. During his short life (as well as the short life of the First Republic), he managed to express his informed opinion on an unusually broad range of social problems. He was concerned with questions of justice and the contradictory verdicts of jurists; he wrote about the dangers of nationalism, about the threatening symptoms of mass behavior and totalitarian tendencies in society; he wrote about American overemphasis on technology, about Czech political machinations, about the attempt to lessen the importance of parliament to the detriment of the ruling parties' interests, and of course about many cultural problems. The rise in Germany of Hitler and his totalitarian regime occasioned brilliant and impassioned essays on the importance of culture and the treachery of the intelligentsia, and on the twisted theories of nationalism and racism. We can say without exaggeration that nothing of significance happened in either his country or the world that did not attract Čapek's attention and lead him to formulate his opinions. It is a testimony to the acuity of his judgment that many of his political reflections have lost little of their relevance.[5]

Newspapers offered Čapek a unique platform, a platform he inherently needed and greatly respected, and he felt a great responsibility for how it was used. Čapek expressed his opinion of journalistic work, or calling, time and time again, even writing several humorous essays on what newspapers should look like, how they are produced, and how the journalist's trade differs from all others. He formulated his journalistic credo extensively in a 1934 article; the emphases are mine.

> A man who writes conscientiously over the years for newspapers becomes accustomed to thinking of the people for whom he writes; he looks upon his responsibility more as something like baking bread for everyone rather than mixing cultural cocktails for an elite circle of café regulars. It isn't just that he is writing for a great number of people, but something much more serious: he is entering a much wider and more complex world, a world in which there is room for all manner of experiences, interests, and motivations. I say that it's a poor newspaperman and a poor *writer for newspapers* who restricts himself to narrow specialization of any kind. To be a journalist and write for the newspapers means above all to have an affinity for everything that is, to take a lively, direct, democratic interest in the whole of reality, without the intellectual snobbery that fastidiously turns up its nose at the interests and motivations of those others who play soccer, breed canaries, swear at the government and the weather, or scowl over the financial section ... To go into newspaper work feeling in any way exclusive is like expecting to plow a field with a silver fork. It is harder to speak to everyone than to

a select set; it's even harder if we don't want to become hucksters, demagogues, or public liars. I consider the way in which newspapers are done immensely "important for the nation": important that they're done well and responsibly, not poorly or by culturally and morally base means. I won't ask whether it's literarily loftier and more sublime to write poems instead of feuilletons and news items, but I will ask whether such feuilletons and news items have brought something worthwhile into the lives of newspaper readers, be they conductors, cleaning women, or chief counsels. Don't forget that a journalist can do more *harm* than what some circle of cultured friends in their cloistered kingdom thinks worthy of consideration.

It's true: a man who writes for the newspapers, to appear on newsprint, fixing his eyes on the people for whom he writes, doesn't feel that he's performing some exquisite task worthy of handmade paper in a limited edition; he thinks of himself more as a workingman, which I assure you is not the least bit demeaning.[6]

19. Mary and Martha

In February 1925, Čapek published in the journal *Přítomnost* a rather short article entitled "On Relativism." It was a defense of his theory of knowledge against any and all theories making claims to the absolute truth.

> Socialism is good when it comes to wages, but it tells me nothing when it comes to other questions in life that are more private and painful, for which I must seek answers elsewhere. Relativism is not indifference; on the contrary, passionate indifference is necessary in order for you not to hear the voices that oppose your absolute decrees ... Relativism is neither a method of fighting, nor a method of creating, for both of these are uncompromising and at times even ruthless; rather, it is a method of cognition. If one must fight or create, it is necessary that this be preceded by the broadest possible knowledge ... One of the worst muddles of this age is its confusing of the ideas behind combative and cognitive activity. Cognition is not fighting, but once someone knows a lot, he will have much to fight for, so much that he will be called a relativist because of it. The only way not to be a relativist is to be a monomaniac. Choose the better part: Mary, who listens to the only truth, or Martha, who "was careful and concerned about many things." Of course, "many things" includes things that are trifling and odd, unknown and rejected; it includes the whole of reality.[1]

Several years later, Čapek used the New Testament story about these two followers of Christ as a topic for one of his Apocryphal Tales. But while in the evangelist's version Jesus reproaches Martha and praises Mary, who "chose the good part," Čapek sides with Martha, who was diligent in her service. To be diligent in one's service became the credo of Čapek's life, and he therefore supported anything that would give people a zest for work, for life, for creating a free society. His philosophy called for each individual to seek the positive in this world, so that he can "'lift himself' with every step taken under his own power."

Certainly the current situation contributed to this position. The war, as horrifying as it had been, was now part of the past, the revolutionary mood had subsided, and people had begun to couple their hopes with the flourishing of the new nation. Although certain sections of the population continued to be poor, the majority began to fare better and life calmed down, ruffled only on occasion by some political scandal.

Čapek's life had also changed and calmed down. He moved with his brother into a two-family house they built together. Behind the house was a garden, to which Karel, especially, was devoted. And because all that he did, he did passionately and meticulously, he soon became a skilled and well-informed gardener, as can be seen by many of his articles and the book *The Gardener's Year.*[2]

Gardening was, of course, not the only hobby that occupied him then. He also devoted himself to collecting oriental carpets and gramophone records of ethnic music from around the world, taking photographs, drawing, and raising dogs and cats.

People who knew Čapek emphasized his extraordinary curiosity, his wonder at the richness of life, his exceptional talent for seeing what remains hidden from most people. For example, J. B. Kozák, a visitor to Čapek's Friday evening gatherings, remembers that "he was like a child in the playfulness he brought to even his most important work, which was filled with joyful as well as painful discoveries. He could spend an hour watching what some tiny bug might be up to in his garden or how an ant was going to deal with its burden, or an hour examining an old rug some Bedouin family must once have lived on, or waiting till a cactus flower opened..."[3] These attributes also served as background material for his feuilletons and stories.

He was able to write about things as if they were living beings, of whose secret and mysterious functioning he was frequently in awe; at other times he would write about them with captivating humor and an extraordinary ability to discover their hidden aspects. This is how he wrote about the first crystal sets, the loudspeaker, airplanes, the telephone, the automobile, doorknobs, the American coke stove, a box of matches, about all sorts of hobbies and activites such as reading, growing cacti, and the cultivation of tobacco, about human qualities such as schadenfreude, envy, and hatred; he discovered unusual "laws" according to which books get lost, the streetcar you're not waiting for always arrives first, and things disappear at the very moment you're in a hurry and absolutely need them. He praised artisans and men "who are right where they belong," doing work they're well suited for; he paid homage to the heroism of a roofer who, sixty meters above the ground, held his colleague on his shoulders and didn't budge even as molten metal ran down his arms, and he wrote about repossessors and tax officials and domestics, about jurors and defendants.

In the early 1930s, several books were published that brought together the best of his feuilletons and essays, such as *In Praise of Newspapers and Other Essays* (1931), consisting of his witty, informed reflections on literature, for the most part concentrating on those genres considered to be on the margins of literature or sometimes even beneath it: proverbs, the lyrics of anonymous Prague folk songs, detective tales, anecdotes, the popular fiction found in almanacs of the time, fairy tales, pornography, and the romantic stories then termed "women's" literature (Čapek called them novels for housemaids).

A year later, *Nine Fairy Tales* was published, one of the most beautiful modern fairy-tale books in world literature, and not long after that another book for children: *Dashenka, or The Life of a Puppy*. Also appearing in 1932 was a tiny collection of Čapek's first five Apocryphal Tales (the complete version was assembled only after Čapek's death). And finally, in that same year, his *Letters from Holland* was published.

In his lengthier works, Čapek was concerned about what threatens humankind, what pits one person against another, and in them he expressed his anxiety about the way civilization was evolving. In his shorter works, we hear a desire for mutual understanding, for hope, for a positive vitality. It was as if he had decided to seek out everything that might connect people with one another. And what better way to connect people than the common, ordinary experiences that serve their daily needs? Anecdotes and proverbs don't give rise to conflict. (Another reason, surely, was that folk wisdom, as he pointed out, is truly relativistic, because for every assertion, there's another that contradicts it: "Yes, 'A lame tongue brings nothing but pure misfortune,' but don't forget that 'Speech is silver, silence is golden,' and, 'Speak only when a louse coughs.'")

In his fairy tales, the protagonists are good, ordinary people, such as a letter carrier, a logger and a doctor, a detective and a chauffeur. The fairy-tale creatures themselves are every bit as good-natured and kind-hearted as the people, they understand each other, and when in difficulty they fall back on each other for help.

Čapek's friend and literary colleague František Langer explained this tendency to search for what unites rather than divides people. Small things bring people together, he wrote.

> Big ones also bring people together, but at the same time they separate them. And they separate them cruelly. In the shadow of something as great as God, entire races have exterminated each other. There are wars between people with differing concepts of order in the world ... But never would associations of people who breed long-haired rabbits fight against associations of people who train carrier pigeons. Never would a class revolution arise between collectors of the stamps of Central Europe and collectors of stamps from around the world. Around small things is an atmosphere of sacred calm ... Roses, pigeons, dahlias, chess, cameras, radios, canaries, gardens on the outskirts of town, pipes, books, and who knows what other small pleasures, these are the areas of life where the bourgeois rubs shoulders with the proletarian, these are the dominions of the international and the equality of religions. Over small things a sacred peace hovers...[4]

The fact that he had given up on having a family life understandably influenced the rhythm of Čapek's daily life. Relationships with friends would at least partially substitute for a family environment, and so he began to organize gatherings at his house. From these originated the remarkable institution called the *Pátečníci*, or Friday Circle, a fairly good-sized group of colleagues and friends who met at Čapek's house every Friday evening. Together, these men comprised the intellectual elite of the interwar republic: the writers Šrámek, Langer, Kubka, Kopta, Poláček, and Vančura, the painters Špála and Rada, professors and journalists and, often, even President Masaryk.[5] Many of the Friday Circle, especially Čapek's contemporaries, such as Langer and Peroutka, as well as those almost a generation older, such as Šrámek, were among his closest friends; among those less close to Čapek personally were the Catholic writer Durych, the leftist painter and caricaturist Hoffmeister, and the communist writer Vančura.[6] The Friday Circle became an informal gathering of democratically-oriented intellectuals, and from its midst flowed important political initiatives and even advice to the nation's president.

At a 1925 reception that Masaryk organized for writers, he asked Čapek whether he would look over one chapter of his memoir *The Making of a State*, which he was just then preparing for publication. Čapek agreed and received the chapter the next day. "It contained an analysis of a novel by an overly honored Czech literary demigod," recalled Čapek, "and in it, the grand old reader picked the book apart thread by thread, demonstrating that the writer knew nothing about life, that the characters were cardboard, and that they and the plot were arbitrarily constructed..." (At issue was a novel by the critic F. X. Šalda, who was in truth a very poor writer of novels and plays.) Whereupon, Čapek writes, he replied to the president: "Don't publish this chapter under any circumstances. First of all, the writer you've reviewed is a sick man; second, it isn't typical of Czech literature; and third, you have enough political battles as is; why have a literary polemicist turn against you, too?"

"'Gracias,' the old gentleman replied. And he left the chapter out.

"Perhaps that was how the president acquired a certain degree of trust in a forty-years-younger scribe,"[7] Čapek concluded. Masaryk indeed felt an affinity with the younger man, and Čapek was inspired by the president's favorable regard.

After Masaryk's first visit to the Friday Circle, Čapek wrote him a letter with considerably more feeling than would be dictated by mere politeness toward the head of state.

> I can say for almost all whom you saw on Friday at my house that without you ours was a deprived youth; you had stopped teaching by the time we entered the university, and thus we were deprived of the sole philosophical personage who would have been able to engage us directly and vitally. How we found you in spite of this, not only through books but also in life, is another chapter; but I would like to tell you, with sincere gratitude from all of us, that last Friday you compensated our generation, at least on that one evening, for our earlier deprivation. We all beg you – if it is not presumptuous – not to let this be your last visit...[8]

A friendly relationship developed between the president and the young writer; Čapek repaid the president's friendship with lifelong devotion and always tried to be available for "the old gentleman," as he called him, whenever it seemed that he might be of use.

"Manage your authority meticulously," he exhorted the president, "and to the extent that you can, make use of us – there are so many of us who wish only to do something for you. When we met with you, we felt a certain sense of shame: that you might fling yourself alone into battle, feeling you're on your own, that it is up to the rest of us, that we must try harder, in order that you won't have to expose yourself so much."[9]

In August 1926, when the Czech fascists were about to attempt a coup, Čapek informed Masaryk:

> Yesterday at my house ... the editors-in-chief and political editors of the 'left bloc' met to agree on a common line. It turned out very well, I think; they promised to stay out of each other's way, and they intend to create a 'democratic bloc' of the press (that is, not leftist), which does not exclude tradesmen or perhaps members of the Agrarian Party. We cannot let a left bloc vs. right bloc situation arise in the nation, because the President cannot be the candidate for any single bloc, but for a broad democratic majority, and moreover it is necessary to keep in mind a future coalition of 'farmers and workers,' as you say.[10]

Tomáš Garrigue Masaryk was unquestionably a charismatic personality, but Čapek's relationship with him went beyond the conventional level of admiration: the writer became his faithful pupil, helper, and an important popularizer of his ideas and politics. It seems likely that Čapek, whose work up to that time had been full of skepticism, at least concerning the future of civilization, was attracted to the vital optimism and élan of the old gentleman. Čapek deeply wished to believe in happy endings, but his intellect dissuaded him from excessive optimism. The great authority of the president, his extraordinary solidity and integrity, were something on which he could lean in his search for hope and a way out for humankind. It is apparent in Čapek's writing during the second half of the 1920s that he was turning away from his postwar skepticism.

Out of this long friendship and from an intensive effort during the seven years between 1928 and 1935, came *Talks with T. G. Masaryk*, surely the best book ever written about the man. Gradually, over three volumes, Čapek captured Masaryk's life – his youth, his scholarly career, and his leading role in the Czech resistance and in the political battle for the creation of the republic. Čapek dedicated most of the space, however, to philosophy, to the president's outlook on life, religion, and questions of Czechoslovak national existence.

Without a doubt, Masaryk found in Čapek an outstanding biographer. Unlike most of the other biographies, *Talks* is not a hagiographic work; rather, it is an account of the meetings between two remarkable personalities who were close, despite their great age difference, in terms of both their humaneness and their ideas. Even if Masaryk dismissed Čapek's pragmatism, even if he was a man of deep religious belief while Čapek was, at most, tolerant in matters of faith, Masaryk's philosophy agreed with Čapek's on many points. Both emphasized the necessity of evolutionary social development, the importance of ordinary, everyday work, and the responsibility of each individual for the spiritual, political, and cultural state of society. Both were also dedicated to the idea of democracy, and they saw its development in the newly-founded republic as their life's mission. Both were prepared to serve the republic, to carry out the difficult struggle for its existence in such an unstable postwar Europe.

In *Talks with T. G. Masaryk*, Čapek succeeded in something which, for such an eminent author, was certainly not very easy: to be subservient to the person he was drawing a portrait of. This meant not only being subservient to the content of what Masaryk said, but also to the president's way of thinking and expressing himself.[11]

Friendship with Masaryk brought Čapek the disparaging designation of "Castle writer," and it certainly contributed to the fact that many literary and journalistic colleagues and critics had little fondness for him. It was easy to explain Čapek's relations with the head of state on the grounds of personal gain. For instance, the publisher and journalist Karel Horký (in his journal *Stopa*, which the Brothers Čapek had helped found) falsely charged that Čapek benefited by having Masaryk secure entrées abroad for him. "It would be truly unjust," he wrote, "if Masaryk, for whom Dr. K. Čapek has done so much in our nation, were to do nothing for Čapek in America and Great Britain."[12]

In general, Čapek's effort to find the positive in life, his opposition to generalizations and all revolutionary efforts, and his "state-forming" activities led some some critics (mainly on the left) to accuse him of effeminacy, of being conservative or reactionary, and of trying to idealize contemporary society. And they attacked his philosophy as shallow, as too intellectually lax, or as opportunistic. "He just sits by his fire, the cautious steward of his literary profits, avoiding every battle and every blow," wrote the critic F. X. Šalda.[13] However, this condemnation did not extend to Čapek's *Talks with T. G. Masaryk*, which Šalda praised (although the praise came only after publication of the third and final volume of the *Talks*, that is, shortly before Masaryk's and, not long afterwards, Čapek's death.)

The Marxist critic Václavek, in a long essay published in 1926 in the journal *Tvorba* (Creativity), accused Čapek of a conservatism that "wants to have calm, balance, happiness, and primarily: peace and quiet. He gets most angry with those who disturb his peace, no matter how serious their motives. Basically, however, he has taken a positive attitude only toward the meaningless, trivial lives of the bourgeoisie ... In his pessimism about civilization, Čapek demonstrates his kinship with the dying bourgeois culture and its feeble vitality, which cannot keep pace with modern times ... Čapek's relativism stands in diametrical opposition to the effort of our generation to attain a supra-individual but nonetheless humane order."[14]

Despite these personal and biased attacks, it is actually possible to find in Čapek's work from this period an almost exaggerated effort to discover in everyday life the greatest possibilities for seeking satisfaction, joy, and personal happiness. He looks for this even in Masaryk's life, and Masaryk's statement that he had lived a happy life brings to a close both the first two volumes of the *Talks*.

In the years between the wars, overflowing with ideologies, Masaryk's adversaries were seeking ideological explanations for such a serene depiction of the world, which is surely one reason why Čapek came down with such fervor on ideologies. Yet I am convinced that his stands resulted more than he himself would admit from his efforts to overcome his personal troubles. No matter that his relationship with Olga had developed according to his wishes, this plus his wrecked relationship with Věra Hruzová meant capitulating to life or, we might say, to life without a woman. Just as for Franz Kafka the prospect that what was most essential to his life would not be realized, that he would not start a family, that his destiny would not be like that of others, just as this was a determining factor for the majority of his great works, a similar prospect led Čapek to try to find substitute goals and substitute positives in life.

After all, people usually have a need to hide from others as well as from themselves their inner suffering, their inadequacies. It is necessary to seek an explanation for what he did to meet this need, for his frequent displays of lightness, humor, joking about serious matters, for his need to present himself as fastidious in his service, for his seeking out the broadest possible circle of friends, even for his flitting from theme to theme. At the same time, we cannot help but observe a degree of pained, even unbalanced oversensitivity in some of Čapek's reactions to criticism, in his refusing membership in the Czech Academy of Arts and Sciences,[15] and in resigning from all functions of the PEN Club, an organization whose Czech chapter he had founded and chaired for many years.[16]

20. The Stolen Document and Other Tales

Čapek was a master of short literary forms, but surprisingly, after *Wayside Crosses* and *Painful Tales* he did not return to the short story for nearly ten years. Then, in the years 1928 and 1929, he wrote and published in the newspaper forty-seven short stories, which he compiled in two volumes: *Tales from One Pocket* and *Tales from the Other Pocket* (in the first volume he also included one story from 1919).

The short story is the most difficult genre in literature. In our country, there was practically no short story tradition at all, no one comparable to Gogol, Chekhov, Twain, or Maupassant. With the exception of Jan Neruda and Jaroslav Hašek, it would be difficult to name a Czech author who had succeeded in writing short realistic stories. Just as with his plays, it's unlikely that Čapek would have found in their stories a national tradition to carry on. It's not even possible to say that he might have been very influenced by any contemporary international author, even though he knew and greatly respected Chesterton, Shaw, and his French contemporaries. He created his own genre – often on the borderline between short story and feuilleton. The Pocket Tales appeared first in the newspaper, which limited their length, required a certain simplicity and readability (a Joycean story is hard to imagine in the newspapers), and sometimes even had a simulated journalistic realism, with references to contemporary life.

What surprises and, to this day, charms readers of Čapek's stories is the multitude of ideas, the variety of situations, the breadth of life these stories encompass. I would say that, in these stories, Čapek succinctly summarized all of his knowledge and essential life experiences. Their protagonists include collectors of carpets as well as of cacti, a passionate gardener, a journalist, a poet; there are new variations of Čapek's favorite motifs, such as mysterious footprints and desperate people besieged; there are observations he had already made in his columns (such as how wrong it is to judge people according to their handwriting instead of their actions, or how difficult the decisions of jurors are), a balladic story about murder in Subcarpathian Ruthenia (to reappear in another form in *Hordubal*, the first volume in his trilogy). There is also a collection of stamps, something he had devoted himself to in childhood, and the idea that people live only one of many potential lives, which he developed in the last volume of the trilogy, *An Ordinary Life*.

Most of the stories – especially in the first volume – have criminal or detective themes, but they are notably nontraditional in terms of the mystery genre as it was at the time. Their protagonists are not usually private detectives, ingenious masters of deduction, but workaday police officers or scruffy police inspectors who pride themselves on being old-fashioned. "Look," one of the police protagonists says, "the thing is, I'm simple-minded the same way a murderer is. Whatever I think of is just as ordinary, everyday, and stupid as his motive, scheme, and deed. And by and large, that's exactly how I catch him out."[1]

Čapek himself saw, in this same "how to catch him out," one of the unifying elements of the first volume.

> My principal interest, as a writer, in detective stories is in the noetic problems of how to know, how to detect a fact, what is real. *Tales from One Pocket* are therefore noetic tales. As soon as I began to occupy myself with the world of crime, I became captivated almost involuntarily by the problem of justice. You will probably find a turning point halfway through the book. The question of how to know what's real gives way to the question of how to punish.[2]

In the first half of this volume, various means of knowing reality play an important role. Three stories feature, respectively, a clairvoyant, a graphologist, and a fortune teller, and each of them has a different way of determining what is real. In "The Poet," a poet notes down the details of a car accident in metaphors because he perceives not outer reality, but an inner reality based on associations. (Čapek returns to the means of cognition of a clairvoyant and a poet in *Meteor*, the second volume of his trilogy.) In "The Experiment of Professor Rouss," a scholar exposes a murderer on the basis of associations he uses to penetrate the man's subconscious. At the end of the story, the method that exposed the murderer fails because of a journalist who associates every word the professor gives him with some journalistic cliché – evidence of the fact that many of the Pocket Tales are, on another level, satires. Čapek let the fortune teller's predictions come true, let Professor Rouss expose a murderer within just a few minutes, and let the poet subsconsciously record through his metaphors the license number of the car that knocked down an old woman – but the outcomes from these three methods of cognition are so bizarre that it is hard for the reader to accept them in all seriousness.

In a brilliant essay, "Holmesiana, or On Detective Stories," he compares the heroes of classic detective stories, who do not deign to check fingerprints or police archives, with real policemen.

> In actual practice, a policeman normally proceeds by classifying a new case as part of a group of cases they're familiar with; that is, he looks for a thief among thieves, and not among the owners of villas in Bubenec; or he searches more readily for a robber in Židovské Pece than among members of the Philosophical Union. The police would undoubtedly have solved the murders in Rue Morgue if, on the basis of reliable experience, they could say that such murders, as a rule, are usually committed by apes. The police have their own, somewhat melancholic belief that all cases are old and hackneyed, and they all proceed in accordance with customary rules. Strangely enough, they are usually right.[3]

Čapek developed this same slant in several of his tales, one of which, "The Stolen Document 139/VII Sect. C," is a perfectly constructed story. A great espionage scandal is reduced to the level of an ordinary household robbery, solved triumphantly by an insignificant police inspector named Pištora, who, on the basis of experience, has marked out this robbery from the very beginning as the work of one of his "regular customers." This tale also has an ironic twist: at the moment the affair descends from the heights of suspected espionage, the reward for the stolen goods' recovery also drops, from a height of several thousand to a paltry tip.

The same method employed by Inspector Pištora is used by police officer Pitr in "The Death of Baron Gandara." "I don't have a head for mysterious things," says Pitr. "I like plain, ordinary murders, like a tobacconist's murder. Look, I'm not about to learn new methods. Since they gave the case to me, I'm going to handle it my way; and as far as I'm concerned it's an ordinary robbery and murder. If they'd given it to you, it would have turned into some kind of crime sensation, a torrid romance, or a political scandal."[4]

Čapek devised splendid plots to support the idea that almost everything that appears mysterious could be reduced to something banal or everyday, or simply not brought to a conscious level. He even returned to his mysterious footprint in the snow, over which he once engaged in philosophical speculation; this time, a policeman is called in to look at a row of footprints, and his words apparently argue Čapek's conception of the miraculous in life. When a man discovers five footprints leading into the middle of a snowy street and then simply coming to an end, with no continuation whatsoever, the policeman explains to him:

> "There's this strange notion that the police, especially detectives, are interested in mysteries. We don't give a damn about mysteries; what interests us is disorderly conduct. Sir, crime doesn't interest us because it's mysterious, but because it's against the law. We don't chase crooks out of intellectual curiosity; we chase them so we can arrest them in the name of the law. Listen, streetcleaners don't run around the streets with brooms so they can spot people's traces in the dust, but so they can sweep and tidy up all the filth life leaves behind. Law and order aren't a bit mysterious..."

> "But Captain," Mr. Rybka objected, wriggling with dissatisfaction, "is that really enough for you? What happened here is ... is such a strange thing ... is something so mysterious ... and you..."
>
> Captain Bartošek shrugged his shoulders. "And I just brushed it aside. If you like, sir, I'll have the footprints removed so they don't interfere with a good night's sleep for you. But I can't do more than that..."[5]

Although he constructed the first volume of stories brilliantly, it's clear that Čapek didn't take all of them completely seriously. An author so rational certainly did not believe in mysterious footprints, nor did he think that the shape of a crime depends upon who is investigating it. Also, the theft of a document stored for safety in a macaroni canister is just as unlikely as a poet writing out an automobile's license number in such poetic metaphors as "swan's neck bosom drum and cymbal." From these tales we can conclude that, in great part, Čapek sided with the old-fashioned approach to cognition, expressing, as he did, a distaste for anything that seemed too fashionable, sensational, or snobbish. And as a writer, he was attracted to life's paradoxes, the unexpected twists with which he surprised and sometimes even confused his readers.

In the ambiguous conclusions to certain of the stories, we can detect Čapek's relativism, his desire to demonstrate that there are several ways to grasp reality. He preferred one of them, but he did not consider any to be infallible or exclusively correct. His relativistic stance is even more obvious in questions of guilt and punishment, as can be seen in tales appearing in the latter half of the first volume. In "The Last Judgment," people in heaven are judged by human judges, because God cannot judge – he knows everything and understands far too well the causes of each criminal's behavior. In "The Crime on the Farm," Čapek allows an opposite view to prevail: God should be the judge, because only he could impose "the great and terrible punishments" appropriate to the crime.

A third approach to the question of punishment is suggested in "The Crime at the Post Office." Because people can only punish, there must be someone, above man, someone who is the most just, who can forgive. Because "truth and higher justice are just as strange as love."

Finally, there are tales in which human justice is powerless, as in "The Disappearance of an Actor." The murderer goes unpunished, because the murder cannot be proven. The only justice, the only punishment, is that the murderer will never find peace, will live in fear till his dying day, because someone knows what he did. A similar motif of unpunished crime haunting the criminal's soul can be found in a tale from the second volume, "The Confession."

As much as we can find a deep meaning in most of the tales, we should not overemphasize their philosophical messages. First of all, many of the stories were written simply from the joy of telling a story, from the joy of spinning unbelievable tales. Čapek pretended, however, that the stories he was telling were absolutely true, even though, at the same time, paying very little attention to their likelihood – as is the case with "The Blue Chrysanthemum," "The Record," "The Receipt," "The Tale of the Missing Leg," and others.

In their entirety, the tales created a special world in which the majority of people are ordinary (even the majority of the criminals are merely "ordinary" people), and even extraordinary events can have ordinary explanations. Despite the crimes, mysteries, and enigmas, the predominant elements are kindness, forbearance, even compassion for the criminal.

The second volume is a sort of decameron, in which individual narrators take turns imparting their interesting tales to one another. It sustains an atmosphere of friendly storytelling that seemingly takes place around a table in a tavern.

In both volumes of stories, above all in the second volume, Čapek brought his mastery of language to perfection, suggesting to the reader that, like Jaroslav Hašek's, his narration is incorporating the language actually spoken by ordinary people in conversation. As opposed to Hašek, however, Čapek employed highly stylized language, avoided vulgarisms and, above all, did not use the careless "Prague" Czech, with its deformed word endings. He achieved the colloquiality of his langauge chiefly by syntax, interjections, verbal filler, and the stressing, heard in everyday speech, of certain demonstrative pronouns – resulting in expressions and figures of speech that are often difficult to convey into another language.

Tales from Two Pockets represents the best of Čapek's storytelling art, and (along with the stories of Bohumil Hrabal) belong to this day, in my opinion, to the best of Czech short stories.

21. The End of the Robber

Between the end of 1932 and the summer of 1934, Čapek wrote three novels telling three very different stories. *Hordubal*, *Meteor*, and *An Ordinary Life* (collected as *Three Novels*) were also his first lengthy works without fantasy or science fiction premises. In an afterword that followed the third novel, Čapek called these works a trilogy, in spite of the fact that the novels have no common protagonist or even setting (Subcarpathian Ruthenia, the Greater Antilles, and Bohemia, respectively). The author explains that the novels form a trilogy because they all deal with means of cognition, ways in which we perceive and make judgments about the world. The critics who accepted Čapek's explanation termed the trilogy noetic.

Čapek, as I have already mentioned, accompanied nearly all of his works with frequently surprising explanations, as if he chose to deflect attention from the story and to emphasize that he was not only the author of entertaining fiction, but also an author conveying philosophical messages. But the attraction, specificity, and the essential value of literary works consists more in their singularity, effectiveness, and manner of narration than in the philosophical conclusions we can obtain from them. Paradoxically, therefore, I seek in Čapek's work something other than what the philosophizing author prompts me to find.

The immediate stimulus for writing *Hordubal* came from a courtroom report by Čapek's newspaper colleague Bedřich Golombek, on the murder trial of Jiří Hardubej, a farmer in a small village in Subcarpathian Ruthenia, the far eastern part of Czechoslovakia, which was ceded to Ukraine after the Second World War. After eight years in America, Hardubej had returned with a considerable amount of money, and he became a topic of interest to the entire village – with the exception of his wife, because, as Golombek wrote:

> [I]n his absence, she had compromised her reputation with the hired hands and especially with twenty-three-year-old Vasil Maňák, to whom she betrothed her eleven-year-old daughter, Hafia. After some time, Hardubej started putting his household in order: he canceled the betrothal of his daughter and threw Maňák out. But that was not the end of the matter. Polana Hardubejová, eleven years older than her lover, continued to meet with him, and Maňák found his brother-in-law out in the fields and promised him a pair of oxen if he killed Hardubej. His brother-in-law said that he would do no such thing, not even for a hundred oxen. Maňák therefore decided to carry out the deed himself, and he did so on the night of October 27, 1931. Apparently Polana Hardubejová opened the door of the hut, and then Maňák either by himself or together with his lover used a long basket-maker's needle to stab through Hardubej's heart.[1]

Čapek borrowed practically all of the basic facts surrounding this tragic event, preserving even the manner of murder by basket-maker's needle. The newspaper report of this senseless murder gave him the opportunity to write a balladic story set in what was then the most romantic corner of the Czechoslovak Republic.[2] His major addition was having the main exhibit at the trial – the pierced heart – become lost at some point during the proceedings. Another change involved the betrothed eleven-year-old, Hafia. The kindhearted Hordubal, in order to protect his wife's reputation, himself arranged for the betrothal of his little daughter. Moreover, Čapek, who liked having his main characters seriously ill, allowed Hordubal to be murdered while already in a coma.

Čapek divided *Hordubal* into three parts of unequal length. In the first and longest part, he related the story as if from the point of view of Hordubal himself; in the second part the story is presented from the police investigator's point of view; in the third and shortest part, events are seen as if through the eyes of the court and the witnesses. This method of storytelling enables the author to give a fuller and (perhaps only seemingly) more objective view of the events he is describing. In Čapek's explanation, this variety of views is the most significant characteristic of his narrative. *Hordubal* is about

> a conflict between a man who, out of solitude, turned completely inward, and the simple, we might say brutal facts he was faced with. But that isn't it, that isn't the real tragedy of Hordubal. His real and most bitter lot comes only with what happens to him after his death. With how his story becomes coarse in the hands of men; how the events, which he lived in his way and according to his inner law, become obscure and oblique when policemen reconstruct them by means of objective detection; how it all becomes corrupted and entangled and contorted into another, hopelessly ugly picture of life ... Yes, among those human proceedings Juraj's heart was lost; that is the real, tragic story of Hordubal the farmer – and, more of less, of us all ... How differently the same people and the same facts appear in Hordubal's version, in the eyes of the policemen, and in the moral preoccupations of the court![3]

Čapek closes his explanation with his customary reference to the complexity of truth. In *R.U.R.*, Čapek did not dramatize a story about differing truths, but about robots and their revolt against their creators. Similarly, in *Hordubal*, he did not tell a story about how the truth becomes lost in the hands of the police or the court. First and foremost (and fortunately), the story he told was about passions, blindness, betrayal, murder and its investigation; he drew a picture of a Subcarpathian village; above all, he wrote a balladic story about people caught up in tragic events. It had taken him nearly ten years to start another novel. Why did he choose this story? Was it only because he wanted to show the complexities involved in seeking the truth about an event that, at first glance, is entirely unambiguous? Was there nothing personal in this apparently abstract theme?

When I spoke about the hero of *Krakatit*, I attempted to point out the connection between Čapek's fate and the fate of the main character of his utopian tale about the Robber, which seem, at first glance, to have nothing in common. I am convinced that all authors project into their protagonists their own characteristics, their ideas of what they would like (and, conversely, would not like) to live through, their longings and fears, their experiences, their fate. If we understand an author, we will also have a better understanding of his characters and of the stories he tells. Conversely, from his characters we are often better able to understand an author. Čapek, like so many authors, tried as best he could to conceal his kinship to his protagonists; and in their external traits, their vocations and social standing, his characters were entirely different from him. Beneath these disguises, however, we can recognize the author, and in their struggles and dilemmas his own. In the trilogy, especially in the third volume, we find, not too surprisingly, many autobiographical traits.

What could a Subcarpathian farmer who has toiled eight years in American mines have in common with a frail Prague intellectual? Čapek described Hordubal as a man who, out of loneliness, turned entirely inward. In this way he could portray Hordubal as different from the customary image of a farmer and miner. Hordubal returns from America to his wife, and she openly rejects him. He, however, accepts this, with almost unbelievable forgiveness; he doesn't object to the fact that a young hired hand has moved into his house; he refuses to talk with people about his wife and her infidelity. In Čapek's conception, Hordubal is an odd man who stubbornly believes his wife still loves him. He is a man who passively accepts everything that happened in his absence, including the fact that his wife and her lover sold a field as well as some cattle. His actions are driven by a single motive: to defend the reputation of his wife. Only when his almost limitless patience becomes exhausted does he throw his rival out of the house (and even then, he immediately summons him back).

But Hordubal, in spite of his external peasant-farmer traits, has within himself elements which in many repects remind us of the traits of the one who created him. In his relationship to his wife, for example, he expresses a precisely Čapekian ambivalence: a woman is a princess, a rare, noble, and simultaneously threatening being one must look up to, protect, honor, and also accept as inaccessible. (Four years later, he would endow with exactly these same traits the miner Adam in the novel *The First Rescue Party*.)

Čapek's protagonist yearns for only one thing: to produce and make public a sworn statement that Polana, his wife, was and is faithful. He goes up into the mountains to see an isolated shepherd and asks him to testify, if necessary, that Polana has always been loving and faithful to her husband; he goes to a lawyer and, in his last will, which he writes ten days before being stabbed in the heart, he rewards his unfaithful wife "for her fidelity and love" by leaving her all his property.

And the murder itself? It appears to be both stupid and useless; much more significant is the illness slowly taking Hordubal to his death. Čapek's protagonist is murdered senselessly, right when he's dying anyway. Excessively concerned with his health problems, Čapek created characters who were excessively ill.

If we do not accept Čapek's interpretation as the sole key to understanding this tragic story, we can only conclude that he must have had a deeper reason. Something had changed over the years. The Robber, as well as his successor, Prokop, in whom Čapek had at one time embodied his yearning, has left the stage – another protagonist has pushed into the place of the one who used to be (by coincidence or subconsciously, exactly eight years previously) a robber, a strong man, a fighter who wins the love of women. Now he has become older, has given up his claim to love, is full of humility, is ready to love and forgive even when deceived, even when he's a laughingstock to others. As a reward, the author lets him die a double death: the one at the hands of the murderers is especially cruel, for, as much as Čapek in his explanation of the novel (not in the story itself) cast doubts, undoubtedly the wife took part in the murder as well, the wife whom the protagonist was prepared to forgive everything and shower her with everything he had.

As if the author subconsciously was demonstrating that there is no place among the living for an overly delicate man. For that matter, he completed *Hordubal* five years before his own untimely death.

22. The Story of a Man Hurrying Towards Death

In the second volume of his trilogy, Čapek, who had never traveled outside Europe, chose an even more exotic locale than backward Subcarpathian Ruthenia: the Greater Antilles. But *Meteor*'s frame story takes place in a hospital apparently somewhere in Bohemia. In a rather peaceful atmosphere barely affected by the storm outside, a surgeon is talking with two patients, a poet and a clairvoyant. At that moment a seriously wounded man is brought in, a man who has been freed from a wrecked, burning airplane. The plane was not flying on a regular air lane, the pilot is dead, and the only passenger, whom they have just brought to the hospital, is in a deep coma. Since all his papers have burned, there is nothing to help determine his identity. In the pocket of this unknown man they find French, English, Dutch, and American coins. He has scars in his groin area from an injury evidently caused by a large beast of prey. Moreover, he has a tropical disease, most likely yellow fever (this tropical disease seems to have interested Čapek: he had one of the main characters in his play, *The Mother*, die of it). In his unconscious state, the new patient mumbles words in English and Spanish; on his left wrist an anchor is tattooed; his heart, considering his presumed age, shows too much wear and tear. That is all that can be learned about the man who fell from the sky – therefore, in the hospital, they refer to him as Case X.

The author of course is not particularly concerned with what is happening with the patient in the hospital: Case X, like Hordubal, is doubly sentenced to death. The characters we've met at the beginning of the story are perturbed by the anonymity of the man. Where was he coming from? Why was he flying in such windy weather? What was he hurrying after?

One by one, the two patients and one of the nurses use their imaginations to try and reconstruct the story of Case X and thus restore his identity to him. The tripartite *Hordubal* was an attempt to play with the novel form in an interesting manner; *Meteor* is less a novel than a trio of stories, two shorter and one longer, in which three narrators – a nurse, a clairvoyant, and a poet – imagine the story of the unknown man. The nurse's story is based on a dream, the clairvoyant is guided by his intuition, and the poet, in obedience to his imagination, writes down a lengthy tale.

In his explanation of this novel, Čapek again tried to emphasize his aim of showing the different ways in which we come to know.

> And then we have *Meteor*, the second phase of the trilogy. Here, too, the life of a man is portrayed in a triple, or quadruple way, but the situation is inverted: in every possible way people try to find the lost heart of a man; they have only his body, and they try to fit to it a corresponding life. But this time the point is not how far they diverge in their explanations, which, after all, they had to conjure out of their own wits (we may call it intuition, daydream, imagination, or whatever); what is so striking is that here and there, in some things, they coincide with or hint at a probable reality – but even this isn't so much the point. Each one places the given fact – the unconscious body of a man – into a different life story; each time the story is different, depending on who is telling it; each one includes himself, his experiences, his trade, his methods, and his inclinations ... These stories all have in common the fact that in them is mirrored more or less fantastically the one who is telling them ... Whatever we look at is one thing and, at the same time, something of us, something of ours, something personal; our knowledge of the world and of men is like a confession. We see things differently according to who and what we are; things are good and evil, beautiful and dreadful – it depends upon the eyes with which we look at them. How terribly big and complex, how spacious is reality when there is room enough for so many different interpretations! But

> it is no longer a chaos, it is a distinct plurality; it is no longer an uncertainty, but a polyphony...[1]

Some of the critics of the time saw in this declaration merely new formulations of Čapek's old relativism. But it can be argued that Čapek was merely summing up basic information about the essence of narration. All the same, there is no doubt that the narrator's personality and point of view are mirrored in every story. And in the long run, the one telling the stories through the mouths of a nurse, a clairvoyant, and a poet is the author himself.

Čapek subscribed to the tradition of epic narration. "People's literature will never be other than epic," he wrote in 1920, in an article entitled "In Place of Criticism."

> Of course, I refer here only to prose writing. I would like at this point to expand upon matters regarding the young: people remain boys who are fascinated by heroism, great and robust characters, the simple passions, and strong and even fantastical tales. Their relish for literature lies in intense complicity, involvement in what is going on; they want not to look upon something, but to live it, to experience something out of the ordinary. This isn't romanticism; this thirst for powerful experiences is older and more primitive than any division of literature into period or movement. Indeed, if literature does not evolve once again into epic, it will be a literature read by fewer and fewer people.[2]

In *Meteor,* Čapek strove to present his own art in thrilling, exotic stories, and just as a musical improviser plays variations on a few notes, Čapek too could produce brilliant variations on a few motifs. In addition, he nearly overwhelmed the reader with exotic details of the smells, fragrances, sounds, and names of dozens of exotic plants (this was the erudite gardener speaking) in dialogues that pretended absolute knowledge of local details.

More interesting for us is how, behind the exotic details and artful disguises, we find their author, and how, in descriptions of seemingly faraway worlds and relationships, his world and his relationships show through.

The innermost connection between the unknown men portrayed by the three *Meteor* narrators is loneliness. "He sought out solitude," it was said of the unknown man in the clairvoyant's story, "so that there should be no conflict between himself and his surroundings. He tried to melt his internal desolation, like a piece of ice, in the immense solitude of the sea or foreign lands."[3]

In the other two stories, he takes this rash and tragic flight because he is on the run from loneliness, from his failure to find a woman he had earlier abandoned or with whom, for some reason, he could not stay. "There was in me a violent, anxious aversion to anything that would bind me," the unknown man says of himself in the nurse's story, "and this cowardice I felt to be an expression of my liberty. I was terrified by how demanding and committed she was in her love; although she was above me, I was frightened that I would be bound forever. I felt that I must decide between myself and her, and I decided on myself."[4] How can one not hear in this the author's lifelong dilemma? At the end of this story, the unknown man realizes the error and immaturity of his decision, and he finds himself when he recognizes that no person should belong to another.

A less probable motif accounts for his loneliness in the longest story, that of the poet: after being wounded, the hero loses his memory and therefore his identity and is given a new name. Love plays a decisive role in this story, too, but this time its fulfillment is impeded by an external obstacle: the father of the young woman he loves. He tries to obtain the wealth needed to clear the path to his beloved, but does not succeed. Then, at the moment of utter failure, when the hero is writing his love a letter of farewell, his memory returns, and with it the hope that he might win his beloved after all. In an emotionally extravagant finale, he declares his boundless love.

> For God's sake, don't mention her hand! Say hand, and already my fingers and chin are trembling. How she took me then by the hand – I am thinking of her smooth fingers, stop! stop!

> Are you immensely happy?
>
> Yes, no, wait, it will pass. Damn these tears! How is it possible that a man can love someone beyond all reason![5]

Yet even this story must have a tragic ending, because in the frame story the unknown traveler dies.

Death plays a very important role in the trilogy (as, for that matter, it does in all of Čapek's works). "But strange enough, however much I thought about it," we read in the nurse's story, "I could not imagine death as an end, snip, like cutting a thread. I looked at it up close enough and it seemed to be something vast and enduring, I can't say what, but a tremendous span of time, for death endures. I will tell you that it was its endurance, its permanence, that frightened me so terribly..."[6] The author himself is speaking directly here, and in his words we also hear the anguish of modern man, who has lost faith and, along with it, any hope that his existence will continue after death. In all of his works, Čapek was searching desperately for some kind of hope. And so he continues his contemplation as, again through the words of the nurse, he professes Bergsonian[7] hope in at least the continuation of life. "And I began to understand that life, like death, has the elements of permanence, that in its way, and with its own small means, it has the will and the courage to last forever."[7]

The first and third stories of *Meteor* also demonstrate how, in Čapek's work, one of the most fundamental human relationships changed. His women have turned into beings more angelic than human; affectionate relationships have taken the shape of romantic ones. For women, love is noble, pure, unmarred by lust – it is resigned and patient. For men, true love seems unattainable, unfulfillable, whether for internal or external reasons.

Even in his most exotic stories we find reflections of the author's personal story, and it is worth noting the long passage which Čapek gave to the poet's explanation of the process that went into the creation of his story.

> Such are we, we fabricators of the imagination: to extol or improve a man's life, we bring upon it a hard fate, we overburden him with conflict and adversity. But after all, doesn't it bring with it a special glory of its own? ... If I follow the road of the imagination, I will choose some striking and unusual event; like a butcher appraising a cow, I appraise whether a feeling is duly plump and ample ... To the devil with the imagination; it's no use to us, it won't lead us even to the tips of our noses if it isn't shaking with the fever of interest ... I can imagine anything I like, but only at the cost of my believing in it myself. As soon as my trust that it really might have been like that is shaken, my imagination appears to me as just puerile and deplorable bungling.[8]

In this we hear the voice of the man who wrote *R.U.R.*, *Krakatit*, and *The Makropulos Secret*. At the conclusion of the poet's story, we hear him say that the life he has been describing was not imagined, was not fiction, but is identical with his own life, is merely the recording of one of his own life's possibilities in his own life: "[T]o make it clear, it is me, I am the man who did not finish his flight."[9]

Readers are unlikely to perceive the three stories of *Meteor* as the outcome of varying kinds of cognition. It is much more likely that they read them as exotic stories from faraway places, the first engendered in a dream, the second in a vision (which, if it could not be substantiated, could at least be passionately experienced), and the third from the rich imagination of a poet. Readers perceive them also as wonderful variations on several basically minor motifs, and as a struggle to maintain individuality, to leave a human footprint in life, when a human life itself cannot be salvaged.

Meteor was received by most critics with great praise. The interwar period placed almost exaggerated emphasis on innovations in form. The way Čapek conceived of to tell the stories was original and effective. Some of the critics drew comparisons to the new storytelling approaches of Joyce, Proust, Dos Passos, and Gide, and contended that *Meteor* was an important creative act in the development of the European novel. František Götz, an important Czech critic who in the past had carried on a passionate dispute with Čapek, wrote a long eulogy on the novel. According to him, in a work of enormous poetic elevation Čapek had succeeded in overcoming nihilism, a feeling chronic in modern man.

> It is futile to seek meaning and content merely in decomposed forms. It is necessary to create substance, meaning, and an objective – out of oneself, out of a deep spirituality of the soul, which is being filled to the brim with others' pain and horror. This is the word of poetic redemption. Čapek advances toward the objectivity of fate by presenting it from four subjective perspectives. Thus he shows contempt for epic unity, because it would lead to sterility and cardboard characters. He shows contempt for the use of common novelistic illusion, he observes the unalloyed ingredients of life always from new, singular perspectives, and he analyzes the case from four points of view and with an effort to know – that is, to create anew.[10]

Unquestionably, in *Meteor* Čapek proved once again that he was not only a master of small forms, but also an author seeking new forms for more extensive, epic plots. Additionally, he showed that his poetic imagination and superb language had not been diminished by his daily work in journalism. And in the first two volumes of the trilogy, he attempted to depict characters which most authors up to then had avoided. In the third volume, he progressed still farther with this effort.

23. Looking for Love

Even more theoretical than the explanation of the meaning of *Meteor* is the author's explanation of the meaning of the trilogy's third volume: we can come to know other people only because hidden in us are many other, unrealized lives.

Čapek wrote this novel during part of the summer of 1934 (he always wrote very quickly and easily) and called it *An Ordinary Life*. In contrast to the previous two volumes, this time the story not only takes place in Bohemia, but its protagonist, a minor railway official, himself tells the story of his thoroughly run-of-the-mill life. That his ordinary life is meant to be symbolic is underlined by the fact that the protagonist (just as in *Meteor*) has no name. The first half of the novel (nineteen of the thirty-four chapters) deals with the absolute ordinariness of the man's life. In this placid section, he remembers his childhood and his brief period of university study, when he got involved with a bohemian crowd, and wrote and published poems. When his father, a small-town cabinetmaker, refused to support him in this style of life, he left his studies and became a civil servant in the Ministry of Railways. But he unexpectedly began to cough up blood, and his superiors wisely transferred him from Prague to a small railroad station in the mountains, where his health gradually improved. After a while he was transferred again, to a busier station headed by a good-natured German stationmaster. The protagonist fell in love with the stationmaster's daughter and married her. For some time during the First World War, he supplied information about his station and military train transport to the anti-Austrian resistance; after the war, he was transferred back to Prague, to the Ministry of Railways. As with the majority of Čapek's protagonists (excepting Hordubal), he remained childless, and his wife conferred her maternal solicitude on him. The first half ends with the protagonist contending that his was "an ordinary, but in its way complete and consummate life."

In the next part of the novel, the protagonist returns to certain stages in his life and discovers that his narration was incomplete, that he did not actually think through the meaning of many of his experiences. Now he discovers that many moments and events seem quite at odds with how he views himself, and it seems as if there were beings in him whose pasts are entirely different from his own. Gradually he discovers in himself a poet, a brutal animal, a romantic, a hypochondriac, a hero of the resistance, a man with ambition – he discovers in himself a crowd of various beings, and he recognizes that this crowd might be even larger, because we bring into actuality, we realize, only a small portion of our possibilities. It is in just this realization of possibilities that, in the novel's moving conclusion, the protagonist finds a reason for tolerance, understanding, and the love of others. We are all of one blood, he now understands, all of us could be any of the others, and thus we can consider one another brothers.

> Each of us is a crowd that dwindles off out of sight. Just look at yourself, you're nearly the whole of mankind! That's what's so frightening about it: when you sin, the blame falls on all of them, and that huge crowd bears all your pain and pettiness. You mustn't, you mustn't lead so many people along the path of humiliation and vanity. You are me, you lead, you're responsible for them, you were supposed to lead them all somewhere.
>
> ... But you don't even know what you have in common with them; just look – indeed, their life too is one of those countless possible ones that are inside you! You could be what the other is, you could be a gentleman, or a beggar, or a day-laborer stripped to the waist...
>
> Look, look carefully so as to see at last all you might have been; if you pay attention, you will see in everyone a fragment of yourself, and then, with amazement, you will recognize in him your true neighbor.
>
> ... Whoever you are, I recognize you, for we are on the same level, each of us lives one of the other's possibilities. Whoever

> you are, you are my innumerable self, good or bad, you are inside me. Even if I hated you, I would never forget how terribly near to me you are. I will love my neighbor as I do myself, and I will fear him as I do myself, and I will oppose him as I do myself; I will feel his burden, I will be vexed with his pain, and I will groan under the wrongs that are done to him. The nearer I am to him, the more I will find myself.[1]

While the conclusions at which Čapek's protagonist arrives certainly contain humanistic pathos, the way he arrives at them could be considered overly theoretical – and an attempt to find one's way to others by discovering innumerable beings within oneself could be considered somewhat pathological. To the extent that we consider the protagonist's account of the other beings within him merely metaphorical, we are back at the concept of cognition, of how one comes to know oneself, and the importance of this process to knowing and understanding others. But still I find the story more impressive than the philosophical message.

In *An Ordinary Life* more than in Čapek's other works, we find a great deal of autobiographical material and the highly effective use of childhood experiences. Even if the protagonist's father is a cabinetmaker, not a doctor, he has many of the characteristics of Čapek's father, and the protagonist's mother resembles Čapek's mother even more.

> I loved my father because he was strong and straightforward. Touching him gave me a feeling like leaning against a wall or a strong pillar ... and his powerful build filled me with a pleasant sense of safety, solidity, and strength ... Mother was not so straightforward ... Because she was supremely emotional, she dramatized everything; small family disputes ended with swollen eyes and tragic silences; Papa banged the door behind him and set to work with fierce tenacity, while from the kitchen an awful accusatory silence rose into the heavens. She cherished the idea that I was a weak child, that some misfortune might happen to me, or that I might die...[2]

With great love and understanding, Čapek described life in a small town from the point of view of a child. The boy has a somewhat forlorn childhood. He is excellent in school, "a quiet and diligent pupil" who very much longs for the friendship of the greatest rascal in his class. And because he is such a good student, and out of loneliness and lack of sociability buries himself in books, his father sends him to university. "And I was a shy country boy who felt he cut a poor figure with the plucky little masters from the town ... Because I could not find any way to be close to them, I made up my mind to excel in school; I became the drudge who finds sense in life, revenge, triumph, in progressing from class to class to summa cum laude..."[3]

The prominent literary historian and critic Václav Černý, who accepted the author's philosophical interpretation of the trilogy without reservation, expressed the greatest admiration for these autobiographical passages. "Perhaps I have read little, but I do not know of any more truthful and – despite the light irony – more heartfelt pages than this ballad of student life in chapters VII and VIII."[4]

On the basis of these passages, we can better understand certain aspects of his nature: his oversensitivity, his extraordinary industry, his need to excel intellectually, an attempt to gain love by emphasizing physical weakness and suffering. Čapek was aware of this latter connection, and he allowed his protagonist to make full use of it:

> Then it comes out that the other one was seriously, terribly, gravely ill; if it was like that, she could hold him maternally by the hand and fervently give him a talking to: You must take care of yourself, you must not be ill; I should like so much to look after you! ... If I fell ill now, no elderly clerk would come to me, reckless, looking like a black beetle; I would lie pale and feverish, into the room would slip a maiden with tearful eyes, and I would pretend that I was asleep; and she, leaning over me, would begin sobbing and say: My only one, you must not die! Yes, like my mother. For the maiden it is also good to be a mother and weave round the other her pained solicitude; her eyes

> full of tears, she is thinking, If he fell ill, how well I would look after him! She doesn't realize how, with such a feeling, she appropriates him, how she seeks to subject him; she wants him to be hers, to be unable to defend himself, to submit to the terrifying self-sacrifice of her love.[5]

Čapek's protagonist returns once again to the identification of love with the need to be pitied, and in so doing explains the origin of such a morbid connection.

> Mother was obsessed with the notion that I was in danger, that I was a weak and ailing child ... By all the love she gave me, she fostered in me the idea that I was something delicate, more delicate than other children ... it was Mother who fostered in me my lifelong timidity and lack of self-confidence, that physical feeling of inferiority I grew up with. It was Mother's pathological love that led me to regard myself as the object of endless nursing and coddling, an inclination I nestled up to, practically indulged, whenever the first tap of a real illness gave me the opportunity.

Slightly earlier he recalls, "To be ill, that was an important and solemn thing."[6]

To the extent that we can accept the protagonists of *The Robber* and *Krakatit* as projections of the author's dreams about his own masculinity, the protagonist of *An Ordinary Life* is, on the contrary, more the author's self-projection, with all his weaknesses and anxieties, with his longing for a love more maternal than a lover's love, with the anxiety he felt about exactly that sort of devouring love, with his fear of the erotic and with his longing for a rational – and peaceful – love. It is for this reason that the first part of *An Ordinary Life* must be counted, for its psychological development, as one of the most successful works Čapek ever wrote. It is not without interest that this analysis of the negative influence of a mother's devouring love was written about a year before Čapek decided to marry, despite his illness.

These three novels, produced in close succession, constituted a milestone in Čapek's literary development. Until then, he had written only shorter works, except for two novels that belong more properly to the field of science fiction. Now he had tried a novelistic work in which the plot takes place in realistic, contemporary settings. And wheras Čapek had always been set on endowing his longer works with a philosophical message, in the first two volumes of the trilogy and also the first part of the third, this aspiration receded into the background to such a degree that he felt a need to call attention to it with additional explanatory material.

In the majority of Čapek's works, the protagonists are men. Women – even when, as in *Hordubal*, a murder is committed for one – play merely secondary roles. In Čapek's view, they are loving, devoted beings who are themselves in love. That is true of both female characters in *Meteor* and also of the protagonist's wife in *An Ordinary Life*. Even Hordubal sees his unfaithful wife as innocent and loving, and Čapek was apparently partial to this view. And then there is suffering: "great and difficult is love," writes the protagonist of *An Ordinary Life*, "and even the happiest love is horrible and its excessiveness overwhelming. We cannot love without pain; if only we would die of love, if only we could measure its vastness with suffering..."[7] Woman, in relationship to man, is the bearer of love, solicitude – and suffering.

Čapek's protagonists suffer from loneliness, and this loneliness is not only explicitly mentioned, but is emphasized by the structure of each story. It is as if Čapek's protagonists, with the exception of a short moment when they become inflamed with love, cannot establish genuine relationships with women, cannot relate to them either as adversaries or as partners. The protagonist in *Hordubal*, who in his loneliness travels up into the mountains to see the simple, taciturn Míša, has no such relationships, nor does the protagonist of *Meteor*. And the protagonist of *An Ordinary Life* has encounters with women that are merely episodic. Symptomatically, in the latter's childhood, his most ardent relationship is with an unknown girl whose language he doesn't know and with whom he therefore cannot communicate. Nevertheless, *An Ordinary Life* is an attempt, at least theoretically, to overcome loneliness and alienation.

It should not be overlooked that the protagonists of all three novels fall victim to illness and death. Hordubal is dying and, while dying, is murdered. The unknown protagonist of *Meteor* is dying from a tropical disease, in addition to being mortally wounded. The protagonist of *An Ordinary Life* writes his memoirs just before he dies; we could even explain the ecstatic tone of its final passages as a presentiment of death.

All three novels develop the motif of return. Hordubal returns from his eight-year stay in the United States; in all three parts of *Meteor* the protagonist returns, as does, in his own way, the protagonist of *An Ordinary Life*, for he revisits the more consequential moments of his life. All three are stories of taking stock; face to face with death, the protagonists evaluate the meaning and importance of their acts, of their virtues. In the three parts of *Meteor*, above and beyond this taking stock, there is a desperate desire to change the course of the unknown man's life up to that time, to give to his frantic flight, or return, a value it had been lacking.

Of course, most of these motifs relate to the author's own life, to his bachelorhood, to his illness (which engendered in him a fear of the end as well as the need to take stock of his own life), to his conception of love, and to his ambivalent relationships with the women who came into his life – beginning with his mother and ending with the woman he finally married. In this respect, we can consider the trilogy to be the most authentic of all Čapek's writing, and it is also the most successful of his longer works.

In his trilogy, Čapek proved himself to be a master of original composition and an outstanding storyteller in command of a great imagination, thanks to which he was entirely convincing in describing even the most exotic environments. I have chosen not to emphasize the trilogy's philosophical level, which Čapek himself called attention to with such insistence and about which contemporary critics spoke sometimes approvingly, sometimes with displeasure. I think that, just as in *R.U.R.* and *Krakatit*, the excellent storyteller won out over the philosopher. Čapek's attempt to give the stories a further dimension did, however, lead to the singularity of his creative methods. Each story in the trilogy was told several times, always from a different point of view, and that, in his day, was a technique unquestionably original and intellectually stimulating.

24. The Failure of the Intellectuals Will Make Barbarians of Us All

In 1932, Čapek published a book entitled *On Public Matters, or Zóon Politikon*, in which he gathered together his important articles on social and political topics from the previous eight years, including the essays "Why Am I Not a Communist?" "On Relativism," and the previously-mentioned articles on the dangers of technology and on Americanism. The final third of the book consists of a series of articles published that same year in the weekly *Přítomnost*, containing more personal essays on political and civic issues, collectively called "On Myself and Weightier Matters," from which the following excerpts are taken.

Čapek had always spoken out on contemporary political morals, political schemers, strong partisanship, and all attempts to circumvent democratic principles. In these essays he most succinctly criticized the contemporary political atmosphere, identifying its predominant features as "mutual mistrust, disloyalty, uncooperativeness, blind partisan selfishness and fury, connivance for personal gain, lack of interest in big ideas, an inability to conceive larger solutions, and an unwillingness to take personal responsibility. Political twilight."[1]

He differed substantially from those who responded to political problems by calling for the elimination of democracy and the introduction of either a Soviet system (there were many such critics, especially in the Czech Lands) or a strong-hand government along Italian lines. Čapek emphasized that people shape politics – and whatever people are like, so will their politics be. "Democracy derives not from people's rights, but from people and their actions ... You can bring any kind of system into existence: if done by half-hearted, disloyal, small, cowardly people, it will be an inadequate, chaotic system." And he concluded, as he had many times before, that no sort of radicalism can save a society, that what is necessary is to educate people and improve their relationships with each other as well as their relationship to democracy. Influenced by the centuries-long lack of freedom, the attitude of the republic's citizens toward democracy was one of irresponsibility.

> Psychologically, we are still living in a state of serfdom, of being governed, of bondage. Look at the more advanced democracies, at nations more mature in their character: how much less servility and snobbiness, rage and reluctance, officialism, disrespect, and irritability is apparent in their person-to-person relationships ... Take note: opposition to democracy is usually coupled with chronic name-calling, with passive pessimism; the opinion that democracy has become outdated usually arises from the gloomy insistence that it's all a lot of dirty dealing. If so, how do you want to improve it? A pile of garbage remains garbage even if you turn it upside down...

Then he turns directly to the communists:

> You want to change the order of things without changing people – least of all yourselves.[2]

In another piece, he analyzes Czech nationalism and concludes that, essentially, it has been constructed on pure negativism, on a distaste for democracy, an anti-German mentality, and the rejection of socialism.

Towards the end of this section of the book, Čapek formulates his civic program.:

> First of all, to make sure that people experience neither material nor ethical injustice ... to increase the value of everyone's life by striving for a better social and world order; and to tackle it practically, without any messianism and without blinders on our eyes. To not take away faith from people, but rather their pain, ennui, despondency, and isolation. To see that people maintain a state of cordiality, mutual loyalty and goodwill, joy and respect, in a word, morality; in a word, optimism; and in a few more words, clear-headed, empowered human life.[3]

One could certainly fault this agenda for consisting of too many generalities or for its strained optimism, but it is more as if this essay brought to a close a period in Čapek's thinking when he elevated tolerance above all else, emphasizing that there is room in this world for many views and truths, and denouncing the bad habit of generalizing as well as the destructiveness of all negativisms. But only a year later, without having to revise his position, he felt the need to be far less universal, much more to the point. In January of 1933, in Czechoslovakia's backyard, things took a fateful turn. Adolf Hitler came to power, a man to whom nothing was more foreign than democratic discourse, than tolerance, than morality of any kind.

No writer in Czechoslovakia (and very few elsewhere in the world) reacted with such accuracy and at the same time with such passion to the Nazi takeover, which, unfortunately, the majority of intellectuals and politicians in the democratic world considered at first to be merely an episode unworthy of getting worked up over. "As we can see," Čapek wrote a few days after Hitler's accession to power, "right before our eyes a piece of Europe is reverting to one hundred years in the past ... It's not enough to shake our heads over Germany; when all is said and done, this is about European culture..."[4]

In 1934 he published several perspicacious essays on the mission of culture and of the intelligentsia in an era he labeled one of the greatest cultural debacles in the history of the world – so labeled because "one entire nation, one whole Reich has come around, spiritually, to believing in animism, racism, and similar nonsense; an entire nation, if you please, with university professors, priests, writers, physicians, and lawyers."[5] Čapek, unlike many intellectuals, was less interested in the economic, class, and political causes of totalitarian upheavals. For him, the fact of most consequence was the failure of educated people, their willingness to serve totalitarian systems. He continued:

> What happened there was nothing less than an immense betrayal by educated Germans, and it gives you a frightening idea what educated people are capable of. I could give you more examples,

> and not only from that one country. Wherever violence is used against civilized humanity, you will find intellectuals by the dozens collaborating and furthermore brandishing their ideological reasons for doing so. This is not about a crisis of or helplessness on the part of the intelligentsia, rather it is about a silent – or else extremely active – complicity in the moral and political shambles of Europe today.[6]

He therefore considered it desirable to assign a role to intellectuals in the current crisis. Since intellectuals tend to be weak and dependent, rather than discussing how they could make use of their resources, it made better sense to lay down what they must not do. They should not, they must not be false to their intellectual disciplines. In an essay on Ortega y Gasset's *The Revolt of the Masses*, Čapek made some modifications to the Spaniard's philosophy:

> It is not the revolt of the masses, but the mass failure of individuals. If we speak of a certain decline, the phenomenon is not that of the masses struggling upward, but that of the headlong, downward rush of those who, given their mission, should stand higher, that is, be intellectually superior ... Those who can and should go after knowledge run after the masses and think they are leading them ... No cultural value can be vanquished until it has been abandoned. The true danger lies not in the revolt of the masses, but in weak minds and characters, in the shameful failure of those who have their lot and their mission as individuals.[7] *and elsewhere:*
>
> Let me put it this way: if a culture fails, the "average" person, the simple and decent man, the farmer, the factory worker, the tradesman with his common sense and moral code, will not be heard, but will instead accept into his life something far beneath him, a barbaric and violent element that will start making a hash of the civilized world ... Destroy the hierarchy of the intellect and you clear the way for the return of savagery. The failure of the intellectuals will make barbarians of us all.[8]

This was, assuredly, a perceptive analysis of the phenomenon accompanying the birth of all totalitarian regimes in Europe at that time. Čapek was particularly horrified by the fact that a significant portion of the Czech intelligentsia professed various totalitarian ideologies and were willing to betray their culture – that is, their civic mission.

At the moment when it seemed that Europe was gradually turning into a group of totalitarian regimes, Čapek tried to define what he meant by "culture" and what its role should be.

> We are not speaking here about culture in the sense of forming a culture, but in the sense of education, spiritual possessions, and intellectual standards. I would say that all our education probably has this as its purpose: to know at least something about the kinds of experience, knowledge, and values that humankind has already formed – and not to lose them, not to lower ourselves below what we are now ... education, in this sense, is the conservation, preservation, and defense of what people who came before us achieved by means of enormous effort. That is why revolutionary eras more or less hate education: precisely because of its mission, of preserving a whole armful of legacies. No use in trying to pass this over without comment: above all, culture represents continuity with every human endeavor, and we must not lose it; no matter what it creates that is new, it is a continuation of the work that has been done before.[9]

Čapek continues in another of his series of articles:

> Culture must have the courage and strength to stick to its guns and not surrender to anything that confines it. It will not be the tool of any spiritual one-sidedness, it will not serve anything other than spiritual integrity, than man's totality.

Culture means struggle without hope of victory, struggle for one's own spiritual freedom, struggle against an environment that wants to orientate thought. "Everyone comes to know by means of his own individual mind, but the truth he hopes to find is valid for all. What is valid only for one side, one faith, one nation is not the truth that is the eternal goal of the human spirit. The entire truth lies in the endless human striving for truth."[10]

Much of what he emphasized might seem self-evident to us today, but on the eve of the Second World War these were claims that many found difficult to accept. The times favored unambiguous, ideological stands. The principle of not lowering oneself below the experiences, knowledge, and values already formed by humankind was violated not only on the eve of the war and during it, but in Czechoslovakia, just as in the Soviet Union and the rest of the communist bloc, it was still being violated many decades after the war had ended – and continues to be violated in many countries today. At the same time, it cannot be denied that the role of the bearers of culture, and thus also their responsibility for the state of the world, is on the rise.

More than thirty years later, long after Čapek's death, Václav Černý wrote with admiration in his memoirs, "Čapek's devotion to democracy was something internal and intrinsic, at one with his entire personality; it was not an opinion, it was a credo. The three basic components integral to, permeating his being were: advocacy of Masaryk, of course; knowledge of world cultures and cultural development; and still deeper, an ardent love of humankind and fear for it."[11]

25. The Third Report on the End of Civilization: War with the Newts

The essays in which Čapek responded to the upsurge of totalitarian systems in Europe were excellent, and his analyses of the spreading downfall of democracies were original and distinct from the schematic analyses of leftist intellectuals, who refused to see the totalitarian horrors in the Soviet Union and who blamed the Nazi victory first and foremost on the intrigues of the capitalist powers and on the treachery of the social democrats, whom they persisted in calling social-fascists. In his essays, Čapek was able to speak out, without an ideological bias, on the dangers that threatened peace and democracy in Europe. But as a writer, he knew that a literary work can speak to readers more effectively than even the best of articles.

By 1934 he had already written several Apocryphal Tales on themes similar to those he pursued in his political essays. In the longest of these tales, "Hamlet, Prince of Denmark," he played with Hamlet's famous soliloquy and had the prince vacillating over whether to simply do the deed or choose a career that might amplify the deed, raise it to another level:

> To be an actor. Or to write? Or speak
> And stir the people? This or that? Oh, hell!
> Which shall I choose? What then shall Hamlet be?
> What I could achieve, accomplish
> If only I were something! – Yes, but what?
> That is the question![1]

In that same year he also published in his newspaper column a set of aphorisms entitled "Fables from the Future," his ironic response to the news that an architect thought some cliffs on the outskirts of Prague suitable for building underground shelters for the city's residents. He applied his sense of irony, paradox, and exaggeration, along with his aphoristic skills, to express people's widely shared anxiety about a new, even more horrific war than the one they remembered.

> Building Commission: From the standpoint of health, your cave is defective. It lets in air.
>
> Mother: That was your boy who did it? Why, that rascal almost crawled up to the surface of the earth!
>
> Diver: Wife, hand me my diving suit; I'm going on up.
>
> Reminiscence: It's already been a year now since we buried dear old papa up there.[2]

Yet small forms such as the aphorism or Apocryphal Tale did not provide enough space for a more analytical depiction of the world. In the spring of 1935, therefore, he began a lengthier prose work which, as always, when he wanted to address a weighty social problem in his art, had a science-fiction premise. In Čapek's words:

> At that time – it was last spring, when the world was looking unbelievably bad economically, and politically still worse – on some occasion or other I wrote this sentence: 'You mustn't think that the evolution that gave rise to our form of life was the only evolutionary possibility on this planet.' And that was it. That sentence is to blame for my writing *War with the Newts*.[3]

Čapek's Newts remind us, in many ways, of his Robots, which were living beings and not machines as we understand the term "robot" today. The danger lay in the fact that they became the object of a ruthless, rigidly logical business, and that their utilization served utopian and technocratic visions. It was this process, the exploitation of industrious and easily reproducible beings, that Čapek tried to capture even more dramatically and colorfully in his utopia about the Newts.

While the play about Robots starts out with a lengthy explanation of this remarkable invention and the wonderful possibilities for exploiting it, the novel about Newts begins more like a classic adventure novel. A Czech sea captain named van

Toch discovers somewhere in the Pacific a remarkable species of newt that lives in the shallow waters near islands, walks on its two hind legs, seems to be very docile, and offers pearls in exchange for various tools, above all knives, which it very quickly learns to use. The captain makes his way to an industrial magnate named Bondy, who happens to be an old schoolmate, and proposes a magnificent scheme for obtaining a prodigious quantity of pearls. Understandably, Bondy doesn't believe the captain's story, but from some combination of sentiment and romantic boyhood memories, promises the captain two ships in which to transport the Newts to various sites where pearls can be found.

Thus, romantically and harmlessly, begins the story of the Newts. Great societal catastrophes begin similarly: from small peripheral stirrings, from the delirious visions of a future leader, from small troops of fanatics.

The entire first section of the novel radiates with ironic wit – it appears that the book will consist of the kinds of satirical references to contemporary society's vices with which Čapek was so lavish in *The Absolute at Large* and *From the Life of the Insects*[1]; there is nothing to suggest that the world will soon be standing on the edge of catastrophe. People encounter the first Newts and begin to take an interest in them. The animal is scientifically classified as newt Andrias Scheuchzeri. A winsome film starlet encounters some Newts and is afraid of them, they disgust her, but she wants to make a film in which Newts fall in love with her and carry her away to their underwater kingdom. A guard at the London Zoo teaches a Newt to talk and also to read newspapers. This latter incident naturally attracts the attention of scientists, who then begin to conduct research on the Newt. They conclude that the Newt can talk, has four hundred words at its disposal, and says only what it's heard or read. "It's interested in the same things as the average Englishman and reacts to them in a similar manner, i.e., in the direction of established general views. Its intellectual life – insofar as one may speak of any – consists precisely of ideas and opinions current at the present time. ... There is absolutely no need to overrate its intelligence, since in no respect does it exceed the intelligence of the average person of our time."[5] It was precisely the consequences that followed from such averageness that Čapek saw as a source of danger for contemporary society.

At the close of the first section, the story returns to the magnate Bondy, who has convened an extraordinary meeting of the board of the Pacific Export Company, which he heads. Čapek informs us of the reason for this meeting by quoting from its minutes, thereby initiating the series of wonderful parodies of a variety of literary genres with which he moves the action forward in the second part of the novel. Since the era of trade in pearls is coming to an end, Bondy tells the board members of his plans for a new phase in the firm's development: a Salamander Syndicate. The Newts have proved themselves to be excellent underwater workers, and because they multiply with such tremendous rapidity, the Syndicate will be in a position to supply an unlimited number of workers, thus making possible the realization of any number of grandiose projects. The Salamander Syndicate will see not only to the breeding and sale of Newts, but also to their tools and food.

> It will supply plans and ideas for control of the seas. It will promote Utopias and gigantic dreams. It will supply projects for new coasts and canals, for causeways linking the continents, for whole chains of artificial islands, for transoceanic flights, for new continents to be built in the oceans. That is where mankind's future lies. Gentlemen, four-fifths of the earth's surface is covered by seas; that is unquestionably too much; the world's surface, the map of oceans and dry land, must be corrected. We shall give the world the workforce of the sea, gentlemen ... We can speak today of a new Atlantis, of ancient continents which will stretch out further and further into the world's oceans, of New Worlds which mankind will build for itself. Forgive me, gentlemen, if this strikes you as utopian. Yes indeed, we are entering upon Utopia. We are right in it, my friends.[6]

This is the same technocratic vision we've already heard from the mouth of Domin, director of the Robot-producing firm R.U.R.; it is also the temptation to which Prokop, the protagonist of *Krakatit*, was exposed. The moment a man finds he is able to realize utopia, humanity is threatened by catastrophe.

In the second part of the novel, capitalizing on his experience in journalism, Čapek reconstructs the Newts' history out of a colorful collage of fictitious newspaper clippings of wildly varying types: articles, commentary, scientific papers, and even the results of a survey asking whether Newts have souls. (The answers given by famous intellectuals are, understandably, supplemented by those from film and sports stars.) But as the Newts implement people's utopian conceptions, rebuilding the globe, their story takes a more menacing turn. Having preserved their amphibious fertility – now numbering in the billions – the Newts construct underground cities and factories, and for their energy needs they utilize differences in water temperature. People continue to supply them with food, raw materials, weapons, and explosives. The Newts themselves invent nothing, but

> what else is civilization than the ability to make use of things invented by someone else? Even if, for the sake of argument, the Newts have no original ideas of their own, they can perfectly well have their own science. True, they have no music or literature of their own but they manage perfectly well without; indeed people are beginning to think that this is marvellously modern of them. So there you are – already humans can learn something from the Newts. And small wonder: what other example are people to follow if not success? ... Real, self-assured Newt Age people will no longer waste their time meditating on the Essence of Things; they will be concerned solely with numbers and mass production. The world's entire future lies in a continually increased production and consumption – so we need even more Newts to produce even more and consume even more.[7]

In his remarkable metaphor, Čapek successfully formulated an outline for a philosophy of mass consumption and mass thought.

In the third and final part of the novel, Čapek takes his fantastical story to its logical conclusion. Demoralized humankind can no longer resist the constantly growing demands of the Newts. The Newts need more shallow areas, because they are able to live neither on dry land nor in deep sea. People need to produce more, to sell more, because this is the principle upon which their economic philosophy is based; therefore they need the Newts as irreplaceable consumers. Rather than extending the continents to meet their needs, however, the Newts begin to blow up the coastal lowlands, changing them into shallow water. They follow proper procedure, are willing to pay for every inch of destroyed land, and give timely warning so that coastal inhabitants can move onto higher ground. The Newts and their leader, Chief Salamander, increase their demands, and a larger and larger portion of the land mass disappears into the seas. Humankind or, more correctly, nations and their representatives, are unable to agree on a common course of action against the growing Newt danger. In the novel's final chapter, "The Author Talks to Himself," Čapek sums up:

> They all wanted to have Newts, commerce wanted them, and industry and engineering, the statesmen wanted them and the military gentlemen too ... Let me ask you this: you know who *even now*, with one-fifth of Europe inundated, is supplying the Newts with high explosives and torpedoes and drills? Do you know who is feverishly working in laboratories night and day to discover ever more efficient machines and substances to blow up the world? Do you know who is lending money to the Newts, do you know who is financing this End of the World, this whole new Flood?
>
> I do. Every factory in the world. Every bank. Every country.[8]

In *R.U.R.*, Čapek warned against the unbridled desire for affluence, against utopian visions based on the unlimited possibilities of cheap production. The play also recognized that this particular utopian vision was supposed to be implemented at the expense of Robots, creatures without feelings, without demands, creatures reduced to the level of machines. In the end, the experimental Robots, the ones endowed with feelings, recognize their situation, revolt, and exterminate humankind. One could say that *War with the Newts* contains much the same ideas and even a similar structure. Yet the world has made advances – in technological development, in the expansion of mass society, and in the upsurge in totalitarian regimes. One-fifth of Europe's democracies had already been submerged.

Čapek developed his science-fiction premise logically and with impressive breadth, tracing the Newts' history while simultaneously, as if mere background information, developing a picture of humankind. In his vision, human civilization is dashing after profits, success, material progress. Its ideals have become wealth, entertainment, and pleasure, and so it worships everything that helps them implement these ideals. It does not even notice that, on the road toward their goals, it is quickly losing what engendered them: individuality, culture, intellect, soul. It has exchanged inquiry and reflection for journalistic twaddle, individual participation in common social efforts for the passive taking in of sensationalism, and for thought it has substituted slogans and clichés. "Your work = your success." "He who doesn't work shouldn't eat!" All this has contributed to the world becoming inundated with masses of people dangerous in their averageness and in their readiness to accept any kind of belief whatsoever, adopt any kind of goal. The masses were becoming more like the Newts and the Newts more like the masses.

> The most terrible thing is that they have multiplied that half-educated, brainless and smug type of civilized mediocrity on a vast scale, in millions and billions of identical specimens. But no, I'm wrong: the most terrible thing is that they are so successful. They have learned how to use machines and numbers, and it has become obvious that that is enough for them to become the masters of their world.[9]

Everything that was happening to humans in this Age of the Newts had the appearance of a natural disaster, not because the overmultiplied Newts had become a part of nature, but because no humans could be found who felt personal responsibility (today we would say global responsibility) for their own actions, their own behavior, for the common enterprise that is civilization. Or, more accurately – and Čapek's irony is most brutal here – the only person to accept responsibility was the most insignificant person of all, a man who used to answer the door at the Bondy mansion. Not one of the powerful or the chosen considered the long-term consequences of the direction civilization was headed. Culture became sterile, art was displaced by the production of kitsch, philosophy declined to the point of justifying and even celebrating destruction, politicians were incapable of rising above local, mostly nationalistic considerations. Granted, civilization had spread to all corners of the planet, but people were incapable of being governed by anything other than their own particular interests – they were unable even to consider, let alone control, the consequences of their own actions. Modern civilization proved to be so destructive and egotistic that it tainted anyone who came in contact with it. This was true as well of the Newts, who adopted the basic characteristics of human behavior. This is why they began, without restraint, to destroy the land masses, whenever they found it to be in their interest. And since they had relinquished the right to participate in their own fate, people helped the Newts do this, right to the last moment.[10]

As the story of the Newts and people gradually developed, Čapek included in it more and more realities of the contemporary world. He parodied Spengler's *Decline of the West*, the hymn of the Nazis as well as of Hitler's demand for lebensraum. "Hello, you humans! No need for alarm. We have no hostile intentions towards you. We only need more water, more coasts, more shallows to live in."[11] He also lampooned diplomatic negotiations, cowardly even when face to face with destruction, and presciently named Great Britain as the only European country to behave bravely and honestly in the face of mortal danger. At the conclusion, he makes it clear that the dictator who speaks in the name of the Newts is not a Newt, but a man. "His name was actually Andreas Schultze, and during the world war he was a rank-and-file something somewhere." (Čapek obviously selected the first letters of the actual name of the Nazi leader, who, though illegitimate, used Schickelgruber, the name of his biological father; the noncommissioned rank also corresponds to Hitler's rank during the war.)

War with the Newts was the first of several works by Čapek intended to warn against the dangers of Nazism, and therefore it is a very direct response to the political situation in Europe at the time, which was growing more and more critical. In it, he united the best of his authorial and journalistic art, constructing the story magnificently, gradually crossing from a light, humorous tone to one more serious and even moving, formulating world problems generally and at the same time in concrete, convincing forms. The linguistic and stylistic skill with which he parodied and lampooned dozens of literary and journalistic genres is remarkable.

Despite its origin as a response to the political situation of the 1930s, *War with the Newts* depicted the basic characteristics of our civilization with such perceptiveness that it still engages and urges readers even so many decades later. Instead of destruction by war, humanity is threatened by ecological destruction, toward which it reacts with similar frivolity and shortsightedness.

"Your satirical view of the abysmal craziness in Europe," Thomas Mann wrote about the novel, "has something absolutely magnificent about it, and one suffers this craziness with you in following the story's grotesque and horrible events."[12]

26. Do You Wish Merry Me?

It seemed that Čapek's personal life was unlikely to change anymore. His circle of friends was broad but at the same time closed, which is common at the age of forty-five. After he decided not to marry Olga Scheinpflugová, and his second love, Věra Hrůzová, got married, no other woman appeared in his life, and it seems that he was avoiding them. Women form only a minuscule fraction of the addressees in the preserved correspondence,[1] and his relationship with his brother was much warmer than that with his sister. Olga Scheinpflugová remained his friend however, and when Čapek was away, he wrote her regularly, and he reported to her on his major works. Olga is said to have received his writings with uncritical enthusiasm, which would have been satisfying and encouraging for Čapek, so often bitterly attacked by Czech critics. That they looked upon their relationship as a friendship is also supported by the fact that Olga had several affairs with other men and didn't hide them from Karel in any way. One such intimate friend was Jan Masaryk, the son of the president, one of the most interesting and also contradictory personalities of the era's political life. Jarmila Čapková, Josef's wife, left interesting testimony about the way in which the circle of people close to Čapek viewed his relationship to Olga. "I know from Karel that Jan once asked him if he should marry Olga Scheinpflugová. And his answer was: I can't advise you about that, that you must decide for yourself."[2]

Olga was apparently aiming for marriage with Jan Masaryk and was disappointed when she failed. Evidently, she couldn't find anyone else she'd want to live with permanently. What is certain is that no one close to Čapek expected what happened in the summer of 1935.

Olga wrote in *Český román* about how things came together, but perhaps it would be better to listen to someone who was only indirectly a participant. The events were described in the memoirs of Julius Firt, the general director of *Lidový noviny*'s publishing company and a friend of Čapek's.

> In 1935, Karel Čapek's life took a turn that surprised us all. It all began inconspicuously. He called me to say that Olga Scheinpflugová urgently needed a car. For one thing, she truly wanted one, and for another, after her evening performances it wasn't good for her to walk home alone. He could offer her money, but he knew in advance that she wouldn't accept it...

Firt indeed arranged for Olga to receive a car from *Lidové noviny,* to be paid in monthly installments, to which Čapek secretly contributed. The car's owner then told Čapek that she was going to take her new car on vacation to Austria.

> Čapek asked her if she would take him with her; in any case, he told her he had some business in Vienna, and it would be very convenient for him. He didn't tell her what he would be doing in the Austrian capital, he didn't reveal that Vienna was where he wanted confirmation that his spinal disease had stopped progressing. In Hotel Gnadenwald, in the Alps, he asked for her hand. Their rooms and balconies were adjacent. At dawn, Čapek suddenly said, in English: 'Do you wish merry me?'
>
> When Čapek told me that, I couldn't hold back, I asked him why in English? I knew that Olga didn't really know any language other than Czech ... 'You know,' Čapek answered, 'I thought that a Czech "no" would sound a little too harsh, too merciless, decidedly less pleasant than an English "no." And then I told myself that perhaps she wouldn't even understand.' Olga understood and said "yes," whether in Czech or in English, I no longer remember. When they returned to Prague, they didn't confide their marital plans to anyone. Čapek was of course entirely changed, he sparkled with wit, ideas, jokes directed at his friends.[3]

Understandably, Olga Scheinpflugová described it all in greater detail. After his proposal, she wrote, Čapek told her:

"I've always let someone else make you happy, but I haven't seen much of that happiness, so perhaps it will be better if you suffer with me."[4] Olga also says that Čapek was happy, that he changed, he became fifteen years younger and was suddenly interested in other people's personal lives.

His family had a somewhat different view of the marriage's influence on Karel. That they had little love for Olga can be deduced from their many references to her, above all by Čapek's niece, Helena Koželuhová, an estimable journalist. According to her, Olga had many talents,

> many gifts, and many merits. One thing, however, she lacked. Delicacy and sensitivity. She was not only emotional, but primitively sentimental and impulsive. She was unacquainted with nuance, she jumped from flamboyant grief and compassion to equally flamboyant humor. God knows that there was nothing subdued or mysterious about her. She never knew the anguish of loneliness or unanswered questions. Everything about her was noisy and cheerful, or dramatic, just like a country fair. She never paused in contemplation or silent admiration. She wouldn't have known how to even if she'd wanted to a hundred times over, but she didn't ... For her, life, as she saw it and as she observed it in herself, was simple, with a satisfactory well of things to discover ... Olga dramatized everything and thus arrived at half-truths. Everyone supposed that a creature with such tempestuous feelings must be consumed by passion, and Olga sincerely believed this herself. But she proved to be divided, desperate, even wretched, or, on the other hand, crazily happy, and yet not one iota changed in the breadth of her other interests. One simply can't imagine her ever thinking anything through...[5]

Those closest to Čapek were convinced that Olga was not a good influence on him, and moreover that she too uncritically adored his writing, and that this harmed him. Even though this opinion, as well as the attributes reported by Helena Koželuhová, might have been biased, or explained by a certain degree of jealousy, we cannot deny that Čapek's last works were indeed threatened by superficiality, and that critical evaluation by those close to him could have helped the author. Karel was aware of his family's attitude toward Olga, and either from defiance or from fear that they would try to talk him out of the marriage, he did not announce his decision to his siblings until after the ceremony. Josef's wife, Jarmila, recalled that they learned about the wedding from the newspaper. "That same day we got a postcard from Karlový Vary with the usual greetings, and then the signatures of Karel and Olga Scheinpflugová bracketed together. And below that, a brief note: 'No mushrooms growing.' We were astonished. Peča [Josef] went to the post office and sent a telegram: 'We congratulate you on your marriage. No mushrooms growing here either.'"[6]

Karel's sister Helena sent her own congratulations, and he is reputed to have thanked her "with a letter several lines long that was downright threatening: 'If you ever say a word against my wife, I shall break with you forever. I could never forgive you nor could I bear it.'"[7] Josef's view of his brother's decision is obvious from his letter to his sister, written after he learned of the wedding.

> Of course marriage is not an excursion, and the serious question is not what has already happened (it's already happened), but what it will be like if, three years from now, they're disenchanted and tired of each other, and there's a crisis, which would undoubtedly affect Karel very seriously.[8] He doesn't need us now, but in the future he's likely to need us very much, and then we want him to be able to trust us. We must accept things as they are, be level-headed and decent about it, so that now, when he has his wife and the rest of us aren't of that much concern to him, he won't be too estranged from us. I worry about Karel, but I worry about you too, Helenka; by no means do I feel that in doing this he was doing anything for himself, for his work, or for his peace and happiness, that it was the best thing he could have done at his age. But an overpowering urge drove him to it; maybe it will give him more inspiration for life and literature than we might suppose. She was full of praise for the novel he's writing [*War with the Newts*], saying there are magnificent and

> ingenious things in it, it's one of the best he's ever written, and he was just beaming. We are much more severe with him, and admittedly he takes it hard. It certainly won't benefit him artistically, but it didn't benefit him earlier, either; it was undoubtedly her (and also sometimes Langer's) influence that every so often Karel preferred to think of himself as a man of letters rather than as an artist.[9]

There is more evidence that Josef feared his brother would waste too much of his talent on topical commentary and political polemics. According to Josef's wife, he was angry with Karel for writing even *War with the Newts*.[10]

Worse was the way the relationship between Karel and his sister developed, and she refused for some time to visit her brother. For that matter, his siblings fully reconciled with Karel only when he lay dying.

Čapek received a most unusual wedding gift. His sister's second husband was the poet Josef Palivec. Palivec' brother was a well-to-do landowner (he even owned a castle), and he gave the newlyweds, for their lifelong use, a spacious house in the picturesque landscape between Dobříš and Stará Hut'. The house had an enormous garden with a brook flowing through it. The passionate gardener and lover of the countryside, who until then had had at his disposal only his small Prague garden, suddenly found himself with plenty of space and a flowing stream, to boot. He also gained a spot in which, at least once in a while, he could take refuge from Prague, where the atmosphere was becoming more and more oppressive. According to his contemporaries, Strž, as the house was called, became the site of daily get-togethers for many of Čapek's and also Olga's friends (even though Čapek asked for help with improvements to the brook as well as the garden as repayment for his hospitality). The couple spent much time there, and it is also where Čapek wrote most of his last works.

Although the newlyweds had already taken their honeymoon prior to the wedding, in July of 1936 they nonetheless left on a grand tour of Scandinavia. Čapek wrote his last travelogue about this trip, *Travels in the North*, accompanied by two hundred and fifty of his own drawings. The way in which Čapek assembled his travel notes was not very different from what he had done before, except that there was less about culture (the north was not as rich in artistic sights as was Italy or Spain), but the book is richer in its enthusiastic and almost unbelievably erudite descriptions of nature. The author made a few brief references to the situation in Europe, but these were the exception – as if, in northern seclusion, he had charged himself with forgetting everything that had disturbed him back home, as if he wanted to take his readers to a place where, as yet, the sounds of Hitler's shouting and the gunfire from Ethiopian battlegrounds had not yet reached. As if he himself had forgotten and so was merely setting before his readers the thoughts of an onlooker charmed by sea, fjords, crags, nature resisting the elements, and people who lived their lives far from civilization.

Something had changed, however – he did not take this particular trip alone. And only from his wife's account of their long journey, published ten years later, do we learn that Čapek was completely silent about one aspect of their trip, about how warmly he was received in Scandinavia.

> Even though it was vacation time and everyone had gone off to the forests or the fjords, Karel Čapek was received cordially all over. The entire North knew his plays and books; they were welcomed at every railway station with film crews and bouquets. There wasn't even time after the tiring trip to straighten their clothes or wash their faces, the hotels' corridors quickly filled with journalists and curious onlookers. The world was living under a political strain, and the author of the Robots and Newts had something to say to them.
>
> It was touching how uneasily he bore this avalanche of attention in front of his wife; modest and embarrassed, he was helped again by his unique sense of humor and as always, whenever he was interviewed, he turned the conversation to his nation and his people ... He always declined questions about personal matters, but about the Czech question he could talk forever!...

> Karel Čapek had already been a candidate for the Nobel Prize several years before, but his last book, *War with the Newts*, was too aggressive, and made too clear a reference to the leader of a certain political movement. Word came to him to furnish a novel of about three hundred pages attacking nothing and no one. 'Thank you for your kindness,' he told the man who was serving as go-between, 'but I finished my dissertation long ago.'[11]

The idyllic northern journey came to an end, and the couple returned home. At the very end of his travelogue Čapek complained:

> A gray and cold dawn is beginning to break; it is a bit as if one were opening a damp morning newspaper and looking in it to see what had happened in the world. We have not read a newspaper for such a long time, and nothing has happened, only a few weeks of eternity have passed, the Norwegian mountains were reflected in the water of the fjords, the Swedish forests closed in above our heads, and the gentle cows gazed at us with peaceful, saintly eyes. The first ugly, barbarous news, that will be the true end of our journey.[12]

At the end of the journey the news reached Čapek that civil war had broken out in Spain. As had become more and more obvious with the passage of time, a clash between the adherents of two militant ideologies was taking place on Spanish territory. It was the overture to the greatest conflict humankind had ever experienced. It was a war Čapek did not live to see but which he tried with all his power to prevent, up to the last moments of his life.

27. Artist v. Newspaperman

The Spanish Civil War had begun. People like Karel Čapek, who were intrinsically preoccupied with politics and distressed at the direction it was taking, could not help but see that on the Spanish battleground something monstrous was coming into existence, something which threatened to outgrow the borders of a single country and a single civil war.

In the lead article in *Přítomnost*'s first issue of 1937, Ferdinand Peroutka described Europe's situation with his extraordinary analytical skills: "In 1936 there were no solutions to any of the problems that were to the calm of Europe as a burning fuse is to a keg of gunpowder. We have no more right to feel safe in the world at the end of the year than we did at the beginning. We have all sorts of hopes for peace, of course, but we have no clear evidence of peace." Peroutka then mentions Hitler, who had entered the European scene four years previously: "since the moment he arrived, he has been in control of the plot; he as well as others are sharpening their swords; the drama is not yet over on this stage; there will have to be some sort of ending..." Like Čapek, Peroutka took exception to claims that European culture had disappeared, that only civilization remained, "but never have we seen so clearly as we do today that civilization without culture is a tower built on sand, that technology without compassion or morality is destruction." Democracy and liberalism should be the two pillars of European culture, but "all the pillars on which the vault of European culture, in its classical form, was resting have somehow crumbled..." Of course, fascism was not the first attack on democracy. "The first attack was communism; with pleasure, fascism appropriated the results of its work. Indeed, Mussolini and Hitler only had to do half the work on the masses: the first half was done for them by Lenin and Trotsky

… a Europe not weakened or turned over by communism would have had far greater inner resistance against fascism … 'When a forest is cut, splinters fly,' said Lenin. 'When wood is planed, sawdust falls," says Göring. Behold the son beside the father! Bolsheviks and fascists alike jeer at humanity."

The Czechoslovak Republic was wedged between the domains of father and son – what hope was there for it?

As a journalist, Čapek did everything he could in defense of democracy, even before the Nazi victory in Germany, and afterwards he concentrated even more on political topics. And his late literary works were also directly influenced by the dangers a totalitarian system posed for democracy, and therefore Czechoslovakia. This includes the novel *The First Rescue Party*, and the plays *The White Plague* and *The Mother*. Leftist critics (their heirs retained the final word in Czechoslovakia until 1989), who had never respected Čapek and who accused him of defending a class-bound society with his relativism and of celebrating petit bourgeois coziness in his shorter prose and feuilletons about his garden and his cats and dogs – these same critics praised these late works, along with *War with the Newts*, as the pinnacle of his creation.[1]

But what was immediate and urgent in a short essay, newspaper article, or feuilleton was frequently too declarative and therefore less convincing in a literary work. Čapek was a master of the short form, and successful at finding metaphors for his ideas and expressing his opinions figuratively and aphoristically. He astounded his readers by his wealth of ideas and observations, as well as by his unexpected interpretations of events from both the present and the past. In 1936 and 1937, he published many excellent short works, among them two series of short essays, *How Newspapers Are Produced*, and *How They Make Films*, which belong among the most humorous and also most well-informed that he ever wrote. He continued to make use of the feuilleton for pursuing everyday concerns, but he began more and more to focus his interest on the dangers of the war that was threatening to engulf Europe.

In one particularly short piece, he commented on the news that fifty-two children had been torn apart by the aerial bombing of a school in the Catalonian town of Lerida.

> No doubt we will never know the name of the successful bombardier. Perhaps it was a patriotic Spaniard from Franco's army, perhaps a young German, perhaps an Italian; what we can assume, with near certainty, is that it was not a professional murderer of children, but a soldier simply fulfilling his orders to bomb a town ... We do not blame the aircrew for this crime. The responsibility lies higher up. With those who command. With those who lead. With those who finance the massacres of these shameful years.[2]

Some of his short verses for *Lidové noviny* sound downright prophetic today, including this one, published in August 1936:

> When this century collapses, dead at last,
> and its sleep within the dark tomb has begun,
> come, look down upon us, world, file past
> and be ashamed of what our age has done.
>
> Inscribe our stone, that everyone may see
> what this dead era valued most and best:
> Science, progress, work, technology
> and death – but death we prized above the rest.
>
> We set new records, measuring men and deeds
> in terms of greatness; thus we tempted fate.
> In keeping with the greatness of our needs,
> our heroes and our gangsters, too, were great.
>
> The XXth century, buried; nonetheless,
> world, see what eras yet to come will gain:
> Great new records, great inventions. Wretchedness.
> Dictators. War. A ruined town in Spain.

Čapek also responded to the political situation of the time in several of his Apocryphical Tales. "The Death of Archimedes" speaks most directly. In Čapek's topical conception, Archimedes is visited by a Roman centurion, who tries to talk him into constructing war machines for the Romans. Čapek has the thinking of a scientist confront the great-powers thinking of a Roman centurion. Archimedes doesn't understand why he should cooperate with the Romans.

> "Because you live in Sicily, and we need Sicily."
> "And why do you need it?" asked Archimedes.
> "Because we intend to control the Mediterranean Sea."
> "Aha," Archimedes said, and he contemplated his tablet. "And why do you want to do that?"
> "Whoever is master of the Mediterranean," said Lucius, "is master of the world. That's clear enough."
> "And must you be masters of the world?"
> "Yes. The mission of Rome is to be master of the world. And I'm telling you that it will be."[3]

It's understandable that a scientist and philosopher, true to his mission, can hardly reach an understanding with a centurion who thinks in terms of power. At the end, Archimedes is killed. "Later it was reported that the learned Archimedes had met his death through an accident," the author concludes his story, parodying the official language of totalitarian regimes. In a short story modifying a tale from antiquity, this parody of Nazi rhetoric is very effective.

Also effective in their brevity are the aphorisms with which Čapek commented on the Spanish Civil War and, later, his disillusionment with Czechoslovakia's presumed allies after the Munich Agreement was signed. Even when, as is clear from some of his public appearances and writings, Čapek sided with the republicans (supported by socialists and Trotskyites) against the rebel army of General Franco (supported by Hitler and Mussolini), his aphorisms concern above all the absurd brutality of civil war as an unacceptable solution to a country's internal conflicts.

> Civil War: Hurrah! In the name of the country, we will annihilate ourselves!

> National Success: Our brave foreign legions have crushed the cowardly hordes of our domestic enemies.
>
> Before the Battle: Soldiers, fire on your brothers. The homeland's eyes are upon you.
>
> Appeal to the Besieged: Further resistance is futile. Allow us to execute you instead.[4]

At the end of 1936, after a ten-year hiatus, Čapek returned to playwriting. As with all his plays, with the exception of *The Robber*, Čapek based the plot on a fantastical premise. A white plague, a sort of leprosy, appears and snowballs around the globe. The disease progresses very fast; over the course of a few weeks, the patient completely decomposes. The disease has one peculiar property: it attacks only people who have reached middle age, that is, those in relatively influential positions. *The White Plague* takes place in a nearby, unspecified totalitarian country which is at that moment preparing to begin a war against its neighbors. The country is governed by a field marshal who is surrounded by sycophants and revered by the masses. In his diction as well as in the attitude of those surrounding him, and also in the name of the chief arms dealer, we find obvious allusions to Hitler's Germany, to Čapek's traitorous intelligentsia, to the masses turned to fools under the assault of ideological propaganda.[5]

The medical establishment is unable to deal with this new disease, and the censors attempt to suppress any news about it, but the disease is spreading and threatening those who govern. At this point, Doctor Galen[6] appears on stage, a doctor known to none of the officials, modest, seemingly shy and naïve, yet tenacious in his convictions. He announces to the chief medical official that he has at his disposal medication that can cure the disease. He is, however, willing to make it available to the public only when all governments pledge to renounce the use of violence. Wars kill people just as the white plague does, and he therefore considers eliminating war just as important as curing people. Until the governments accept his condition, he will treat only those patients who are poor and powerless. His suggestion seems hopelessly naïve, but when Baron Krüg, the arms manufacturer, and finally the dictator himself eventually become ill, Galen's hopes for accomplishing his pacifist ideals seem more realistic, especially when, in spite of threats, he agrees to treat the Marshal – but only on condition that he stop the war he's just begun against a small neighboring nation, which is courageously trying to defend itself. The Marshal hesitates, but finally his fear of death (and perhaps also failure on the battlefield) induce him to accept Galen's condition, even to the extent of being inspired by the magnitude of the mission being offered him: to be the one to bring peace to humanity.

Galen therefore hurries to see the dictator. In front of the palace, however, he comes up against a mob of people demonstrating their allegiance to the Marshal. When the doctor refuses to shout belligerent slogans with them, the inflamed mob of fanatics kills him and also destroys the vials with his miraculous medication.

Galen's stand sounds very naïve, but it was meant symbolically. Čapek's doctor was intended to personify the responsibility of intellectuals for their acts and the stands they take. The play raises the issue of responsibility for the fate of the world in an absolute way, and the fate of the doctor is tragic – for to refuse anyone a medicine that could return him to health is contrary to medical ethics, to the Hippocratic oath.

Some contemporary criticism objected to Galen's stand as being completely unethical, some considered him as fanatical as the fanaticism the pacifist doctor opposed. That's why Čapek's protagonist consistently, even though hesitantly, defends his decision not to treat the rich.

> Reporter: Would you refuse treatment to the rich?
>
> Galen: Regretfully, but ... I couldn't. The rich have so much influence that... If the rich and powerful really want peace ... they know how to get it.
>
> Reporter: But doesn't that seem a little unfair to the rich?

> Galen: It is. I know it is. But doesn't it seem a little unfair to the poor that they're ... well, poor? Everyone has the same right to life, yet every time a war comes along they're the ones who do the dying. And it needn't be that way, it needn't be that way. If the money spent on warships went to hospitals...[7]

But the majority of critics accepted Galen's stand. After all, the play was responding to a concrete political situation. Humankind was threatened by a real war and the republic by its aggressive neighbor, whereas the malignant disease was only a fantastic fiction. The goal of the play is obvious: to show that war is not only the gravest of crimes but also the greatest of dangers for humanity. At the same time, Čapek was accurately depicting how totalitarian regimes represent this danger (differing in this regard from fashionable Marxist analysis).

More substantial objections can be raised against the play's excessive idea orientation. I've already mentioned that proficiency in delineating characters was not among Čapek's strongest talents. His protagonists in *R.U.R.*, for instance, were more representatives of certain attitudes than they were dramatic characters, and the characters' development had no effect on the play's ending. In *The White Plague*, the situation is different. Galen's dilemma is a dramatic dilemma, and the same can be said of the Marshal's dilemma. Čapek circumvented the inner conflicts of his characters and substituted for them proclamations, the controversy over two conceptions. When the pugnacious dictator allows himself to be convinced of the harmfulness of war and begins to dream about becoming a peacemaker, thus saving millions of people who have the plague, you have the sense that this is not a dramatic character, but merely one that is obedient to the author's will, which calls for this transformation. The secondary characters, too, revel in proclamations; they are merely illustrations of sociological observations about behavior symptomatic of certain social strata. Similar artistic misdemeanors frequently accompany works written in direct response to a societal situation. An author like Čapek had to respond to the danger of war; expounding his views on conflicts in the ideological and political spheres was more important to him than being occupied with the personal dilemmas of individual characters or the development of their individual natures. The majority of Czechs, and even of the world public, understood and accepted this. According to contemporary accounts, a half-hour of applause followed the Prague premiere – something uncommon in the history of Czech theater. That people understood the play as a depiction of the approaching political conflict is witnessed also by the fact that the most frequent criticism Čapek received, supposedly even from the republic's new president Edvard Beneš, was that the play was too pessimistic. (This is nonsense, not only in light of what the following years brought, but above all because optimism and pessimism are not attributes by which one evaulates a work of art.)

The White Plague was certainly a topical work, an expression of both civic responsibility and political courage (the censorship office tried, up to the last minute, to stop the premiere). It was also a work written by an experienced playwright. Čapek knew supremely well how to construct dramatic predicaments within which he could develop philosophical, moral, and topical political themes, but in this play much was sacrificed to its very topicality, and with the passage of time and in a changed political situation, we realize that the artist too often gave way to the journalist, who was thinking about the causes of the contemporary crisis as well as the ensuing dangers.

But the Čapek expert František Černý considered *The White Plague* among the best of Čapek's works, in the company of the greatest works of world drama.[8]

28. It Could Have Been a Book About Soldiers or the Crew of a Ship

The political situation in Europe was coming to a head as Czechoslovakia's neighbor, Hitler's Germany, behaved more and more aggressively. At the beginning of 1937, Hitler announced in the Reichstag that he did not recognize Germany's signature on the Treaty of Versailles – a matter of fundamental concern to Czechoslovakia, since the republic's birth originated under that treaty. The war in Spain was assuming international dimensions. At the end of April, German bombers destroyed Guernica, in the Basque region. The more than three million Germans in Czechoslovakia were increasingly subjected to Nazi propaganda. That summer, the second volume of Heiden's biography of Hitler appeared (it was published in Czech before it was published in German). Heiden predicted that the only country he considered a target for a blitz attack by the German army was Czechoslovakia, because of its strategic importance and also the spectacular political success such a conquest would bring Hitler. At a time when the more far-sighted suspected that a new great war in Europe was already difficult to avoid, T. G. Masaryk, the first president of the republic, the man on whom Čapek had focused his attention for many years and whose political ideals he accepted as his own, passed away.

The situation in the neighboring Reich necessarily had an echo in Czechoslovakia. On the one hand, Czechoslovak nationalism was gaining strength; on the other hand, more and more people were impressed with Hitler's method of governing, and they considered democracy a vanquished political system with no future in Europe and no hope of resisting the dynamic totalitarian regimes. They intensified their attacks on those who embodied democracy, among whom Karel Čapek was at the fore. One of the most treacherous attacks against him was led by the prominent Catholic writer and military physician Jaroslav Durych (he had carried on arguments with Čapek since the 1920s). One example is the polemic he wrote against Čapek's "Civil War Fables," which he used merely as a pretext for accusing Čapek of unmanliness:

> I am an army doctor. For me, men are divided into three groups, A, B, and C, according to their fitness for military service. Over many long years I have come to realize that each of these groups, A, B, and C, has its own morality. When I read Karel Čapek, it is as an army doctor, not as a writer. I recognize him as a C, and I am afraid. I am afraid of everything that is C. I can imagine what would happen if C morality were to be favored by a large part of the nation.[1]

Čapek responded with a short and poisonous, even if entirely factual, article in *Přítomnost*. It is likely that it was this attack on his physical weakness, along with criticism from those who denounced *The White Plague* for its tragic ending, and the increasingly obvious signs of approaching war, that led him to write a heroic story with a Czech setting. As the protagonists of the novel, which he called *The First Rescue Party*, he chose miners.

Shortly before he began the book, *Přítomnost* ran the results of a survey asking whether people agreed or disagreed with the statement, Modern literature avoids manly characters. Čapek answered, in part:

> Modern psychology, which literature accepts as a matter of course, has a tendency towards the problematic; a manly or heroic character is, however, basically simple, nonproblematic; he reveals himself more in action, in an objective and factually presented plot, than in his inner state and contradictions. Clearly, literature aiming for subjectivity cannot very well consort with the simple and objective word 'masculinity.'[2]

The First Rescue Party was written only a few months after *The White Plague*. Unlike the play, which had been accused of being pessimistic, the novel sought hope and encouragement in the solidarity and heroism of men facing a common danger. The story is narrated from the point of view of a poor young man, an orphan named Standa Půlpán. He is unable to finish his studies for lack of money and so, after five years at a technical secondary school and two years working for a building contractor, he becomes a coal miner. He moves into the small house of another miner, Josef Adam, where he platonically worships Adam's wife, Marie. The relationship between Adam and his wife is, in the usual Čapek style, odd. "He sleeps in the kitchen, and his wife – in such a tiny room, nothing but curtains which she sewed herself. For all Standa knows, Adam has never set foot in that tiny room. He comes home from work, takes his coffee from the stove, and eats slowly, sitting on a coal box. In the tiny adjacent room, Marie lets her hands, with their sewing, drop into her lap, and sits – lifelessly, you might say, except that sometimes her shoulders heave forcefully with a sigh."[3]

Standa is an immature young man, he loves Marie, he worships the Swedish mining engineer, Hansen, and his wife, and he dreams of becoming a leader of the miners who will defend his comrades' rights, but in his job pushing a coal car, he's awkward and ineffective. Everything begins to change, of course, when an accident occurs, burying several miners. Standa is the first to volunteer for the rescue team and thus becomes, along with Adam, a member of the first rescue party.

After a short exposition, the entire remainder of the novel describes in detail the work of the first rescue party and the relationships among its members. It also attempts to sketch the individual characters. Common danger, awareness of the magnitude of the task, and exceptionally difficult working conditions change the relationships among the team members. Old animosities disappear, and the hot-headed supervisor, Andres, known for his cur-like meanness toward his subordinates, is finally accepted as one of the team – as is Standa, despite his lack of experience. Marie's attitude of spurning Adam also changes, even if Adam in his clumsiness is not able to respond. Čapek, in great detail and with ever-increasing pathos and emotion, describes the work of the rescue party, its visit to a tavern after the party returns to the surface, the reactions of individual miners to a newspaper article about the accident and their rescue work. Then finally he describes the second day of rescue work. Standa is hurt, and Adam loses his life.

Three of the buried miners die, but their fate was not of concern to the author; rather, he was concerned with the team's resolve to save them even at the cost of self-sacrifice. Male heroism is important, as is the new-found solidarity which bridges personal disputes as well as social differences.

Čapek himself admitted that he claimed no right to do a book about miners, even though he had been born in a mining town and had heard about miners and mining life since childhood.

> My concern was actually something different, entirely universal: I wanted to write a book some day about male bravery, about the different types and motivations of what we call heroism, about male solidarity, in short, about certain physical and moral values that we honor whenever a people or a nation needs real, whole, authentic men. It could have been a book about soldiers, but deep down inside I'm too much of a pacifist for that; or about a ship's crew, or a team of men on a dangerous expedition, about any situation where I could follow a handful of men as they exert themselves to the full extent of their strength, courage, and camaraderie. I chose a rescue team at a mining disaster because mining is such a large part of our Czech world ... It's a book about about a small group of upright men, ordinary fellows who happen to be miners. Nothing more, nothing else should you expect from *The First Rescue Party*.[4]

Thus Čapek candidly admits that he wrote the novel to advance a thesis, which his story and main characters were meant to illustrate. This method, in my opinion, can give rise to good reportage (Čapek in fact went down into a pit for several hours), but only with difficulty can it give birth to convincing literature. In this instance, it didn't work. The thesis dominates all else, the manly heroes are characterized primarily by a single dominant attribute or often by some detail repeated ad nauseum, all of which is supposed to make the characters believable, but which instead has the opposite effect. Every gesture, even the most trivial action, such as handing someone a small shot of brandy or offering a cigarette, is intended to have far weightier meaning than usual, and Čapek made this excessively plain – surprising in an author so experienced. Some critics of the time found at least the very young Standa believable, but even he was drawn only sketchily, characterized by a few attributes only, the most visible being exaggerated shyness in the presence of the female characters and a virginal admiration for them.

Adam is from the same tribe of Čapekian protagonists as, for example, Hordubal – at peace with the fact that their wives, whom they look up to as untouchable creatures, refuse them. But Adam has nothing of Hordubal's stubbornness, of his willpower; Adam vacillates between humility and rash action.

Certainly other works by Čapek were inspired by ideas, but it is more acceptable to base a utopian or fantastic story on ideas than it is one that strives to be realistic and tell about the lives of contemporary people. And there is no question but that in *Krakatit*, for example, notwithstanding its utopian theme, Čapek's portrayal of his hero was much more personal, involved, and authentic. Čapek's characterization was personal in *Hordubal*, as well. In *The First Rescue Party*, however, the journalist was victorious over the creative writer. Keep in mind that Čapek's newspaper articles and essays were excellent. In them, Čapek knew how to be personally involved and convincing. But in *The First Rescue Party*, his writing hovers halfway between the journalistic and the artistic: too impassioned and sentimental for journalism, too superficial and schematic for a work of art.

It says much about this book that Čapek gained favor in the eyes of at least some communist critics. The young literary critic Julius Fučík, a leading Stalinist ideologue, reviewed the book with admiration. According to him, Čapek had proved that he was indeed a poet, that he was entirely familiar with the psychology, speech, and thoughts of workers, and that "he did justice to it all with poetic vision, conveying it in strong, poetic language such as we find too seldom in Czech literature. It is a beautiful song about worker solidarity, about worker heroism, a heroism which we fail to appreciate as such."[5] This praise could hardly have pleased Čapek, so redolent of the official Soviet critics' enthusiasm over dull, doctrinaire works about the working class.

The First Rescue Party might not be the most convincing of Čapek's works, but in the eventful time in which it was written, the story spoke directly to its readers. Times of crisis are more inclined to accept thematic or oversimplified messages. A narrative about the bravery of ordinary people who, in a difficult moment, forget everything that has divided them could, on the eve of catastrophe, bring people solace and hope. One can judge his play *The Mother*, the last major work Čapek completed, in much the same way.

29. Anyone Can Go to His Death, But to Lose Someone...

On February 12, 1938, the premiere of Čapek's last play took place at the Stavovský Theater in Prague. *The Mother* portrays the fateful dilemma of a mother whose soldier husband and physician son are dead and who gradually, in the course of the play, loses her other three sons as well. The mother cannot understand what motivates their actions and cannot accept that they would willingly sacrifice their lives for their goals and ideals. In the end, she is left alone with only her youngest son, but he too wants to leave, to defend his homeland that has just been attacked by an enemy. The mother desperately tries to hold him back, until the moment she hears on the radio that the enemy is also killing children. Only then, with a grand gesture, does she send her last son off to war.

Čapek emphasized on several occasions that the play's topic was suggested to him by his wife, who originally had wanted to write the play herself. The theme of a mother losing her children for reasons she can't understand, and therefore cannot accept, is an age-old theme. The classical myth of Niobe has often been treated in plays, poems, and numerous works of visual art. At more or less this same time, Bertolt Brecht was writing a one-act play with a similar theme, Señora Carrar's Rifles.

Čapek treated the theme in an original way. Those who have died continue to live on in the mother's mind; bodily present on stage, they talk with her, intervene in the plot, and appraise the family's and their country's dilemma. According to Olga Scheinpflugová, Čapek confided to her his feeling that "he who dies for something fine and decent does not die and disappear, but remains here with us, along with his moral values and his accomplishments." And he added, she wrote, "The devil knows what draws me so suddenly in the direction of the dead."[1]

As if by these statements he were readying the words for his own epitaph.

In *The Mother*, just as in *The White Plague* and *The First Rescue Party*, Čapek wanted to express his opinions on the current political situation, on the predicament of a Europe threatened by war. He is said to have written this play with unusual enthusiasm, and with its ending he was clearly turning to his fellow citizens, challenging them to defend their homeland in the event it was attacked.

Some critics saw in the play a fundamental change in Čapek's beliefs, primarily his abandonment of his pacificism and abstract humanism. But this was a superficial judgment. Čapek remained essentially himself even in *The Mother*, no matter how unusual the clear, militant closing line was for him. Here, too, the clash is more between principles than between characters. The men are willing to die for some higher ideal, for honor, or even to set a record. The mother stubbornly defends her right to have her family live rather than offer their lives for ideals she doesn't comprehend.

> Each of you does something just the opposite, and then afterwards you tell me: these are important matters, Mother, you couldn't possibly understand. One of you will build something, and two others will tear it down. And you say to me: These are tremendous things, Mama, we *must* do them even if it means an end to our lives. Life! You talk about life! To die oneself, that's easy enough to do; but to lose a husband or a son, if only you could know what that's like – If only you could know–[2]

The Mother repeats her truth in many variations, just as the men in her family repeatedly explain to her that they had to do what they did: fight on in a hopeless battle, find a cure for yellow fever, break an altitude record in an airplane, even at the cost of their lives. Čapek wrote in his commentary to the play.

> I imagined all of the play's characters as noble people following their convictions. The two elements, masculine and feminine, do not and cannot find consonance or harmony: the Mother simply

does not understand, she resigns herself; she does not understand and does not agree that those whom she loves have the right to go off to their deaths for their various causes.

I see the center of gravity from the female point of view in the Mother's sentence: Anyone can go to his death, but to lose someone…

As long as the world looks as it does now, this conflict can be neither ignored nor resolved. It's simply here…[3]

Čapek wrote his play while the Spanish Civil War was still going on and when Hitler's invasion of Czechoslovakia seemed more and more imminent. The play's protagonists are therefore acting against the backdrop of a bloody civil war which, towards the end of the play, changes into the defense of a country being attacked by a powerful neighbor. The twins, Cornel and Peter, represent not only the two sides in a civil war but something more universal: a fanaticism willing to murder its adversary. One side is black, the other white – the one revolutionary, the other reactionary. Two main ideologies dominated the political situation of 1938, both of which were highly aggressive and dangerous: Hitler's nationalism, with its racist and nationalistic hatreds, and communism, with its theory as well as practice of class hatred. (Stalin's communism displayed to an astonished world the horror of staged trials and of the executions that followed.) Because Čapek wanted to demonstrate that fanaticism of any stripe is dangerous, he avoided specifics about either side's goals, and for the same reason had an imaginary country as the story's locale. "I set the play in a fictitious coastal state with colonies – it is merely an artificially-created environment necessary to the dramatic design of the play."[4]

The Mother tries to convince her sons of the senselessness of fanaticism. When she protests that she cannot understand how anyone could imprison her son when he has harmed no one, Cornel explains:

Forgive me, Mama. You don't seem to realize that what's happening here is … civil war.

Mother: Oh? And we have to just accept it?

Cornel: We do. Because people are divided into two factions, and only one side can rule, do you see? And this is the fight, Mama, that will decide which side rules.

Mother: And that's why you're shooting at each other?

Cornel: Yes. It can't be any other way.

Mother: Tell me, does it matter so terribly much which side rules? Don't both sides have families? They should be worrying about their families!

Cornel: Families aren't everything.

Mother: They are, Cornel. They are to me. And don't tell me that Peter wants to rule over anyone. I know him; he couldn't even give orders to his dog – Maybe you, Cornel, but not Peter. Telling others what to do isn't his nature.

Cornel: That doesn't matter, Mama; his side wants to take charge of everything; they want to turn everything upside down, according to their own ideas. – It would be a disaster for the whole country, do you understand? Why, they're nothing but a gang of criminals and traitors, Mama! They would take over and ruin everything.[5]

Cornel objects when his mother sides with Peter, and it's not difficult to recognize in his opinions the old Čapekian idea heard at the end of *The Absolute at Large* and repeated many times over in his political essays: "Then I must be the one who believes in something false, Mama. Either his side is right or … we are. Damn it, one of us must be wrong!"[6] Čapek has the second of the twins, an executed member of the revolutionary forces, speak even more fanatically in defending a massacre:

It's the only way to make room for the new world. Andrew, George, it's worth it! Even if thousands and thousands of lives are… Do you hear those shots? It's beautiful! If only I could be there … Comrades, don't give up! Let the city be destroyed! Let it happen, it doesn't matter … Blacks, to war! For our freedom! For our victory! For a new world! Comrades, comrades, don't give in! Let the city fall, let the nation go under, let the whole world crumble: if only our cause is victorious! Better for everyone to be slaughtered than have those white dogs come out on top.[7]

What we have here is Fanaticism speaking through the mouths of characters, an inability to see even in one's own brother a man who can also be right, who can have his own truth. It's a conflict between two principles, not two characters, and they are more than brothers – they're twins. So their fanaticism should have had an even more absurd effect, more destructive and more barbarous.

Fanaticism at that time was reaching truly disastrous dimensions; thus someone intrinsically a democrat, as Čapek was, could not stand in either camp. In order to remain above the realities of the European conflicts, he limited himself to universal symbols: black against white, revolutionary against reactionary, fanaticism against fanaticism, good and honest people held captive by inflammatory ideologies. And in opposition to all of these is a mother who has no interest in political conflicts, who sees only her children, who knows them, who believes they could do nothing evil, and who sees that the world wants to take her children away from her. It is through her lips we hear a basic principle of motherhood: "I am too old," she says of herself. "Thousands and thousands of years old, my child." And elsewhere: "I feel like a she-wolf. Nothing in the world is as fierce as motherhood."

The difference beween political commentary and a play, however, consists in the fact that commentaries concern a particular external situation. Arguments that are convincing in a newspaper article sound far too declarative on stage. The external danger Čapek wanted to address was a possible attack by Hitler's Germany. And so he combined the predicament of civil war with the predicament at the close of the play, where the country, shaken by internal strife, is attacked by an external enemy. While civil war is monstrous, Čapek considered defense against external aggression necessary and just. Near the end of the play, the Mother hears on the radio that enemy airplanes have attacked the city, that hundreds of civilians, most of them women and children, have died, and that "our ancient castle, our beloved national monument, was reduced to ashes...," and at that moment she decides to send her last son out to fight the enemy. Even the play's conclusion, then, is declarative. Justification for the Mother's abrupt turnabout, her fateful decision, hovers on the verge of cliché: "What are you saying? Children? Why would anyone kill children?"

I would say that in *The Mother* Čapek intended to connect what cannot be connected: he wanted to state yet again that no one can find the whole truth and therefore no one has any right to violently force what he considers truth upon others, that fanaticism and negativism lead to murder. At the same time, he wanted to call on people, in the event their homeland is threatened, to be prepared to fight for it. Of course "the homeland" belongs among the most abused of concepts, and it is totalitarian ideologues who use the word most frequently. When only different kinds of fanaticisms are facing each other, the argument that women and children are dying cannot be resolved – an argument that has always appeared in news from the front on all sides of a conflict. It is an emotional argument that can be – and always is – misused, over and over. Because Čapek set up conflicts that were too universal, he was unable, at the play's end, to use any arguments other than those he had already used before. Consequently, the Mother's transformation at hearing a news bulletin on the radio follows not from her nature, but from the need to tell all mothers how to act when the nation is threatened.

Shortly after the war, Čapek's friend Ferdinand Peroutka tellingly characterized Čapek's last works as agitprop:

> At the onset of Hitlerism, Čapek changed from a playwright and novelist into a propagandist who wanted to break through the crust of human indifference and lack of foresight, and point to the approaching danger. His *White Plague, Newts*, and *The Mother* – they shout: People, pay attention, defend yourselves! These days writers are exhorted from one side and the other to tendentiousness, to writing 'agitprop.' Will we remember the agitprop Čapek wrote for us?[8]

At the time *The Mother* was first performed, people understood Čapek's urgent appeal. They were aware that, despite valuing peace above all else, it was right to resist aggression, even at the cost of human life. The play thus made reference to off-stage reality, counting on the fact that, by the end of the play, the audience will have recognized the unnamed coastal nation as democratic Czechoslovakia under the threat of Nazi aggression. There are exceptional periods in history where a drama of precisely this type can speak to people with startling urgency.

The situation to which *The Mother* referred has passed and we hear too much rhetoric as well as pathos in the speeches of its characters, but the play's principal problem is that the author did not allow his eponymous heroine to work through her suffering in order to reach her fateful decision. A director choosing to stage a Čapek play today probably would prefer *The Robber* or *The Makropulos Secret* to *The Mother* or *The White Plague*.

30. We Are All Increasingly Alone

The political situation quickly moved towards a pan-European catastrophe. The first victim of Hitler's aggression was Austria, and it was to be expected that the second would be Czechoslovakia. The majority of the country's German population supported the pro-Hitler Henlein's Sudeten German Party, which was obviously directed from Berlin and which, patterned on Hitler's operations, began organizing its own storm troopers. Weapons were smuggled across the border from Germany. Clashes occurred more and more frequently between people of Czech and German extraction. In 1938, the traditional May Day celebrations in the majority of ethnically German towns were transformed into massive demonstrations of citizens greeting their leaders with "Aryan salutes" and speakers escalating their demands on the Czechoslovak government.

While there is no question that the course of events was influenced by the situation in Nazi Germany, some far-sighted Czech democrats, such as the philosopher Emanual Rádl, called attention to the fact that, even as early as the 1920s, Czech policy in regard to the country's German citizens had been short-sighted and nationalistically narrow-minded, if not outright insulting. Čapek, too, repeatedly came out against nationalistic and anti-German excesses. "Certainly we do not and will not have much influence on what is or is not happening north of Podmokly," he wrote in the spring of 1937, referring to areas where ethnic Germans were a majority, areas called by the Germans the Sudetenland. "But the question is whether we might not have had a bit more influence on what was happening to and with our Germans. We took more interest in how a Czech roadmender somewhere in Kraslice was doing than in the political and cultural developments of the three million Germans in our nation."[1]

He analyzed the Czech-German problem in greater depth in his article "History Lesson," published in *Přítomnost* at the end of April 1938. Hitlerism, in Čapek's view, was the culmination of the radical process of German unification begun by Bismarck. Enthusiasm for unification was whipped up to such a level that it spread across the borders historically assigned to Germany, thereby placing the nation in danger by possibly provoking war. This policy resulted in an additional – and very serious – danger for the German people themselves:

> This hasty unification process on the part of the German nation expresses itself with fatal urgency in the way the German nation is now making every effort, including culturally and morally, to 'create itself.' It is unifying itself not only politically but spiritually by its 'German' world view, its teachings, its racist prejudices, its conception of culture and, slowly, its own German God. In other words, in the interest of national unity, it is knowingly and intentionally cutting itself off from Europe, from the spiritual solidarity of European nations.[2]

But no one can be excluded forever, without any consequences, from the community of others. We are obligated to secure for Czechoslovak Germans all civil and ethnic rights, Čapek continued, but it seems they are demanding something more, namely, a special German right, the right of German isolation.

> We're afraid that, while the Czechoslovak state can guarantee them all of their human and civil rights, it simply does not have exclusive, Germans-only rights at its disposal. It appears the government is unable to satisfy them with any of the things it provides to citizens of other languages within the framework of its democracy. As long as they want to be German Germans, there is no prospect of their becoming European Germans ... We, on the other hand, can guarantee only that they may indeed become European Germans. No one can ask more of us than that. Not even them. Even we ourselves cannot undertake so great a task.[3]

Čapek was precise in his analysis. In reality, the adherents of Henlein's party had only one thing on their minds: they wanted to live in the Reich, they preferred a totalitarian regime to life in democratic Czechoslovakia.

Čapek tried hard to influence political developments in a positive way.[4] According to Julius Firt, Čapek and Peroutka together participated in a special political mission. They called several times on the German ambassador, Eisenlohr, who had requested the meetings. Apparently the ambassador's intent was to warn Beneš about the particularly active and thus traitorous members of Henlein's party, as well as about Hitler's plans to destroy Czechoslovakia. Peroutka and Čapek informed President Beneš of the content of their talks. (It is not out of the question, however, that this information only strengthened the president's fears that resisting Hitler's demands would mean the nation's destruction in war.)

To his Friday gatherings Čapek now added Tuesdays, when there was said to be more discussion of the kinds of policies Czechoslovakia should employ in order to avoid German aggression. The events that led to the end of the republic, however, could not be stopped. In June 1938, Prague hosted the tenth annual Sokol Festival,[5] which was perceived as a demonstration of the national will to defend itself. At the same time, the International PEN Club Congress also took place in Prague, at which Čapek, by far the most well-known Czech writer in the world, was perceived by his colleagues from abroad as a representative of Czech culture, as the spokesman for an endangered country. It was he who suggested that Congress participants travel to view a military training exercise in Milovice, not far from Prague. Benjamin Crémieux, one of the participants, made a characteristic observation: "Today we had a choice of visiting library or army. We preferred the army. If someone had predicted this ten years ago, we would have turned away from the fool in thorough disgust. Today, we book people go from books to army, because the army defends the library."[6] Even though the date of the Congress had been determined long before, the presence of so many important personalities in Prague was perceived as a demonstration of solidarity with threatened Czechoslovakia.[7]

Nevertheless, no demonstration of intellectual solidarity was able to alter Hitler's intent nor to convince Czechoslovakia's Western allies that it would be in the interest of peace and democracy to stand up to Hitler's demands. During the days when Britain's prime minister, Neville Chamberlain, was meeting with Hitler, Czech society feverishly, desperately awaited what developments each day might bring. For Karel Čapek, it also involved feverish exertion. He felt the need to speak to the people daily, to give hope or at least to fortify weakening spirits. "Soon, very soon now, this week of uncertainty will come to an end. For better or for worse, we will at least know where we stand, and we will cope bravely with what, from our point of view, will be acknowledged, prudently and with resolve, as necessary," he wrote in *Lidové noviny* on September 21. "Meanwhile, the grimmest struggle of our young history is taking place. It is not only a struggle for our soil, it is also a struggle for our souls, for the souls of each and every one of us.

"Defend your soul, defend your soul in these terrible, trying days, let nothing make you waver..." A day later, in his article "Prayer for This Evening," he tried to encourage the despairing.

> We have no cause for shame, though fate has struck us with a rod of iron. No, it is not we who were vanquished; no, not we who were lacking in courage. Our nation has lost none of its honor; it has lost only a piece of its body ... God, we do not ask that you avenge us, but that you instill in each of us a spirit of confidence, that you let no one despair, but rather seek how to be of use in the future work of our eternal nation. We have no need for despair. We need inner strength ... No nation will ever be small that does not waver in its faith in the future and in its work for better days to come.

The Munich Agreement between Hitler and the Western powers sliced away the majority of Czechoslovakia's border regions, which meant, in essence, the demise of the republic whose spiritual representative Čapek legitimately felt himself to be. In the first days of October, he was still looking for words of encouragement, but before long, his articles evinced a tone of bitter skepticism. In "The Progress of the Human Spirit," he contemplated progress in all fields of human endeavor. People invented artificial light, they learned how to fly, radio was invented. Science was learning to look for truth in the most complex processes, to weigh and measure atoms as well as stars with increasingly greater accuracy. "But human ingenuity could not be satisfied with slow progress in our knowledge of our world, and that's why it invented lies. Blind, fanatical, superstitious lies about things and people within reach of our hand. It is no longer necessary to discover with certainty what the truth is. Human ingenuity has broken through those narrow confines. This is, until further notice, the latest triumph of modern civilization."[8] Several days later he was reflecting how close we all were to finding ourselves in the midst of war. Death was hanging over the heads of us all. We were given life at a horrendous cost. The only conclusion following from all this: "The life we were given no longer belongs only to us. It belongs to our nation. It belongs to our land. It was extended or granted to us at our nation's expense ... The generation now living, from children to the elderly, is indebted to our homeland for its life. We will continue to pay that debt until the end of our days."[9]

Not everyone shared these views. Many grasped that not only had times changed, but commonly shared values had changed with them. The spirit of totalitarian thought blew quickly across the new borders, and many hurried to demonstrate just how closely attuned to it they felt. This spirit presupposed that those who embraced democracy had no place in the new era. Immediately after the Munich Agreement, Čapek was again attacked by Jaroslav Durych and falsely accused of having fled Prague at the time of Czechoslovak mobilization. František Langer remembered years later:

> After that performance by Durych, as if at a given signal, the street scum and journalistic rabble, with all the hatred and envy that had been stored up for years, understood that Čapek was now fair game, and they dumped sewers of slander and fury onto him. For Čapek, Munich was crippling. He was wounded, beaten unconscious; the personal attacks that went beyond him to strike at everything he loved, all these he bore as the deepest humiliation and disgrace. It was as if he were looking all about him and questioning whether, at a time when his thoughts were most needed, there would be anyone listening to him. This campaign was one more blow added to the other ordeals of his final hours.[10]

It's true that Čapek's voice was heard less often in the newspapers during the weeks following Munich. He was spending most of the time at his summer house, and he had returned once again to writing fiction. In *The Life and Work of the Composer Foltýn*, he attempted – at least formally – to continue along the lines of his best work, the trilogy. The novel is composed of testimony, that is, each chapter consists of a statement by someone who had known Foltýn at one period of his life or another. Together they form a picture of a lazy, uncreative, hedonistic egotist with only one goal in life: to be a celebrated composer. He hoped to reach this goal by compiling an opera about Judith from stolen and purchased snatches of text and melodies.

Unlike the composite in *Hordubal*, however, this one was not meant to prove the impossibility of grasping a man's story in its entirety, or that his story "coarsens" in its telling by others. On the contrary, each of the individual observations and opinions served to round out the picture of Foltýn, and make it increasingly precise.

Literary historians who tried to determine who might have been the model for such an unusual Čapekian protagonist came up with several possibilities. But the identity of a real-life model, if indeed one existed at all, is not important; far more important is the question of why Čapek chose this type of person in the first place. I would say that the answer is readily at hand. The democratic era was ending, about to be replaced by a totalitarian society, and so the times were extremely favorable for political and intellectual swindlers, untalented phonies, and other diabolical sorts who saw this as their opportunity to attain glory, power, and wealth. One can't agree with Helena Koželuhová's assertion that the new novel's subject matter was entirely alien to Čapek, and that he was writing without energy, without joy, only to keep his mind occupied. Rather, the novel was intended to be Čapek's artistic response to one of the essential problems of a society entering upon an era of totalitarianism. While Čapek remained within the sphere closest to him, the sphere of artistic honesty, his dishonest protagonist was a perfect representative of that inglorious era and, for that matter, of the decades that followed.

Čapek's death prevented him from finishing the novel, but it can nonetheless be said that the fraudulent composer Foltýn, that vain, contemptible man and sterile epigone, is one of the best-drawn characters Čapek ever created, and that his story, even if unfinished, is among the best of the author's works.

After Munich, many of Čapek's friends suggested that he emigrate, just as the republic's president, Dr. Beneš, had left the country, and they tried to convince him that he could be more useful abroad. Čapek is said to have refused because he felt he would be needed more at home. But surely the question of how he and his wife could continue their work abroad would also have been an important consideration. Doctors and engineers, musicians and craftsmen may fare well as emigrés, but it is much more difficult for a writer or actor because of the substantial role played by one's native language and by a knowledge of the public the artist addresses.

Thus Čapek stayed and, according to Olga Scheinpflugová, applied himself prodigiously to writing the novel about Foltýn as well as several long newspaper articles. In "Greetings," which appeared in *Lidové noviny* on Christmas Day, Čapek's voice was heard for the last time and almost symbolically: full of reconciliation, simultaneously wistful and weary. In the article, the author passes through countries which he had visited and which were now, in one way or another, actively involved in the present world crisis: England, Germany, France, Spain, and Italy. "A person thinks various things about nations," he begins, "and they are not always things which that particular nation would want to have framed; it has become such a habit these days for a person somehow to identify a country and a nation with its policies, regime, government, public opinion, call it what you like." Čapek then recalled places or situations which had remained fixed in his memory, mostly inconspicuous, unimportant events and places, such as the small red house in Kent where an old gentleman was clipping a hedge; his brief exchange with the regulars at a Swabian inn; the two-wheeled cart in front of a tavern on the outskirts of Paris whose driver, a farmer with a straw hat, sat drinking wine; a train to Rome and the sleepy, generous laborer seated across from him ... It was possible to enter into a mutual understanding with such people and greet them from a distance, but: "What can one do, it is terribly far from one nation to another; we are all increasingly alone. Better, now, never to set foot outside one's home; better to lock the doors and close the shutters and let them all do as they please. I no longer care. And now you can close your eyes and softly, so softly say: How do you do, old gentleman in Kent? Grüss Gott, meine Herren! Grazia, signor! À vôtre santé!"

Several hours after the article "Greetings" was published, Čapek passed away. He died only a few days before his forty-ninth birthday – in other words, relatively young.

The death certificate stated the cause of death as inflammation of the bronchi developing into double pneumonia. According to most of the testimony we have about Čapek's last days, he was in fact so worn down by the circumstances, by the attacks in the press and the anonymous letters and threats, that he lost his motivation to live. According to Ferdinand Peroutka,

Čapek said to him at the time of Munich: "My world has died. I no longer have any reason to write."[11]

Olga Scheinpflugová quotes Čapek's words from that same time: "I feel immensely weak, not physically, but morally and spiritually, weak in hope, weak in reproaches, entitled to neither this nor that, indifferent to both relief and pain ... I am completely torn apart, as if my blood, guts, brain, everything was pouring out of me, as if a herd of stampeding bulls had trampled me over."[12] Dr. Karel Steinbach, the friend and doctor who tended him until the last moment of his life, was of a similar opinion. "As a doctor, I know that he died because there were no antibiotics or sulfa drugs at the time, but surely a large piece of the truth lies with those who say that Čapek was killed by Munich. There is no question but that the Munich tragedy knocked the legs out from under what he believed, and that the wounded, disappointed soul wavered and, in the end, refused to support the sick, fragile body in its struggle...'[13]

Certainly the post-Munich situation was dispiriting for Čapek, as it was for so many of his fellow citizens, and his mental state would have influenced the course of his illness; but surely this was not the reason he died. Despite the abuse heaped on him by the gutter press and Catholic newspapers, he had many close friends who stood by him, a great many readers who trusted and revered him, and a wife with whom, by all accounts, he was happy. In addition, he had a sense of responsibility toward society and his work, and he wanted to finish writing the novel about Foltýn, to which he justly attributed great weight. And finally, it is known that he was very much afraid of death. He thus had many reasons to fight for his life.

The illness that finally destroyed him was caused by several seemingly minor circumstances. That autumn, after severe, protracted rainstorms, the creek that ran through Strž and often flooded part of his garden overflowed its banks. Čapek was devoted to nature and to his plot of land, which he tended painstakingly and with diligence. He worked himself to the point of exhaustion, clearing away the aftermath of the flood. He caught cold while so doing, and the cold became progressively chronic, although he refused to stay in bed, thinking that he could not afford the time. And up to several days before his death, he was still working from morning to night on his novel. Even though the bronchial inflammation was worsening, he invited friends over prior to the Christmas holidays, sitting up with them far into the night and then running out into the icy night to say goodbye at the gate. One could say that, rather than showing symptoms of depression and a disinclination to live, right up to his last moments Čapek displayed an excess of activity – something very characteristic of him. When his neglected cold took a sudden turn for the worse, the doctor who was called in, a relative of Olga's, did not diagnose pneumonia and injected Čapek with morphine, which is contraindicated for this condition. Then everything happened quickly. Each of Čapek's illnesses was aggravated by his stiff back, his congested lungs, and his physical fragility. In addition, Čapek was an exceptionally heavy smoker – very little was said during his time about the effects of smoking on the lungs, but it's obvious that his chest cold and cough were connected to his smoking.

Many of Čapek's friends assumed that he would have been a victim of Nazi persecution anyway, and that for him death was in fact deliverance from far greater suffering. It's also true, however, that many of those who were close to him intellectually and politically were arrested but survived the camps (Ferdinand Peroutka, for example). Unfortunately, his brother Josef died only a few days, or perhaps only a few hours, before the camp in which he was imprisoned was liberated by the American army.

This line of thought leads us nowhere, of course. An excellent writer who symbolized an entire epoch in the history of his country and of Europe, an artist who with his entire being was committed to the young Czechoslovak Republic and its democracy, on which he collaborated so strenuously, conscientiously, and responsibly, who died at one and the same time with it. We might discern in this a certain higher connection.

Vitěslav Nezval accompanied Čapek to his grave with this poem:

> The last candle on the Christmas tree
> burns for thee today.
> So few of us remain,
> so few of us, in pain,
> to leave the task to
> at such a mournful time,
> in this fateful season
> after disaster –
> oh, what grief in the house...
> You knew it, you know
> that the nation lives, that all it can do is drag its cross
> on its drooping, broken shoulders...

Endnotes

KČ = Karel Čapek
Čs = Prague: Československý ('Český' 1993 on) spisovatel

For all references to English translations of Čapek's works, only the title is included; the complete information can be found in the list of works in translation. However, most translations of Czech-language excerpts in this book are by this book's translator, Norma Comrada, and when she has used others' translations, she has edited them.

Ch. 1. **A Trio of Geniuses**

1. Franz Kafka, *Diaries 1910-1923* (N.Y.: Schocken Books, 1965), tr. Joseph Kresh, 75.

Ch. 2. **Mama's Boy**

1. KČ, *Obrázky z domova* (Pictures from Home) (Čs, 1959), 12
2. Ibid, 13
3. KČ, *Three Novels*, 343-344
4. Olga Scheinpflugová, *Živý jako nikdo z nás* (As Alive as Any of Us), (Prague: Hynek, 1997), 11
5. Ibid, 12
6. Josef Čapek, *O sobě* (About Myself) (Čs, 1958), 34
7. Helena Čapková, *Moji milí bratři* (My Dear Brothers) (Čs, 1986), 78
8. Ibid, 113-114
9. Ibid, 113
10. Jan Kábrt, *Krakonošova zahrada bratří Čapků* (The Čapek Brothers' Garden of Krakonoš) (Hradec Králové: KRUH, 1985), 22
11. Helena Čapková, *Moji milí bratři*, 24
12. Ibid, 134, 133
13. Ibid, 130
14. Ibid, 138
15. KČ, *Three Novels*, 342
16. Ibid, 344
17. Ibid, 408
18. Jarmila Čapková, *Vzpomínky* (Memories) (Prague: Torst, 1998), 290

19. František Langer, *Byli a bylo* (They Were and It Was) (Čs, 1963), 92

Ch. 3. **Visual Artist or Writer?**

1. KČ, *O umění a kultuře I* (On Art and Culture) (Čs, 1984), 371-372
2. Ibid, 372
3. KČ, *Francouzská poesie* (French Poetry) (Prague: KLHU, 1957), 312
4. KČ, *Korespondence I* (Čs, 1993), 321

Ch. 4. **Civilized Optimism Swept Away**

1. Josef Čapek, "Podzím 1914" (Autumn 1914), *Lumír* 1915, no. 2
2. KČ, *Korespondence I*, 339
3. KČ, *O umění a kultuře III* (Čs, 1986), 316
4. KČ, *Francouzská poesie*, 194
5. Ibid, 8, 11
6. Ibid, 372
7. KČ, "Elegy" in *Cross Roads*, 31
8. KČ, "The Footprint" in ibid, 16
9. KČ, "The Mountain" in ibid, 63
10. Ibid, 67
11. KČ, "The Lost Way" in ibid, 40-41
12. KČ, *Korespondence I*, 383
13. KČ, "Help!" in *Cross Roads*, 97
14. Jan Mukařovský, introduction to *Výbor z prøzy Karla Čapka* (A Selection of Karel Čapek's Prose) (Prague: Státní nakladatelství v Praze, 1946), 10-11

Ch. 5. **Not Two Sheaves, But Rather Thousands of Stalks**

1. William James, *Pragmatism: A New Name for Some Old Ways of Thinking* (London: Longmans, 1907), 45
2. Ibid, 203
3. Ibid, 222
4. Ibid, 19-20
5. KČ, *Pragmatismus čili Filosofie praktického života* (Pragmatism, or a Philosophy for a Practical Life) (Prague: F. Topič, 1918), 38-40
6. KČ, *O umění a kultuře III*, 316-317
7. KČ, *Apocryphal Tales,* tr. Norma Comrada, 89-90

8. KČ, "Why Am I Not a Communist?" in *Přítomnost* 4 December 1924, also in *Od člověka k člověku I* (From Person to Person) (Čs, 1988), 418

9. Ibid, vol. II (1991), 539-540

Ch. 6. **From Tutor to Editor**

1. KČ, *Korespondence I*, 198

2. Ibid, 378

3. Marie Šulcová, the Čapek researcher who has dedicated the most space to his stay at the castle in Chyše, notes that a terrible explosion, one of the greatest catastrophes in the country, took place in a nearby munitions factory at exactly that time. She finds a connection between this experience and the depiction, in Čapek's novel *Krakatit*, of the explosion of the deadly substance. See the book *Karel Čapek na Karlovarsku* (Karel Čapek in the Karlový vary Region) (Karlový vary, 1990), and Šulcová's novel *Kruh mého času* (The Circle of My Time) (Západočeské nakladatelství, 1989), 55-63. I would like to add that, for his protagonist in *Krakatit*, the engineer Prokop, Čapek used the name of the boy in the castle at Chyše.

4. KČ, "Starý vlastenec" in *Od člověka k člověku III*, 196

5. KČ, "Noviny a vědy" (Newspapers and Science) in *Národní listy* (National Pages), 28 October 1917 (his first article for that newspaper had been published six days earlier).

6. Ferdinand Peroutka, *Budování státu III* (Building the State) (Prague: Fr. Borový, 1936), 2041

7. Ibid, 2097

8. KČ, *O uměni a kultuře, Dodatky* (On Art and Culture, A Supplement) (Čs, 1995), 76-77

Ch. 7. **The Shy Boy as Robber**

1. KČ, *Korespondence II* (Čs, 1993), 85

2. KČ, "Three" in *Cross Roads,* 142ff.

3. Ibid, "Helena" in ibid, 151ff.

4. KČ, *The Makropulos Secret* in *Toward the Radical Center,* 146

5. KČ, *Three Novels*, 377

6. KČ, *Korespondence I*, 295

7. Ibid, 285

8. KČ, *Loupežník* (The Robber) in *Hry* (Plays) (Čs, 1956), 9

9. Ibid, 28

10. KČ, *Poznámky o tvorbě* (Notes on Creative Work) (Čs, 1959), 85

11. František Černý, *Premiéry bratří Čapků* (Brothers Čapek Premieres) (Prague: Hynek, 2000), 88

Ch. 8. **Olga: Love with a Secret**

1. While we have numerous sources that provide a picture of Čapek's childhood and his later professional and social activities, we have only two for his most important adult relationship. Immediately after the Second World War, Olga Scheinpflugová published an extensive autobiographical work, *Český román* (A Czech Novel or A Czech Romance (in the literary sense)), a tempestuous novelized account of her relationship with Karel Čapek. To underline the authenticity of her narrative, she used dozens of quotations from letters he had sent her. She used these quotes too freely, however: the author herself admits in one place (62) that, at certain moments, she "was not able ... to separate facts from lies." Even though her novel received many negative critical responses, *Český román* remained for several decades the only basic source of information on Čapek's personal life. (In their memoirs, other friends, as well as his sister, were demonstrably silent about his relationship with Olga, but their preserved correspondence does not conceal their lack of love for Olga or their fear that this relationship would negatively affect his work. Helena Koželuhová, his sister Helena's daughter, was even less kind with respect to Olga.) Not until the beginning of the 1970s was a voluminous collection published of Čapek's letters to Olga during the eighteen years left to him before his death. These letters differ so much from *Český román* that they cast considerable doubt on Olga's claims of accuracy. Čapek's letters to Věra Hrůzová were also published, allowing the reader to gain a sense of his other powerful romantic relationship.

2. KČ, *Korespondence II*, 37

3. O. Scheinpflugová, *Český román* (Prague: Fr. Borový, 1946), 79

4. KČ, *Korespondence II*, 41-42

5. Ibid, 43

6. Ibid, 45

7. Ibid, 46

8. Ibid, 52. The way this particular excerpt reads in Scheinpflugová's version is typical. To begin with, she changes the situation from Čapek complaining that she neglects him to one in which Čapek despairs over having neglected her. Her addition is in brackets: "I am apparently younger than is written in the birth registry and dumber

than anyone in the world would believe; I would like more than anything to die. If I get out of this hell [of my own suffering as well as the torment I caused], I will no longer be as I used to be." (*Český román*, 161-162). It is perhaps necessary to add, to Olga's credit, that it was she who prepared Čapek's letters for publication, thereby offering a contrast to her own version of reality. It is also true, however, that many of the letters she quoted from are absent from the published correspondence, and it is therefore possible that they were never written.

9. *Český román*, 99
10. Ibid, 101
11. Ibid, 134
12. Ibid, 145
13. Ibid, 152
14. KČ, *Korespondence II*, 94-95
15. Ibid, 96-97
16. Ibid, 98-99
17. Ibid, 99-100
18. Ibid, 100-101

Ch. 9. **The First Report on the End of Civilization: R.U.R.**

1. The Brothers Čapek, *Krakonošova zahrada* (The Garden of Krakonoš) (Čs, 1957), 18-19
2. KČ, "The Footprint" in *Cross Roads*, 15ff.
3. KČ, "Footprints" in *Tales from Two Pockets*, tr. Norma Comrada, 128
4. KČ, "The Man Who Couldn't Sleep" and "The Stamp Collection" in *Tales from Two Pockets*, 335, 341
5. KČ, *R.U.R.: Rossum's Universal Robots*, in *Toward the Radical Center*, 41
6. Ibid, 49
7. Ibid, 51-52
8. Ibid, 65
9. Ibid, 81
10. Ibid, 83
11. Ibid, 99
12. Ibid, 108-109
13. *Saturday Review* (London), 23 July 1923, translator unknown. In Czech, 1966 Čs edition of *R.U.R.*, 165-167
14. *R.U.R.*, 45

15. "Čapek's theater is not a theater of psychological conflict, but of 'the human lot,' the position of man in society and in the universe. A theater not of characters, but of ideas." Alexandr Matuška, *Karel Čapek: An Essay*, tr. Cathryn Alan (Prague: Artia, 1964), 353

16. *R.U.R.*, 63, 65

17. Even more curious testimony comes from Romain Rolland in 1924. "During their latest trip, Vildrac and Duhamel were very much intrigued by this fantastical play à la Wells, and they told me about it. I was not as excited by it. The idea itself is original, some of the staging as well, but the poetic and especially theatrical realization is average, slow, and the recitation old-fashioned. – Čapek, sitting with me in the president's box, explained the dialogue to me and interspersed his explanations with: 'This is stupid, this is stupid. There are a few thoughts here, but it's stupid. Are you bored? It's terribly boring for me ... Do you have enough patience to stay till the end? This, this part is disgusting ... Don't look!' Etc." *R.U.R.*, 1966 Čs edition, 127

18. KČ, 1911 in *O umění a kultuře I,* 166-167. Prague's Intimate/Lyric Theater staged contemporary plays for free, as did similar theaters in Paris, Berlin, and elsewhere.

Ch. 10. **The Second Report on the End of Civilization – The Absolute at Large**

1. KČ, *The Absolute at Large*, 1962 Čs edition, 7

2. KČ, *The Absolute at Large*, 29

3. Ibid, 38

4. Ibid, 58

5. Ibid, 119

6. Ibid, 135

7. Ibid, 219

8. Ibid, 240-241

9. František Götz, *Jasnící se horizont* (Brightening Horizon) (Prague: Báclav Petr, 1926)

10. Bedřich Václavek, *Od umění k tvorbě* (From Art to Creation) (Prague: Svoboda, 1949)

11. KČ, *O umění a kultuře II*, 413

12. In his comprehensive study of utopian literature of the time, the critic A. M. Píša characterized the circumstances it grew out of; his conclusions can be extended to the utopian works of Karel Čapek. "A wave of utopian ideas had already appeared in the restless, nervous atmosphere before the war. Such ideas typically spring from an attempt

to acquire a supportive inner certainty, which cannot be obtained from the given circumstances ... The war's horrors, despair, and delirious hopes swept away man's most delicate and firm spiritual values and confronted him with an ominous view of the future of mankind." A. M. Píša, *Směry a cíle* (Directions and Feelings) (Prague: Svoboda a Solař, 1927), 142, 144-145

Ch. 11. **A Morality Play About Insects and People**

1. "The more obviously hopeless the internal situation of our republic within the limits of today's 'order' and the fate of the 'democratic' system, and the greater the military and diplomatic successes of Soviet Russia, and the more obvious it becomes that Russia is set on a path towards realizing socialism ... the more craftily the colorful coalition of reactionaries, bourgeoisie, and social-patriots tries to obfuscate the meaning and success of the Russian Revolution, as well as Russian methods and government, and argue against the value to us of its example. Every proletarian must hear it: a new world, a new life, a new order is being born in Russia." S. K. Neumann, in the journal *Červen* (Red, or June), no. 11, 1029.

2. "In this transitional period, wages are still being paid in money, but it has lost much of its former importance, and the time is not far off when it will be seen only in museums, where one day the viewers will talk about these little discs and pieces of paper that were once the most holy thing in the world, for or over which people fought wars, strangled one another, prostituted themselves, and committed suicide. Revolution is strong. Strong and hard. Like a storm that sweeps away everything rotten and corrupt and fills the air with ozone." Ivan Olbracht, *Cesta za poznáním* (The Path to Knowledge) (Prague: Svoboda, 1952), 72, 74.

3. Jiří Wolker, "Manifestoes," *Var* (Agitation), vol. II, no. 1 (1922).

4. Jiří Wolker, "Roentgen," in *Výbor a díla* (Selected Works) (Prague: Svoboda, 1950), 374. I remember hearing this programmatic poem of class hatred recited several times in the 1950s.

5. Bedřich Václavek, "O nové umění" (About the New Art), *Var*, no. 10, 15 April 1922.

6. KČ, "In Place of Criticism," in *Přítomnost* (1920), also in *O umění a kultuře II*, 229

7. KČ, "Save Yourself Who Can" in *Cesta* (Journey), also in *Od člověka k člověku I*, 225-226

8. KČ, "Why Am I Not a Communist?" op. cit.

9. Brothers Čapek, *From the Life of the Insects*, in *Toward the Radical Center*, 307

10. Ibid, 300

11. Ibid, 309

12. Ibid, 311

13. Ibid (but unpublished: only Act II of the translation appeared in *Toward the Radical Center*)

Ch. 12. **To Live Briefly But Fully**

1. KČ, *The Makropulos Secret*, in *Toward the Radical Center*, 168

2. Ibid, 170

3. Ibid, 174

4. Ibid, 176

5. Jarmila Čapková, *Vzpomínky*, 197

Ch. 13. **Personal Crisis and Flight to Italy**

1. KČ, *Korrespondence I*, 121

2. KČ, *Korespondence II*, 123

3. KČ, *Korrespondence I*, 135

4. Ibid, 126

5. Ibid, 136-137

6. KČ, *Letters from Italy*, 1960 Čs edition, 40

7. KČ, *Korespondence II*, 144-145

8. Ibid, 147

9. Ibid, 148-149

10. Ibid, 152

11. KČ, *Korespondence I*, 283

12. KČ, *Korespondence II*, 153

13. Ibid, 157

14. Věra's letters to Čapek have not been preserved. Perhaps the most that is known about her relationship with Čapek, and with men in general, is told in a book by her generation-younger relative, Miloslava Holubová. According to Holubová, Věra did not indicate any particular interest in Čapek: "She didn't even take the time to come to his premiere at the National Theater, even though he had asked her to. When she told me this years later, I could not understand her lack of interest in Čapek." Holubová's characterization of Věra also may suggest something about the nature of her relationship with Čapek: "Věra was a delicate plant that needed to be watered by

male adoration, or else it would wilt. Let some old man at a family gathering offer his arm for a stroll in the garden, and she was beaming. At that time, I did not understand her voracious need to be admired again and again, like an actor after each performance." Miloslava Holubová, *Necestou cestou* (Come What May) (Prague: Torst, 1998), 121, 129, 131

Ch. 14. **Return of the Robber**

1. *Dopisy ze zásuvky, Karel Čapek Věře Hrůzové* (Letters from the Drawer, Karel Čapek to Věra Hrůzová), edited and afterword by Jiří Opelík (Prague: Melantrich, 1980). Čapek liked to play with names, and he gave symbolic names to his characters, as already mentioned in connection with *R.U.R.* For that matter, the name Balttin indicates a place on the Baltic Sea, meaning Germany, which for Čapek – and for the majority of his contemporaries – was associated with the idea of bellicosity.

2. This extremely personal motive was not noticed by contemporary critics. Some of them praised the novel's readability and its author's proficiency in telling an exciting tale. "And therefore," wrote the poet Josef Hora, "we praise *Krakatit* in this sense, that its author is not ashamed of including extraneous thrills; indeed, he even makes a system of it. He succeeds not only in utilizing a timely theme but also in applying to an epic that is digestible, thrilling, and almost sportingly democratic literary styles which until now had been used only for sublime visions." (Josef Hora, *Poesie a Život* (Poetry and Life) (Čs, 1959), 340-341) The young writer Marie Pujmanová also praised *Krakatit* for the same reason. Other critics focused on the novel's philosophizing conclusion. Later, critics took notice of Čapek's prescience in the field of nuclear physics, one being Jan Mukařovský, in a postwar essay. "A comparison of Čapek's fiction with the later state of scientific knowledge confirmed for Mukařovský how Čapek, driven by concern for the future of humankind, was able – not that long after the First World War, when atomic research was in its infancy – to anticipate a stage still far in the future of the development of nuclear physics, and further to convey artistically, in a spellbinding manner, the responsibility of scientists for how the results of their work will be used." (Viktor Kudělka, *Boje o Karla Čapka* (The Struggle over Karel Čapek) (Prague: Academia, 1987), 59)

Ch. 15. **A Bad Dream**

1. KČ, "What Machinery Will Never Do" (also known as "Rule by Machines"), *Daily Express* (London), 5 February 1929, 8 (translator unknown)

2. KČ, "We Alarm and Amuse M. Čapek," *New York Times Magazine*, May 16, 1926, 4 (translator unknown)

Ch. 16. **A Protest Against Ideologies**

1. KČ, *Apocryphal Tales*, 58-59

2. In contrast to neighboring countries, such as Poland, Hungary, and Romania, many important writers in Czechoslovakia professed their allegiance to the left and even to the radical left. Among them, for example, was the Čapek brothers' former friend, S. K. Neumann; the poet and Nobel Prize laureate-to-be Jaroslav Seifert; the excellent poets Hora, Biebl, and Nezval; one of the most remarkable prose writers of the interwar era, Vladislav Vančura; and other good writers such as Ivan Olbracht, Marie Majerová, and Karel Konrád, plus a pair of outstanding writers and performers of avant-garde theater, Jiří Voscovec and Jan Werich. I have already mentioned that Jaroslav Hašek, during his stay in Russia, even became a red commissiar. And many important architects and painters also belonged to leftist and avant-garde groups; however, many of these writers and artists later changed their outlook and resigned from the Communist Party.

3. KČ, "Why Am I Not a Communist?" This essay was written in response to a survey by the journal *Přítomnost*. Many writers and democratically-oriented intellectuals participated in the survey. Also included were the warning voices of those writers who, during the time of Revolution, were fighting in Russia as part of the Czechoslovak Legions; their views were, therefore, those of eyewitnesses. Others, such as the poet Fráňa Šrámek, simply stated: "I prefer to hear the word 'freedom' rather than 'dictatorship,' the word 'person' rather than 'mass.'" Unfortunately, Czech society listened very little to voices like these, and so, two decades later, S. K. Neumann's malevolent prophecy was fulfilled. In his response to the survey, Neumann wrote of another Čapek friend, Ferdinand Peroutka, the publisher of *Přítomnost*: "This is a man who every day drenches his shirt with the sweat of witticisms and acrobatic tricks from the school of higher journalism, and he, along with Karel Čapek, represent the 'first-class' attractions of the first 'genuinely Czech' world circus. The audience for this circus are those *future Czech refugees* [author's emphasis],

who will go running after their own Czechoslovak Kerensky till the dust rises on all roads." (*Reflektor*, 10 February 1925)

4. F.X. Šalda, *Literární svět* (Literary World), 1927-1928, no. 1 & 2

5. Alexandr Matuška, *Karel Čapek*, 354

Ch. 17. **How to Warn of Destruction?**

1. In the Soviet bloc countries during the 1960s, a unique version of theater of the absurd arose. Playwrights such as Sławomir Mrożek and Václav Havel created completely fictitious worlds and plots, in spite of which their audiences took the plays as highly topical.

2. KČ, *Bajky a podpovídky* (Fables and Would-Be Tales) (Praha: Fr. Borový, 1946), 20, 23-24, 25

3. "The noetic system of newspapers is actualized realism; anything outside the present does not exist, *extra praesentiam non est existentia*," wrote Čapek in 1925. "A fanatical interest in the present is one of the secrets of life; it is also one of the secrets of newspapers. It must be new, but it must not be raw or unfamiliar. The jungle of events that opens before you every morning in the newspaper must be traversed by familiar and well-trodden pathways ... In summary, one might say that literature is the expression of old things in perpetually new ways, whereas newspapers are perpetually expressing new realities in a fixed and unchangeable way." KČ, "In Praise of Newspapers," in *In Praise of Newspapers and Other Essays*

4. "If I thought seriously about anything while structuring the play," wrote Čapek about *R.U.R.* in the journal *Jevište* (Scene/Theater) in February 1921, "it was about those six or seven people who were intended to be *representative of humankind* [author's emphasis]. Yes, when the robots start to attack, I wanted passionately for everyone in the audience to feel that something infinitely valuable and great was happening, that humankind is we ourselves. This 'we' was the most important, it was the principal idea, it was the slant, it was the essential scheme of the entire work." "Ještě *R.U.R.*" (Still *R.U.R.*) in *O Umění a kultuře II*, 252

Ch. 18. **Important for the Nation**

1. KČ, (1921) in *O umění a kultuře II*, 320-321

2. Ibid, 339

3. Edmond Konrád, *Nač Vzpomenu* (What I Remember) (Čs, 1957), 174

4. Helena Koželhuová, *Čapci očima rodiny* (The Čapeks in the Eyes of the Family) (Prague: B. Just, 1994), 108-109

5. A passage from one such text provides an accurate picture of contemporary (1925) Czech political reality in its condemnation of those leading political parties which were trying to grasp all the state's powers, without regard for basic democratic principles. "We are humiliated by the parliament's lack of dignity. It cannot transact even requisite state business without haggling among parties; we are humiliated by our parliamentary system, in which, without a crudely bought-off majority, the needs of the state cannot be protected. We are humiliated and dispirited by the pedestrian level of political negotiations; the actors in the political arena have no more interest in anything beyond the domestic concerns of their parties than a peasant farmer has in avionics. We are humiliated by the matter-of-factness with which old political hands accept the fact that the state has been handed over to the parties for exploitation. We are humiliated by the personal standards of many whom the parties have turned into rulers over the affairs of state. We are humiliated by the form and spirit of a political establishment that governs with the help of corrupt compromises among ruthless interests ... If we express our dissatisfaction, they tell us: Work within the parties! No, if we need anything, then it is to work against the parties, against the rule of the parties, against party machines, against incompetence, against politics behind closed doors, against the omnipotence of the party committees, against our humiliation, against the degradation of democracy. (KČ (1925) in *Od člověka k člověku I*, 526)

6. *Lidové noviny*, 21 January 1934

Ch. 19. **Mary and Martha**

1. KČ, *O umění a kultuře III*, 26-27

2. "I'm creating a garden," he writes on February 26, 1927, to his former love Věra, "with the help of bricklayers, concrete workers, carpenters, even gardeners; a garden from the ground up, from the foundation, from the lowest level, from the depths of the soil; that's why I interfere, in part, with the work of said specialists, in part study unusually technical books, and in part give orders for everything possible, out of which comes great chaos. To top it all off, I also have eight puppies (the mother is a purebred Airedale, the father a pure, kennel-bred pinscher, the offspring purebred Doberman). Further, I built a small pond with a fountain (!), painted the inside of the house, and in general have complicated my life in a manner till now unprece-

dented ... I even get up an hour earlier and neglect all my sacred responsibilities at the editorial office and in my public and private life ... day by day I made different plans about how I would use this piece of land which, out of sinful pride, I call my garden. I wanted to specialize in rock gardens, then in roses, then in thistles and thorny bushes, then in evergreens; for an entire month I had nothing but these problems in my head. At times I'm even frightened myself at what a witless fanatic I am. You'll see, I'll tire of it all and then with equal passion throw myself into crystallography or the history of guilds or the state of the national economy. God help me! there are still so many things in the world I haven't dabbled in yet." (*Korespondence I*, 170-171)

3. J. B. Kozák, "O Karlu Čapkovi" (On Karel Čapek), *Kritický měsíčník* (Critical Monthly), reprinted in *Zpravodaj Společnost bratří Čapků* 27 (Journal of the Čapek Brothers Society)

4. František Langer, *Kratší a delší* (Shorter and Longer) (Prague: Pokrok, 1927), 14, 17

5. "After the war, he founded the Friday Circle," recalls one of the members, František Langer. "He brought it to perfection, as he did everything in which he found true joy. He improved the Fridays and the group until there rose around him a social configuration of just the kind he liked: a regular, somewhat closed but nevertheless free entity with established customs and ways of doing things, and with a friendly masculine atmosphere. Čapek was the mayor, watching over everyone's favorite corner and diet, showing interest in their work and their troubles. He all but rearranged his house just for them ... Čapek, as we knew him, liked to speak only in dialogue ... Once, only Josef provided him the opportunity of changing monologue into dialogue; every Friday, this was provided by his large, polyphonic assembly." František Langer, *Byli a bylo*, 112-113

6. Masaryk, in a 1932 conversation with Arno Laurin, complained of excessive heterogeneity at Čapek's Fridays: "Well, as to the Čapeks: I go there very little, they speak too openly there, and I also think that gossip leaks out."

Laurin: "I've said that to Foreign Minister Beneš several times. Once I stopped him from further explaining something by putting my finger to my lips, because the company there was too varied – but it can't be changed. Sometimes someone brings a guest no one knows anything about. Then he starts coming there on his own – and now there's this new element no one knows anything about. Then later he merrily lets something drop, if only to brag about what he heard from the president of the republic."

Masaryk: "Perhaps you've noticed how diligent I am about keeping silent there. It's a shame. It's a shame we can't conduct politics there, it could be very useful." *V hluboké úctě a oddanosti ...* (With Deep Respect and Devotion) (Masarykův ústav (The Masaryk Institute), 1999), 53

7. KČ, *Čtení o Masarykovi* (Reading about Masaryk) (Prague: Melantrich, 1969), 16

8. KČ, *Korespondence I*, 248

9. Ibid, 250

10. Ibid, 249

11. In an interesting study, Jaromír Povejšil compared Čapek's *Talks* with Eckermann's *Conversations with Goethe*. He concluded that common to both "is the aspect of serving, popularizing: their goal is to make accessible, to bring the spiritual horizons of both personalities closer to the broad public. This attitude of serving manifests itself in dissimilar ways. Eckermann creates Goethe's image. He reports on his conversations with him. He does not allow the poet to come into direct contact with the reader, but rather introduces him, presenting him as a higher, exceptionally perfect being who should not lower himself by addressing the reader directly, but only through mediation, through the mouth of Eckermann.

"With Čapek, the process is fundamentally different. He doesn't create, he doesn't describe the personality, but rather allows him to speak, to ponder, to create himself with his own words. In point of fact we do not register Čapek in the text, he is completely in the background, whereas Eckermann outright courts popularity. For Eckermann, the process is narration, portrayal, description, psychologizing; for Čapek, it is authenticity, credibility, and the immediacy of testimony and the person." In *O Čapkových Hovorech s TGM* (About Čapek's Talks with TGM) (Prague: Sborník, Academia, 1994)

12. K. Horký, "Slovo k divadelním ústupkům bratří Čapků" (A Word on the Theatrical Compromises of the Brothers Čapek), *Fronta* 1, 1927

13. F. X. Šalda, *Šaldův zápisník II* (Šalda's Notebook), 196

14. Bedřich Václavek, *Od umění k tvorbě*, 41

15. Čapek was elected to membership in the Czech Academy in the spring of 1925, when he was not yet thirty-five years old. He refused the membership, pointing out that it had not been offered to many excellent older authors. Moreover, as Jiří Opelík wrote in his essay on Čapek's refusal and the reverberations it caused, "Čapek was unlikely to be enthusiastic about having been elected not unanimously,

but only by the lowest number of votes absolutely required, meaning six out of nine ... or, by virtue of his election, being placed on the same level as J. Havlasá, E. Tréval, and G. Preissová." (Jiří Opelík, "Aféra z roku 1925, Karel Čapek a Česká akademie" (The Scandal of 1925, Karel Čapek and the Czech Academy) in *Zpravodaj Společnosti bratří Čapků* 27, 12

16. He explained his resignation in a letter dated March 23, 1933 in this, among other ways: "It is in the interest of the PEN Club to be headed by a person to whom our literary public and the majority of the press have a less negative attitude." Olga Scheinpflugová then quotes from his letter to Masaryk: "The positive reasons for my resignation are not personal, or rather are not only personal. I have observed for some years now that a deep estrangement has set in between me and the literary milieu, particularly between me and the younger generation. They consider me an official spokesman for Czech literature, and as you yourself know, officialdom – especially in this country – is something of a curse. No matter what I write or what I do, it is 'official' and, as such, already somewhat out of date. Much of this has to do with common envy – especially because of my so-called successes abroad; it has become routine to judge not my work, but only my official position. In this respect, all of them are against me, old and young, right and left..." *Český román*, 384

Ch. 20. **The Stolen Document and Other Tales**

1. KČ, *Tales from Two Pockets*, 273-274
2. KČ, *O umění a kultuře III*, 276-277
3. KČ, *In Praise of Newspapers*
4. KČ, *Tales from Two Pockets*, 276
5. Ibid, 134-135

Ch. 21. **The End of the Robber**

1. Bedřich Golombek, "Podkarpatská tragedie," in *Lidové noviny*, 14 October 1932

2. Other Czech authors found in this out-of-the-way region a setting for their work, such as two balladic works by Ivan Olbracht: *Nikola Šuhaj loupežník* (Nikola Šuhaj the Robber), published the same year as *Hordubal*, and somewhat later, *Golet v údolí* (Golet of the Valley), both of which have appeared in English translation, respectively, *Nikola Šuhaj*, tr. Roberta Finlayson-Samsour (Prague: Artia, 1954) and *The Bitter and the Sweet*, tr. Iris Urwin (N.Y.: Crown, 1967).

3. KČ, *Three Novels*, 465-466

Ch. 22. **The Story of a Man Hurrying Towards Death**

1. KČ, *Three Novels*, 467-468
2. KČ, *O umění a kultuře II*, 227-228
3. Ibid, 210
4. Ibid, 182
5. Ibid, 309
6. Čapek wrote several essays about Bergson in the 1920s.
7. KČ, *Three Novels*, 187
8. Ibid, 232, 233, 234, 239-240
9. In the margin of *Hordubal*, Čapek wrote to Olga: "In my heart I completely became Hardubej, I am as serious and sad as my character, I very nearly walk with difficulty and a shaky gait, as he does, and I am ashamed of my feelings, as he is, and I am as taciturn as he." (*Korespondence II*, 254)
10. František Götz, *Osudná český otázka* (The Fateful Czech Question) (Prague: Václav Petr, 1934), 71-72

Ch. 23. **Looking for Love**

1. KČ, *Three Novels*, 460-461
2. Ibid, 342-343
3. Ibid, 349
4. Václav Černý, "Románová trilogie Karla Čapka" (Karel Čapek's Novel Trilogy) in *Přítomnost* 50 (1934), 795
5. KČ, *Three Novels*, 374-375
6. Ibid, 407-408
7. Ibid, 377

Ch. 24. **The Failure of the Intellectuals Will Make Barbarians of Us All**

1. KČ, *O věcech obecných čili Zóon politikon* (On Public Matters, or Zóon Politikon) (Prague: Melantrich, 1991), 100; also in *O umění a kultuře III*, 292
2. Ibid, 105-106; 118
3. Ibid, 134-135
4. KČ, "Duch a bota" (Brains and Boots) in *Lidové noviny*, 18 February 1933
5. KČ, "Zima 34" (Winter 1934) in *O umění a kultuře III*, 510. There were of course two cruel dictatorships in Europe at the time. While that of the Soviets was established earlier than that of the Nazis

Čapek reacted more directly and immediately to events in Germany, Czechoslovakia's neighbor. Three million Germans lived within and near Czechoslovakia's border with the Third Reich; Hitler's expansive nationalism therefore constituted a greater and more real threat to Czechoslovakia than did Soviet communism.

6. Ibid

7. KČ "Vzpoura davů" (The Revolt of the Masses) in *O umění a kultuře III*, 522, 523, 524

8. "Co je kulture" (What Culture Is) in *O umění a kultuře III*, 537

9. Ibid, 537-538

10. Ibid, 543

11. Václav Černý, *Paměti* (Memoirs) (Toronto: 68 Publishers, 1976), 420

Ch. 25. **Third Report on the End of Civilization: War with the Newts**

1. KČ, "Hamlet, Prince of Denmark" in *Apocryphal Tales*, 134

2. KČ, *Bajky a podpovídky*, 82-86

3. KČ, *Poznámky o tvorbě*, 109

4. Irony and wordplay were intrinsic to Čapek in his relations with people, as well. The Slovak literary critic Alexandr Matuška, in his outstanding study of Čapek, showed how these characteristics emerged in his work and how they functioned in it. "There is much open as well as hidden irony in Čapek's work; irony was one of the essential underground passages through which he aimed toward reality, one which leaves us uncertain as to whether what we are encountering here is belief or disbelief, agreement or disagreement. Along with irony, we also encounter humor, satire, a taste for parody and the grotesque, that is, means to brighten, illuminate, add airiness, and yet at the same time – and above all – augment, intensify, make more potent. They also cultivate effective social criticism, for they set before deformed life a suitably warped mirror. (A. Matuška, *Karel Čapek, 296*)

5. KČ, *War with the Newts*, tr. Ewald Osers, 85

6. Ibid, 106-106

7. Ibid, 166

8. Ibid, 236, 237

9. Ibid, 205

10. Čapek's contribution to a Soviet publication, *Deň mira* (Day of Peace), is not well known. The book was edited by Maxim Gorky and published in Moscow in 1937. In it, different people from all over

the world describe how they spent the day of September 27, 1935. In the section entitled "The Writer's Day," Čapek wrote, among other things, "Today I completed the last chapter of my utopian novel. The protagonist of this chapter is nationalism. The content is quite simple: the destruction of the world and its people. It is a disgusting chapter, based solely on logic. Yes, it had to end this way: what destroys us will not be a cosmic catastrophe but mere reasons of state, economics, prestige, etc."

11. KČ, *War with the Newts*, 216

12. *Host do domu* (1963), 386

Ch. 26. **Do You Wish Merry Me?**

1. One of his closest friends, František Langer, remembers: "He felt a little uncomfortable with children. He could nevertheless talk with them, say things that interested them, but his chats with them had none of that childish delight that was so evident when he wrote for them. He fetched a sigh of relief when a child had gone, as if it had been stepping on his flowers. He also felt ill at ease with women, and while polite, most attentive and unaffected, he was always glad when the conversation ended sooner rather than later." (František Langer, *Byli a bylo*, 101)

2. Jarmila Čapková, *Vzpomínky*, 296

3. Julius Firt, *Knihy a osudy* (Books and Fates) (London: Rozmluvy, 1972), 216-217

4. Olga Scheinpflugová, *Český román*, 346

5. Helena Koželuhová, *Čapci o Čima rodiny*, 119-120

6. Jarmila Čapková, *Vzpomínky*, 301

7. Helena Čapková, *Moji milí bratři*, 410. In her book, Čapková mentions just that one sentence from a long letter in which Karel conveyed to his sister various bits and pieces of news about his life. When placed in context, the sentence sounds less threatening.

8. According to what we know from Jarmila Čapková's diary about her marriage to Josef, we can conclude that Karel's brother was not (just as she was not) very happy in it.

9. Cited by Oleg Malevič in his *Bratří Čapkové* (The Brothers Čapek) (Prague: Ivo Železný, 1999), 230

10. Also valuable are Helena Koželuhová's thoughts on why the brothers' writing team broke up: "... I know that Josef reproached Karel not only for an excessive lightness in his work, which would surely strike others as petty, envious, and unjust, but also for his efforts to use his art to promote specific goals. But the first of Josef's

objections is not without substance. And even though it may seem almost laughably pathetic, one finds truly persuasive only those experiences one has actually lived through. The fair and just observer must admit that Karel was a victim of professional optimism. This was his mistake. So much talent devoted so often to writing fairy tales for adults. To accuse the author of so many catastrophic visions of professional optimism is, to say the least, unfair. *Čapci očima rodiny*, 48-49

11. Olga Scheinpflugová, *Český román*, 409, 411

12. KČ, *Travels in the North*

Ch. 27. **Artist v. Newspaperman**

1. In 1955, when I was beginning my dissertation work on Karel Čapek, I had to title it "Čapek's Fight against Fascism," but then I wrote about all his works.

2. KČ, "Lerida" in *Lidové noviny*, 5 November 1937

3. KČ, "The Death of Archimedes" in *Apocryphal Tales*, 45, 46

4. KČ, "Bajky o válce občanské" (Civil War Fables) in *Bajky a podpovídky*, 88-89

5. Čapek himself wrote about this aspect of his play: "The dictatorial state ruled by the Marshal is not, for me, Germany or Italy or Turkey, or any one of the European states, but a piece of common European political and spiritual territory. The Marshal's homeland is not a real country, but a certain moral and civic reality demonstrating how much of today's world has become alienated from the great attempts to achieve humanitarianism and humaneness, peace, freedom, and democracy, the great cultural and political tradition of the European people." (*O umění a kultuře III*, 766) One need not take Čapek's statement as the only correct interpretation of the play. He wrote this explanation for several reasons, one being that he did not want to unnecessarily provoke protests from the German Reich. The Nazi ambassador protested anyway, even about the name of the dictator's chief armaments supplier. During the premiere at the National Theater, at the request of the censor's office, the name was changed from Krüg to Krog.

6. Originally, the doctor who discovered the cure for the White Plague was named Herzfeld, and the chief medical officer in the play, Sigelius, reacted with contempt to the fact that he was a Jew. Later, however, apparently for political reasons, Čapek abandoned his intent to have the protagonist be Jewish and chose instead a symbolic name referring to antiquity and not to the present.

7. KČ, *The White Plague* in *Hry*, 302

8. František Černý, *Premiéry bratří Čapků*, 354

Ch. 28. **It Could Have Been a Book about Soldiers or the Crew of a Ship**

1. Jaroslav Durych, "Pláč Karla Čapka" (The Tears of Karel Čapek), in *Akord* 1937, 1

2. "Survey on Literature and Masculinity" in *Přítomnost* 1937, no. 27. Čapek was surely aware of the warning implicit in the response of another Czech writer, Josef Kopta: "May God save us from art that originates only because a novelist one day manfully sets his shoulder to the wheel and says: 'And now, if you please, I will create a hero with a manly nature!'"

3. KČ, *The First Rescue Party*, 26-27

4. KČ, *O umění a kultuře III*, 781-782

5. Julius Fučík, "Čapkova's První parta" (Čapek's *The First Rescue Party*) in *Rudé Právo* (Red Right), 21 September 1937

Ch. 29. **Anyone Can Go to His Death, But To Lose Someone...**

1. Olga Scheinpflugová, *Živý jako nikdo z nás*, 135

2. KČ, *The Mother* in *Toward the Radical Center*, 357

3. KČ, *O umění a kultuře III*, 795

4. Ibid, 794

5. *The Mother*, 365-366

6. Ibid, 366

7. Ibid, 376, 377, 378

8. Ferdinand Peroutka, *Hrst vzpomínek* (A Handful of Memories) (Nadace Čapkova Strž, 1998), 10

Ch. 30. **We Are All Increasingly Alone**

1. KČ, *Od člověk k člověku III*, 329

2. Ibid, 481

3. *Přítomnost*, 27 April 1938

4. Čapek himself wrote about a month before his death: "There is yet another sort of propaganda: personal relationships with foreigners. For an author somewhat known outside his country, especially this year, when there is an avalanche of world interest in us, this has meant receiving at home, in the editorial office, even secluded out in the countryside, at least one foreign journalist or writer or reporter daily, murdering foreign languages and explaining how and

what and where it is all going to lead." (*Lidové noviny*, 26 November 1938)

5. The Sokol (Falcon) organization, founded in 1862 to promote patriotism and physical fitness, has traditionally held a prominent place in Czechoslovak cultural life. By 1938 it had hundreds of local organizations and hundreds of thousands of members; it was banned during the Nazi occupation.

6. *Přítomnost,* 13 July 1938

7. Jules Romains, president of the International PEN Club, ended his introductory speech with these words: "We would be very proud if we could suppose that our presence, dear Czechoslovak friends, gives you at least some strength in this moment, and that it allows you to realize that the world is most attentive to your situation, being in no way inclined to bow before the obvious and brutal injustice that was done to you, despite all the sacrifices that you yourself would be willing to make for the benefit of the rights of those nearest you and for the spirit of justice." (In *Přítomnost,* 6 July 1939) Later, of course, when France yielded to pressure from Hitler, Romains spoke up for the Munich Agreement and made the shameful declaration that it cannot be tolerated for "a higher nation to be subordinate to a lower nation," merely confirming Čapek's observation of how quickly and complaisantly the intelligentsia is willing to betray its mission.

8. *Lidové noviny*, 9 October 1938

9. KČ, *Od člověk k člověku III*, 520

10. František Langer, *Byli a bylo*, 129

11. Ferdinand Peroutka, "Sbohem K.Č." (Goodbye, K.Č.), in *Přítomnost*, 29 December 1938

12. Olga Scheinpflugová, *Český román*, 517, 518

13. Dr. Karel Steinbach, *Svědek téměř stoletý* (Witness to Nearly a Century) (Prague: SPN, 1990), 53

Karel Čapek's Works in English Translation
(With original Czech titles)

**The Absolute at Large* (Továrna na absolutno), tr. Thomas Mark, Macmillan/Macmillan, 1927; Hyperion, 1974; Garland, 1975.

Adam the Creator (Adam stvořitel), tr. Dora Round, Allen & Unwin/Smith, 1929.

**Apocryphal Tales* (Kniha apocryfů), tr. Norma Comrada, Catbird, 1997; as *Apocryphal Stories,* tr. Dora Round, Allen & Unwin, 1949; Harmondsworth/Penguin, 1975.

An Atomic Phantasy. see *Krakatit.*

The Cheat (Život a dílo skladatele Foltýna), tr. M. & R. Weatherall, Allen & Unwin, 1941. Also known as *The Life and Work of Composer Foltýn.*

**Cross Roads,* tr. Norma Comrada, Catbird, 2002, includes *Wayside Crosses* and *Painful Tales* (see below)

Dashenka; or, The Life of a Puppy (Dášenka čili Život štěněte), tr. M. & R. Weatherall, Allen & Unwin/Holt, 1933, A&U 1949.

**Fairy Tales.* see *Nine Fairy Tales.*

The First Rescue Party (První parta), tr. M. & R. Weatherall, Allen & Unwin/Macmillan, 1939.

**Four Plays,* tr. Peter Majer and Cathy Porter, Methuen, 1999. Includes *R.U.R., The Insect Play, The Makropulos Case,* and *The White Plague* (see below).

From the Life of the Insects. see *The Insect Play.*

The Gardener's Year (Zahradníkův rok), tr. M. & R. Weatherall, Allen & Unwin/Putnam, 1931; A & U, 1943, 1946, 1951, 1966; Dover, 1963; Wisconsin Univ., 1984; Modern Library, 2002.

**Hordubal.* see *Three Novels.*

How a Play Is Produced (Jak vzniká divadelní hra), tr. P. Beaumont Wadsworth, G. Blés, 1928.

How They Do It (Jak se co dělá), tr. M. & R. Weatherall, Allen & Unwin, 1945.

I Had a Dog and a Cat (Měl jsem psa a kočku), tr. M. & R. Weatherall, Allen & Unwin/Macmillan, 1940, 1944, 1950.

In Praise of Newspapers and Other Essays on the Margin of Literature (Marsyas), tr. M. & R. Weatherall, G. Allen/Arts, 1951.

**The Insect Play, or And So Ad Infinitum* (Ze života hmyzu), tr. Paul Selver, adapted by Nigel Playfair and Clifford Bax, Oxford Univ., 1923. However, the translation is an incomplete adaptation; see *The World We Live In,* adapted by Owen Davis, Samuel French, 1933, for a superior adaptation; as **The Insect Play,* tr. Peter

Majer and Cathy Porter, Methuen, 1999. Act II (as *From the Life of the Insects*), tr. Tatiana Firkušný and Robert T. Jones appears in *Toward the Radical Center*, Catbird, 1990.

Intimate Things (O nejbližších věcech), tr. Dora Round, Allen & Unwin/Putnam, 1935; Books for Libraries, 1968.

Krakatit (Krakatit), tr. Lawrence Hyde, G. Blés/Macmillan, 1925; as *An Atomic Phantasy,* Allen & Unwin, 1948; Arts, 1951; Arno, 1975.

**Letters from England* (Anglické listy), tr. Geoffrey Newsome, Claridge, 2001; tr. Paul Selver, G. Blés/Doubleday, Page, 1925, Allen & Unwin, 1957.

Letters from Holland (Obrázky z Holandska), tr. Paul Selver, Faber and Faber/Putnam, 1933, 1935, 1944, 1950.

Letters from Italy (Italské listy), tr. Francis P. Marchant, Besant, 1929.

Letters from Spain (Výlet do Španěl), tr. Paul Selver, G. Blés/Putnam, 1931.

The Life and Work of Composer Foltýn. see *The Cheat* (above).

**The Makropulos Secret* (Věc Makropulos), tr. Yveta Synek Graff and Robert T. Jones, in *Toward the Radical Center,* 1990; as *The Makropulos Case,* tr. Peter Majer and Cathy Porter, Methuen, 1999; as *The Makropoulos Secret,* tr. Paul Selver, adapted by Randal C. Burrell, Luce, 1925; Holden, 1927; International Pocket Library, 1965.

Masaryk on Thought and Life. see *Talks with T. G. Masaryk.*

**Meteor.* see *Three Novels.*

**Money and Other Stories.* see *Painful Tales*

**The Mother* (Matka), tr. Norma Comrada, in *Toward the Radical Center,* 1990; tr. Paul Selver, Allen & Unwin, 1939.

**Nine Fairy Tales* (Devatero pohádek), tr. Dagmar Herrmann, Northwestern Univ., 1990; as *Fairy Tales,* tr. M. & R. Weatherall, Allen & Unwin/Holt, 1933.

**An Ordinary Life.* see *Three Novels.*

**Painful Tales* (Trapné povídky), tr. Norma Comrada in *Cross Roads,* 2002; as *Money and Other Stories* tr. Francis P. Marchant, Dora Round, F. P. Casey, and O. Vocadlo, Hutchison/Brentano, 1930; Books for Libraries Press, 1970.

Power and Glory. see *The White Plague.*

President Masaryk Tells His Story. see *Talks with T. G. Masaryk*

**R.U.R. (Rossum's Universal Robots),* tr. Claudia Novack, in *Toward the Radical Center,* 1990; tr. Peter Majer and Cathy Porter, Methuen, 1999; tr. Paul Selver, Oxford/Doubleday, 1923.

**Tales from Two Pockets* (Povídky z jedné kapsy *and* Povídky z druhé kapsy), tr. Norma Comrada, Catbird, 1994; half the tales tr. Paul Selver, Faber & Faber, 1932; Allen & Unwin/Macmillan, 1943; Folio, 1962.

*_Talks with T. G. Masaryk_ (Hovory T. G. Masarykem), tr. Michael Henry Heim, Catbird, 1995; as _President Masaryk Tells His Story,_ tr. Dora Round, Allen & Unwin/Putnam, 1934; Arno, 1971; and extra material in _Masaryk on Thought and Life,_ tr. M. & R. Weatherall, Allen & Unwin, 1938; Books for Libraries Press and Arno, 1971.

*_Three Novels: Hordubal, Meteor, An Ordinary Life_ (Hordubal, Povětron, _and_ Obyčejný život), tr. M. & R. Weatherall, Allen & Unwin/Wyn, 1948; Catbird, 1990.

*_Toward the Radical Center: A Karel Čapek Reader_, ed. Peter Kussi, Catbird, 1990, contains new translations of the plays _R.U.R., The Makropulos Secret,_ and _The Mother_ in their entirety, Act II of _From the Life of the Insects,_ and numerous stories, feuilletons, essays, drawings, and excerpts from the travel books.

Travels in the North (Cesta na Sever), tr. M. & R. Weatherall, Allen & Unwin/Macmillan, 1939.

*_War with the Newts,_ tr. Ewald Osers, Catbird, 1990; M. & R. Weatherall, Allen & Unwin/Putnam, 1937; Bantam, 1955, 1959; Berkeley, 1967; Gregg, 1975; AMS, 1978; Northwestern Univ./Penguin, 1985.

*_Wayside Crosses_ (Boží muka), tr. Norma Comrada in _Cross Roads,_ 2002.

*_The White Plague,_ (Bílá nemoc), tr. Michael Henry Heim, Theatre Communications/Plays in Process, 1988; also in _Crosscurrents: A Yearbook of Central European Culture_ 7, Univ. of Michigan Slavic Dept., 1988; also tr. Peter Majer and Cathy Porter, Methuen, 1999; as _Power and Glory,_ tr. Paul Selver and Ralph Neale, Allen & Unwin, 1938, published in the form of a seriously flawed adaptation.

The World We Live In. see _The Insect Play._

Note: This list includes only book-length works in English. For a more complete bibliography, see George J. Kovtun, _Czech and Slovak Literature in English: A Bibliography,_ European Division, Library of Congress, 1988, for which we give much thanks. Books that are still in print have an asterisk before their names. Certain books are available in library editions, but since these are not generally available to the public, they have not been given an asterisk.

Index